A History of Human Rights Society in Singapore

Singapore is known for its remarkable economic success while its strict laws on freedom of speech, drugs, vandalism, homosexuality and public protest have been legitimised in the name of maintaining public order, racial harmony and internal security for this success. Lee Kuan Yew's 'Asian values' are widely discussed as a key touchstone for debates on universalism and cultural relativism.

This book is the first of its kind to comprehensively document and categorically narrate the evolution of human rights activism in Singapore since its independence from Malaysia in 1965.

Singapore's tough stance on human rights, however, does not negate the long and persistent existence of a human rights society that is almost unknown to the world. It uncovers this under-appreciated society's discourses, main contentions, campaigns, survival strategies, prominent activists and their untold stories during Singapore's first 50 years of independence.

Jiyoung Song is Director of Migration and Border Policy, Lowy Institute for International Policy, Sydney, and a Global Ethics Fellow of the Carnegie Council for Ethics in International Affairs, New York.

Politics in Asia series

New Dynamics in US–China Relations
Contending for the Asia Pacific
Edited by Mingjiang Li and Kalyan M. Kemburi

Illiberal Democracy in Indonesia
The Ideology of the Family-State
David Bourchier

China's Power and Asian Security
Edited by Mingjiang Li and Kalyan M. Kemburi

Sino-U.S. Energy Triangles
Resource Diplomacy under Hegemony
Edited by David Zweig and Yufan HAO

Advancing the Regional Commons in the New East Asia
Edited by Siriporn Wajjwalku, Kong Chong Ho and Osamu Yoshida

Institutionalizing East Asia
Mapping and Reconfiguring Regional Cooperation
Edited by Alice D. Ba, Cheng Chwee Kuik and Sueo Sudo

Singapore
Negotiating State and Society, 1965–2015
Edited by Jason Lim and Terence Lee

Political Survival and Yasukuni in Japan's Relations with China
Mong Cheung

Regional Community Building in East Asia
Countries in Focus
Edited by Lee Lai To and Zarina Othman

Contested Ideas of Regionalism in Asia
Baogang He

Governing Global-City Singapore
Legacies and Futures after Lee Kuan Yew
Kenneth Paul Tan

Negotiating the U.S.–Japan Alliance
Japan Confidential
Yukinori Komine

Chinese Foreign Policy Under Xi
Edited by Hoo Tiang Boon

A History of Human Rights Society in Singapore
1965–2015
Edited by Jiyoung Song

A History of Human Rights Society in Singapore
1965–2015

Edited by Jiyoung Song

LONDON AND NEW YORK

First published 2017
by Routledge
2 Park Square, Milton Park, Abingdon, Oxon OX14 4RN

and by Routledge
711 Third Avenue, New York, NY 10017

Routledge is an imprint of the Taylor & Francis Group, an informa business

© 2017 selection and editorial matter, Jiyoung Song; individual chapters, the contributors

The right of Jiyoung Song to be identified as the author of the editorial matter, and of the authors for their individual chapters, has been asserted in accordance with sections 77 and 78 of the Copyright, Designs and Patents Act 1988.

All rights reserved. No part of this book may be reprinted or reproduced or utilised in any form or by any electronic, mechanical, or other means, now known or hereafter invented, including photocopying and recording, or in any information storage or retrieval system, without permission in writing from the publishers.

Trademark notice: Product or corporate names may be trademarks or registered trademarks, and are used only for identification and explanation without intent to infringe.

British Library Cataloguing in Publication Data
A catalogue record for this book is available from the British Library

Library of Congress Cataloging in Publication Data
Names: Song, Jiyoung, editor. | Container of (work): Song, Jiyoung. Tracing the history of the anti-death penalty movements in Singapore.
Title: A history of human rights society in Singapore, 1965–2015 / edited by Jiyoung Song.
Description: New York : Routledge, 2017. | Series: Politics in Asia series | Includes bibliographical references and index.
Identifiers: LCCN 2016050171| ISBN 9781138694729 (hardback) | ISBN 9781315527413 (ebook)Subjects: LCSH: Human rights–Singapore–History. | Human rights workers–Singapore–History.
Classification: LCC JC599.S427 H57 2017 | DDC 323.095957/09045–dc23
LC record available at https://lccn.loc.gov/2016050171

ISBN: 978-1-138-69472-9 (hbk)
ISBN: 978-1-315-52741-3 (ebk)

Typeset in Galliard
by Wearset Ltd, Boldon, Tyne and Wear

Contents

List of illustrations vii
Notes on contributors viii
Foreword xi
Acknowledgements xiii
List of abbreviations xv

Introduction 1
JIYOUNG SONG

1 Tracing the history of the Anti-Death Penalty Movements in Singapore 17
PRISCILLA CHIA, RACHEL ZENG, AUDREY TAY AND KOH SHI MIN

2 Inhuman punishment and human rights activism in the little red dot 36
PARVEEN KAUR AND YEO SI YUAN

3 Singapore's press for freedom: between media regulation and activism 54
HOWARD LEE AND ANA ANSARI

4 Activism on arbitrary detention, the suspension of law 70
LIM LI ANN, CONNIE ONG, MOHD SALIHIN SUBHAN, BENJAMIN CHOY AND TAN TEE SENG

5 Socio-economic rights activism in Singapore 96
CATHARINE SMITH, KIMBERLY ANG AND BRYAN GAN

6 Shifting boundaries: state–society relations and activism on migrant worker rights in Singapore 114
EVELYN ANG AND SHEENA NEO

7 Against a teleological reading of the advancement of women's rights in Singapore 132
EDWINA SHADDICK, GOH LI SIAN AND ISABELLA OH

8 LGBTQ activism in Singapore 150
JEAN CHONG

9 Navigating through the 'rules' of civil society: in search of disability rights in Singapore 169
WONG MENG EE, IAN NG, JEAN LOR AND REUBEN WONG

Index 187

Figures

4.1	Timeline (before 1963)	71
4.2	Timeline (1963–1977)	73
4.3	Timeline (1977–1987)	77
4.4	Timeline (1987–2001)	79
4.5	Timeline (after 2001)	83
6.1	Number of migrant labour activism-related articles produced per year	126

Contributors

Evelyn Ang is an independent researcher and volunteer with the Humanitarian Organization for Migration Economics. She graduated with a Bachelor of Social Sciences (Hons) in Political Science at the National University of Singapore in 2015.

Kimberly Ang graduated from Singapore Management University in 2016 with a Bachelor of Business Management, majoring in Marketing and Finance.

Ana Ansari is pursuing a Bachelor of Business Management in Marketing, with a second major in Public Policy and Public Management. She studies at Singapore Management University and expects to graduate in 2017.

Priscilla Chia is Director of We Believe in Second Chances, a youth-led advocacy group that campaigns against the death penalty in Singapore. She graduated with a law degree from Singapore Management University in 2015.

Jean Chong was the Vice Chairwoman in Safehaven, Chairperson of the Free Community Church and co-founded Sayoni, a local queer women's organisation with its core activities in LGBTQ research and advocacy in 2007. She is a member of People Like Us (a national LGBTQ advocacy group), executive member of the ASEAN Sogie Caucus (the Commonwealth LGBT Caucus) and member of the ASEAN Women's Caucus.

Benjamin Choy is pursuing a Bachelor of Social Science in Political Science. He studies at Singapore Management University and expects to graduate in 2017.

Bryan Gan graduated from Singapore Management University in 2016 with a Bachelor of Social Science, majoring in Political Science. He is a member of the Humanist Society of Singapore.

Goh Li Sian is Research and Advocacy Coordinator at AWARE. She gained a BA in Jurisprudence at the University of Oxford. Thereafter she studied for an LLM at the London School of Economics where she graduated with the Goldstone Prize for Criminology and Criminal Justice.

Parveen Kaur is currently studying at the Singapore Management University. She expects to graduate in 2017 with a Bachelor of Law degree.

Contributors ix

Koh Shi Min graduated from Singapore Management University in 2016 with a Bachelor of Science in Economics.

Howard Lee is Commentaries Editor for The Online Citizen, one of Singapore's independent online news websites, and also served as a media liaison officer for the FreeMyInternet movement. He lectures in online communication and is currently a PhD candidate at Murdoch University, focusing on media regulation.

Lim Li Ann pursued her undergraduate studies at Singapore Management University. She graduated with a Bachelor of Science in Economics, with a second major in Public Policy and Public Management in 2015.

Jean Lor graduated from Singapore Management University in 2016 with a double degree in a Bachelor of Science in Economics and Bachelor of Social Science in Political Science.

Sheena Neo graduated from Singapore Management University in 2016 with a Bachelor of Social Science in Political Science, with a second major in Corporate Communications.

Ian Ng is studying at Singapore Management University and expects to graduate in 2017 with a Bachelor of Social Sciences, majoring in Political Science.

Isabella Oh pursued her undergraduate studies at the Singapore Management University. She graduated with a Bachelor of Business Management and a Bachelor of Social Science in Political Science in 2015.

Connie Ong graduated from Singapore Management University in 2016 with a Bachelor of Social Science in Psychology, with a second major in International and Asian Studies.

Edwina Shaddick is coordinator at the AWARE Training Institute. She graduated with a Bachelor of Social Science from Singapore Management University.

Catharine Smith has worked as a research associate for various organisations dedicated to studying and addressing issues of poverty and inequality in Singapore. She holds a PhD in Education from Monash University.

Jiyoung Song is Director of Migration and Border Policy at the Lowy Institute for International Policy in Sydney, Australia, and Global Ethics Fellow at the Carnegie Council for Ethics in International Affairs, New York, USA. She holds a PhD in Politics and International Relations from the University of Cambridge, UK.

Mohd Salihin Subhan is an undergraduate at Singapore Management University, expecting to graduate in 2017. He is pursuing a Bachelor of Social Science in Political Science.

Tan Tee Seng is a former student activist of the mid-1970s. He was arrested on 21 May 1987 and subsequently incarcerated under the Singapore Internal

Security Act. He is a founding member of Function 8 and The Opinion Collaborative, both with the mission of opening up more economic, social and political spaces in society.

Audrey Tay is pursuing a Bachelor of Social Science in Psychology. She expects to graduate in 2017 from Singapore Management University.

Wong Meng Ee is Associate Professor at the Early Childhood and Special Needs Education Academic Group, National Institute of Education, Nanyang Technological University. He teaches diploma and postgraduate courses in special education. His areas of research include assistive technology, education for students with visual impairments, inclusive education and teacher education. He also serves on a number of non-profit organisations.

Reuben Wong is Director of Studies at the College of Alice and Peter Tan (CAPT), and Associate Professor in the Political Science Department at the National University of Singapore (NUS). His research interests include the EU's relations with ASEAN and China, ASEAN regionalism, and the politics of disability rights. A Fulbright Scholar (2009), he serves on the Council of the Singapore Institute of International Affairs (SIIA), the EU Centre Singapore, and is Senior Research Affiliate in the EU–China programme at the College of Europe in Bruges.

Yeo Si Yuan is a candidate for a double degree comprising a Bachelor of Science in Economics and a Bachelor of Social Science in Political Science. He is studying at Singapore Management University and expects to graduate in 2017.

Rachel Zeng is an early childhood educator and has been a member of the Singapore Anti-Death Penalty Campaign since 2009. She holds a Bachelor of Science in Early Childhood Education from Wheelock College.

Foreword

This book, *A History of Human Rights in Singapore, 1965–2015*, is an important contribution to the debate on rights and a landmark recording of the struggle of those who courageously challenged the status quo.

I feel honoured to write the Foreword at the request of then Assistant Professor Jiyoung Song and her undergraduate students at the Singapore Management University. Some months ago I spoke to these students, who were doing a module on human rights. They were excited and eager to learn about Singapore's civil society and were preparing to collaborate with human rights activists to write a book on the history of human rights in Singapore.

The term 'rights' is a strong word and the notion that an individual is entitled to certain human rights is very new and contested. Cultural traditions, religious teachings and old civilisations had established standards of behaviour and in some cultures, even now, the individual is seen as subordinate to the family and to the community. For instance it took women's activists, such as myself in the women's organisation AWARE, 15 years of advocacy work for society and the state to acknowledge that a woman has the right to live in safety in her own home, and to be free from fear of violence and abuse.

The first difficulty of rights advocacy is that the vast majority of Singaporeans believe that compliance with social control by this government, under the People's Action Party (PAP) which has governed Singapore for 50 years, is a major factor in the success of Singapore and in the material benefits and political stability they enjoy. For the Singapore state the demands of the economy and the state's capitalist goals take precedence.

The Singapore government in its 2016 report to the United Nations as part of a routine review of the country's human rights record known as the Universal Periodic Review (UPR) reiterates Singapore's supposedly pragmatic and non-ideological approach to human rights. Singapore's way of promoting human rights, the report states, is to build a fair and inclusive society, by enhancing social protection and preserving social harmony.

The UPR further argued that human rights exist in specific cultural, social, economic and historical contexts. It added that stability, security and social harmony are key prerequisites for economic growth, which enables the government to care for and protect Singaporeans.

The other difficulty for rights activists is that the Singapore state contests the principles of the universality of human rights, arguing instead that human rights is in fact a Western concept which the countries in the West are trying to impose upon countries in Asia. The Singapore state demanded the right to determine its own political and societal model, including its own view on human rights and democracy, and that social, economic and cultural rights should take precedence. Other Asian countries, especially China, would follow Singapore's example and redefine the term prioritising economic and cultural development over the human rights of citizens.

Such an attitude by the Singapore state presumes an ideological hegemony, and dismisses other discourses as irrelevant and counterproductive to national unity and well-being. But opposition to the state's view does exist.

The history recorded in this book is a testament to that opposition, the significant civil society movements towards social justice, liberal principles of government and political diversity that have been attempted since the beginning of independent Singapore.

This is a very special book. I see the energy and commitment of its writers to recording this history as yet another act of opposition to the government-held view of human rights, an assertion of rights and an exercise in empowerment.

Constance Singam
September 2016

Acknowledgements

This book is meant to honour the under-appreciated and under-studied human rights society in Singapore's 50 years of history, and to build their capacity and confidence to influence future generations. It is one of the best things I have done in my 40 years of life. Thirty-five individuals took part in the project and more than 50 activists, former detainees, academics and bloggers were interviewed in 2015. It has been a highly collaborative community engagement project that was intended to create synergy between activists and students. For the activists, it was an opportunity to learn how to document their work in a more systematic and presentable way and to write using evidence. For the students, it was a real-life opportunity to practise what they have learned in the class of international human rights by interacting with human rights activists on the ground.

The year 2015 meant so much to most Singaporeans. While the passing of founding father Lee Kuan Yew saddened the public, the ruling People's Action Party regained confidence by winning 70 per cent of popular votes in the General Election. Pioneering generations are appreciated. Singapore's economic achievements are celebrated. Yet, people who have devoted their lives to advocating for the protection of human rights in Singapore are somewhat under-appreciated in the celebratory year.

This book project started with a small group comprising a professor and two of her former students, Sian Lee and Priscilla Chia, over a New Year's lunch. We had a very simple motivation: to celebrate our own community in Singapore for SG50, the fiftieth anniversary of Singapore Independence. We decided to form a discussion group, called the Thursday Club, as we arranged to meet every first or second Thursday of the month. Subsequently, an entire class was designed to document 50 years' history of human rights activism in Singapore. The end result is this volume. My very special thanks go to Sian and Pris.

First and foremost, I would like to thank all 35 individuals who have contributed to this volume. Among the students, Lim Li Ann, Ana Ansari, Tan Yiwen and Bryan Gan helped in the initial format of the manuscript. This project could not have been done without their assistance and generous funding from Singapore Management University for running the innovative SMU-X class, and from the Carnegie Council for Ethics in International Affairs for the book's publication. I would like to express my sincere gratitude to Tan Gan Hup, Grace Koh, Robert Myers and Devin Stewart for their kind support. Many people both inside and outside Singapore have supported the spirit of this book project. Among them were Imesh Pokharel and Jennifer Jokstad at the United Nations Office of the High Commissioner for Human Rights Regional Office in Bangkok who saw the value of this meaningful project to empower and build the capacity of civil society in Singapore.

Finally, I would like to thank the anonymous reviewers who provided helpful feedback and comments, and the Routledge editor, Simon Bates, for his encouragement and kind assistance in enabling this meaningful project to see the light.

Jiyoung Song
February 2017
Sydney

Abbreviations

ABA	American Bar Association
ACMI	Archdiocesan Commission for the Pastoral Care of Migrants and Itinerant People
ADPM	Anti-Death Penalty Movement
AFA	Action for AIDS
AFP	Agence France-Presse
AHRC	Asian Human Rights Commission
AI	Amnesty International
AIMS	Advisory Council on the Impact of New Media on Society
ALIRAN	Aliran Kepercayaan
ALU	Adventurers Like Us
AMP	Association of Muslim Professionals
AWARE	Association of Women for Action and Research
AWWA	Asian Women's Welfare Association
CAT	Convention Against Torture
CCS	Community Chest of Singapore
CDAC	Chinese Development Assistance Council
CDC	Community Development Council
CEDAW	Convention for the Elimination of All Forms of Discrimination Against Women
CHAS	Community Health Assist Scheme
CLTPA	Criminal Law (Temporary Provisions) Act
CNN	Cable News Network
CO	Community Organisation
COE	Certificate of Entitlement
COI	Commission Of Inquiry
Conversation	Our Singapore Conversation
CPF	Central Provident Fund
CRC	Convention on the Rights of the Child
CRPD	Convention on the Rights of Persons with Disabilities
DAP	Democratic Action Party
DPA	Disabled People's Association
DPI	Disabled People's International

DRC	drug rehabilitation centre
EA	Employment Act
Edusave	Education Endowment Scheme
EFMA	Employment of Foreign Manpower Act
F1	Formula 1
FDW	Foreign Domestic Worker
FEER	Far East Economic Review
FIDH	International Federation of Human Rights
FUEMSSO	Federation of United Kingdom and Eire Malaysian and Singaporean Students Organisations
GCC	Geyland Catholic Centre
GRC	Group Representation Constituency
HAB	Hindu Advisory Board
HDB	Housing Development Board
HEB	Hindu Endowment Board
HOME	Humanitarian Organisation for Migration Economics
HOPE	Home Ownership Plus Education
HWA	Handicap's Welfare Association
IAC	Industrial Arbitration Court
IAO	Internal Affairs Office
IBA	International Bar Association
IC	Identity Card
ICA	Immigration and Checkpoints Authority
ICCPR	International Covenant on Civil and Political Rights
ICESCR	International Covenant of Economic, Social and Cultural Rights
ICJ	International Commission of Jurists
ICRC	International Committee of the Red Cross
IDA	Infocomm Development Authority of Singapore
IDA	International Disability Alliance
ILO	International Organisations of Labour
IMC	Inter-Ministry Committee
IPA	In Principle Approval
IPI	International Press Institute
IPS	Institute of Policy Studies
ISA	Internal Security Act
ISD	Internal Security Department
ISEAS	Institute for Southeast Asian Studies
IWRAR	International Women's Rights Action Watch Asia Pacific
IYDP	International Year of Disabled Persons
JI	Jemaah Islamiyah
JIM	Jurong Industrial Mission
KEHMA-S	European Committee for Human Rights in Malaysia and Singapore
KL	Kuala Lumpur

KLSCAH	Kuala Lumpur Selangor Chinese Assembly Hall
KMM	Kesatuan Melayu Muda
LAWASIA	Law Association for Asia and the Western Pacific
LGBTQ	Lesbian, Gay, Bisexual, Transgender, Queer
LTVP	Long-Term Visit Pass
LTVP+	Long-Term Visit Pass Plus
MDA	Media Development Authority
MDU	Malayan Democratic Union
MEC	Malay Education Council
MFA	Ministry of Foreign Affairs
MHA	Ministry of Home Affairs
MHEB	Mohammedan and Hindu Endowment Board
MHPA	Muslim Healthcare Professionals Association
MICA	Ministry of Information, Communication and the Arts
MINDEF	Ministry of Defence
MLC	Media Literacy Council
MNCs	Multi-National Corporations
MoDA	Misuse of Drugs Act
MOE	Ministry of Education
MOL	Ministry of Labour
MOM	Ministry of Manpower
MP	Member of Parliament
MRT	Mass Rapid Transit
MSA	Ministry of Social Affairs
MUIS	Majlis Ugama Islam Singapura/Islamic Religious Council
MWC	Migrant Workers Council
Nanyang	Nanyang Siang Pau
NCMP	Non-Constituency Member of Parliament
NCSS	National Council for Social Services
NGO	Non-Governmental Organisation
NMP	Nominated Member of Parliament
NPPA	Newspaper and Printing Presses Act
NS	National Service
NTUC	National Trade Union Congress
NUS	National University of Singapore
NWC	National Wage Council
OSC	Open Singapore Centre
PAP	People's Action Party
PERGAS	Singapore Islamic Scholars and Religious Teachers Association
PGP	Pioneer Generation Package
PLU	People Like Us
POHA	Protection from Harassment Act
PPO	Personal Protection Orders
PPSO	Preservation of Public Security Ordinance
PTSD	Post-Traumatic Stress Disorder

PWS	Progressive Wage Scheme
REACH	Reaching Everyone for Active Citizenry @ Home
SADPC	Singapore Anti-Death Penalty Committee
SAF	Singapore Armed Forces
SAP	Special Assistance Plan
SATU	Singapore Association of Trade Unions
SAWL	Singapore Association of Women Lawyers
SBA	Singapore Broadcasting Authority
SCCC	Singapore Chinese Chamber of Commerce
SCSS	Singapore Council of Social Service
SCW	Singapore Council of Women
SDP	Singapore Democratic Party
SEPDA	Singapore Ex-Political Detainees
SFD	Singaporeans for Democracy
SIGNEL	Singapore Gay News List
SIIA	Singapore Institute of International Affairs
SINDA	Singapore Indian Development Association
SMRT	Singapore Mass Rapid Transport
SNEF	Singapore National Employers' Federation
SNUJ	Singapore National Union of Journalists
SPH	Singapore Press Holdings
SPS	Singapore Prison Service
STUC	Singapore Trade Union Congress
SUARAM	Suara Rakyat Malaysia
SWD	Social Welfare Department
TAFEP	Tripartite Alliance for Fair and Progressive Employment Practices
TEACH ME	Therapy and Educational Assistance for Children in Mainstream Education
TIP	Trafficking in Persons
TNS	The Necessary Stage
TOC	The Online Citizen
TWC2	Transient Workers Count Too
UDHR	Universal Declaration of Human Rights
UMNO	United Malays National Organisation
UN	United Nations
UNECOSOC	United Nations Economic and Social Council
UNIFEM	UN Women Singapore
UPR	Universal Periodic Review
VSA	Voluntary Sterilisation Act
VWO	Voluntary Welfare Organisations
WEF	World Economic Fund
WICA	Work Injury Compensation Act
WIS	Workfare Income Supplement
WP	Workers' Party

Introduction

Jiyoung Song

The year 2015 was historic as well as emotional for Singaporeans, since it was the country's fiftieth Anniversary for the Independence from Malaysia and the passing of the founding father Lee Kuan Yew. His lifelong commitments to Singapore's success have been remembered, praised and criticised by those from all walks of life who have been influenced by him. To most people outside Singapore, the island city-state is known for its remarkable economic success and strict rules. Former US President Barack Obama attributed Singapore's high GDP per capita status to its "rule-based system [that] invested in people [with] sound management [...] and governance".[1] Singapore has maintained the stable authoritarian political system that attracted foreign direct investment externally while applying stringent regulations internally on free media and speech, drugs, vandalism, homosexuality, public protest and chewing gum. Curtailing individual freedom has been justified in the name of maintaining public order, racial harmony and national security, but has also been legitimised by the majority support from its own people through the means of regular elections. In the latest general election in 2015, for example, the ruling People's Action Party (PAP) won 69.9 per cent of popular votes.[2]

Singapore's tough stance on human rights and individual freedom, however, does not negate the persistent existence of the human rights society and individual activists, almost unknown to the world. This book is about these dedicated individuals who have believed in human rights principles. This is about how and to what extent they have grown into fully fledged competent human rights activists.

Lee Kuan Yew himself was once a trade union lawyer for the postal strike in 1952 at the beginning of his political career (Yeo 1973). The first Chief Minister, David Marshall, projected strong liberal traditions to the PAP which was originally based on left-wing ideologies (Yeo 1973; Hill and Lian 1995; Kah *et al.* 2012; Rajah 2012). The socialist underpinning of the PAP attempted to represent the working masses of Singapore in the early years and influenced some of the highly regulated social policies such as public housing or the compulsory savings scheme. The post-colonial and post-war environments shaped the formative years of Singapore's political landscape, which was a mixture of Marshall's liberal faction, and Lee's and Lim Chin Siong's socialist camps.

Lee's victory and subsequent co-option or purges of potential political forces have largely left local liberals in one of three positions: (1) co-opted to the government (Tanaka 2002; Worthington 2003); (2) negotiable civil society; or (3) overseas exiles. The three groups are not static but have evolved across the three boundaries over past decades. The focus of this book is on the second group of negotiated civil society, or what Terence Chong (2006) calls 'counter-hegemonic' groups. The aim is to systematically document this under-researched society in Singapore that has a long tradition and legacy of respecting universal values of individual human rights – to discover their discourses, main contentions, campaigns, survival strategies, prominent activists and their untold stories since Singapore's independence in 1965 until today. Whether the history of human rights activism reveals the PAP's constant co-opting of new people and fresh ideas, openness to internal dialecticism and allowance of a "marketplace of ideas" (Chong 2006) is tested throughout this book.

Data and methodology

In 2015, 35 individuals – activists, academics and students – worked on this book project called *A History of Human Rights Society in Singapore*, funded by the Carnegie Council for Ethics in International Affairs in New York. It was part of an innovative project-based course run by the School of Social Sciences at Singapore Management University, under which 21 students have conducted literature reviews, collected raw materials, interviewed more than 50 activists, and co-wrote the following nine chapters. It was a truly collaborative community engagement project. We documented primary materials from parliamentary archives and old newspapers from the National Library, letters from the David Marshall Collections in the Institute for Southeast Asian Studies, campaign pamphlets from non-governmental organisations (NGOs) and other audio/video interview data. We discovered new information and learned about untold or lesser known stories about prominent human rights activists, including Marshall's involvement with Amnesty International and political prisoners under the Internal Security Act (ISA). More than 70 personal interviews were carried out by students and activists. Interviewees include Jean Marshall (the wife of the late David Marshall), human rights activists, former ISA detainees such as Poh Soo Kai and Tan Tee Seng, bloggers, journalists, artists and academics. The interviews were recorded and analysed using qualitative data analysis tools such as DeDoose and Atlas.ti.

The book is the first of its kind to comprehensively and systematically document and categorically narrate the evolution of human rights activism in Singapore over the past 50 years. The first question I posed to the authors was to identify the major public debates on various human rights-related issues such as the death penalty, corporal punishment, media independence, arbitrary detention, migrant workers' rights, gender and racial equality, and social security. Understanding who led these discussions in the public sphere and how these discourses and activisms have evolved over the past five decades is the main objective of this project. Each chapter elaborates upon the evolution of the respective human rights communities, how they have negotiated with the authorities in terms of their campaign strategies and languages, and whether their campaigns have had an impact on policies or people's mindsets. The discursive changes in their campaign strategies are the main areas for our analyses. Each chapter offers the details of major events, campaigns or online petitions, organised by members of the local human rights society, who have internalised international human rights principles and adapted to local political environments. We have examined only the civil society that led social movements and existed outside of formal politics and, therefore, do not include opposition parties.

Defining human rights society in Singapore

A few academics have attempted to address civil society and social issues in Singapore. The most prominent work is *State–Society Relations in Singapore* edited by Gillian Goh and Ooi Giok Ling (2000), which is a collection of short essays. The authors of this volume dealt with various civil society organisations that existed up until 2000. Since then, many new NGOs have been formed. This book surveys comprehensively almost all NGOs and individuals who have directly and indirectly campaigned and advocated for the protection and promotion of international human rights in Singapore since the country's independence up until today. Although some chapters, especially Chapter 4, go further back before 1965, we try to focus on the past 50 years, namely 1965 to 2015.

What is civil society in the Singaporean context? Chua Beng Huat (2000) aptly made the distinction between George Yeo's (then Acting Minister of Information and the Arts in 1991) 'civic' society and 'civil' society in the Singaporean context: the former is preferred by the government with the emphasis on civic 'responsibilities' of citizens, whereas the latter has a strong indication of 'rights' of citizens and residents. Chua (2000: 76–77) then identified two groups of civil society in Singapore: one that is 'wooed by the government' to align with the state in furthering their interests and the welfare of specific groups; the other that embodies independent viewpoints and can potentially compete with given policy values of the state. The latter concept is equated to Chong's 'counter-hegemonic' groups in this regard.

Traditionally in the West, civil society is considered as a product of capitalist democracy. This concept was first suggested by Thomas Hobbes and John Locke in their respective ideas on the social contract and state–society relations. It was followed by eighteenth-century Scottish Enlightenment scholars such as Adam Ferguson who linked the idea to the growth of civilisation and urban commercial activities, in contrast to natural or uncivilised human society (Keane 1988; Seligman 1992; Kumar 1993). G.W.F. Hegel considered civil society as a 'system of needs' between the family and the state and the realm of economic relationships that existed in the modern industrial capitalist society (Stillman 1980). According to Hegel, civil society emerged during the age of capitalism and mainly served the interests of capitalists' individual rights and private property. Karl Marx and Antonio Gramsci held the same view on civil society as Hegel. Marx, in particular, defined civil society as a bourgeois institution intended to perpetuate capitalists' material interests.

Civil society as 'civilised' society was suggested by classical liberal thinker Alexis de Tocqueville, who observed that nineteenth-century American society had both political and civil associations (Whitehead 1997). The latter comprised churches, moral crusades, schools, literary and scientific societies, newspapers, and professional organisations. Similarly, Robert D. Putnam and colleagues (1994) argued that civil society is vital in the road to full democracy. NGOs build social capital, trust and shared values among members of society, facilitating an understanding of the interconnectedness of interests within it. Civil society's function is distinct from the state's: it is independent and voluntary. In this regard, it is not surprising to witness the intellectual and political anticipation for the role of civil society in the new social formation of post-Soviet Central and Eastern Europe in the early 1990s (Huntington 1993; Gellner 1994).

In Singapore, since the first mention of 'civic' society by George Yeo in 1991, then-Prime Minister Goh Chok Tong called for the promotion of civil society for Singapore after winning the general election on 1 June 1997. Simon Tay (1998: 244) interpreted civil society as "the layer of institutions and arrangement that lie between the state and the individual" and specifically referred to "voluntary associations citizens form in society that are not political, economic, or assumed to be natural". He concluded that a Singaporean civil society should not parallel the then-ongoing Eastern European experience that had led to the demise of the dominant powers of the state but 'should' imagine a space between cooperating with the state and raising independent voices. Contrary to his rather prescriptive judgement of that time, Singapore's civil society has grown solid in form and substance, not moulded to the state narrative and especially with its younger and educated members over the past decade.

A local political scientist identifies Singapore as an 'illiberal' (Mutalib 2000) or 'authoritarian' (Mutalib 2010) democracy. The growth of civil society in the Singaporean context has been a subject of academic enquiry for some time. Critical scholars focus on the legal constraints imposed by the state upon civil society and insincere gestural politics by political elites. Garry Rodan (2003) observes that the PAP actively and selectively encourages some social organisations over others as 'a way of embedding the regime'. In the lead-up to his inauguration in 2004, Prime Minister Lee Hsien Loong reintroduced the concept of civil society. This was largely seen as 'gestural politics' by academics and activists such as Terence Lee (2005). Lee argued that the state recognised the political necessity of embracing liberal discourse in the new Singapore but this remained largely gestural rather than substantial.

Chong (2006), on the other hand, called for a more dialectical analysis of the interactions and feedback between the state and civil society, which is one of the aims of this book. For the purposes of this book, civil society is defined as a society of private individuals and independent voluntary organisations that advocate for values, the benefits of which would go beyond the material interests of certain groups and improve the well-being of the broader general public. These values have an impact on political, social, economic and cultural affairs that affect public interests. Fairness, equal opportunity, accountability, transparency, accessibility and participatory processes are among those interests and they are all basic tenets of democracy. These issues relate directly and indirectly to fair political competition, minority politics, an independent judiciary and a free press.

Singaporean human rights groups are little known outside the island city-state with a resident population of just over five million. The subject has never been studied systematically and their work is seriously under-appreciated by the general public. Perhaps the most well-known NGOs are MARUAH and the Think Centre, which are active across Southeast Asia. Aside from these organisations, the Humanitarian Organisation for Migration Economics (HOME) and the Association for Women for Action and Research (AWARE) focus extensively on domestic issues of migrant workers and women, respectively. Locally, HOME and AWARE are the two most successful NGOs – and perhaps the only ones – that have managed to survive with strong underpinning messages and campaigns of human rights. Other anti-death penalty activists, free press campaigners, anti-ISA activists and sexual minority groups have not been able as yet to secure wide public support, while racial minorities and disability communities have gained slow recognition from the state since Singapore signed and ratified the Convention of the Rights of Persons with Disabilities (CRPD) in 2013 and the International Convention on the Elimination of All Forms of Racial Discrimination (CERD) in 2015.

New groups are formed by younger generations who are educated, well connected, articulate and competent to run successful campaigns within the country's legal boundaries. Successful campaigns (or rather campaigns run without incurring the wrath of the government) are based on the learning and adaptation from the older generation activists' coping or surviving strategies. Chapters 6, 7 and 9, which focus on migrants, women and the disabled in particular, explain how some strategically minded activists within each community, such as Bridget Tan, Constance Singam and Chia Yong Yong, prioritise their agendas and employ less provocative language to negotiate with the government and deliver their messages to the public more effectively in the given political contexts. On the other hand, no NGOs work actively on areas such as caning, racial discrimination or the right to information, where activists themselves foresee no success in negotiating with the government or in persuading the public to support their causes. These are not what the activists call 'bread-and-butter issues' for ordinary Singaporeans, the majority of whom are not directly affected by the violations.

The roles of the international community, which is made up of the United Nations, international human rights organisations such as Amnesty International (AI) or Human Rights Watch (HRW), foreign embassies or foreign individuals, are discussed in some chapters, especially Chapters 2, 3 and 4, which address torture, press freedom and arbitrary detention, respectively. The First Chief Minister of Singapore, David Marshall, played a huge role in bringing attention to AI on the conditions of political prisoners following Operation Coldstore in 1963. This is discussed in Chapters 1, 2 and 4. He later became the AI representative of Singapore, and went on a mission to Bangladesh to investigate war crimes in the 1960s and 1970s. During Marshall's ambassadorship in Europe in 1978 to 1993, however, his activism was halted and had limited local impact in Singapore. Until today, AI and other foreign human rights NGOs cannot set up an office in Singapore as they are deemed to be interfering in domestic political affairs. There are unofficial correspondences between these international human rights NGOs and local activists who collaborate across borders on important and urgent matters such as executions of the death penalty, for press releases and letter writing. James Gomez (2005) points out that since the mid-1990s, the Internet has contributed to greater access to information by international NGOs that have an impact on civil society in Singapore.

This book is divided into three parts. Chapters 1 to 4 discuss civil and political rights; Chapter 5 discusses socio-economic rights; and Chapters 6 to 10 discuss group and solidarity rights. I must admit that this grouping is old-fashioned and that what has actually happened in reality is that all three generations of human rights activists have been closely interrelated and inseparable. However, as this volume is the first attempt to systematically document and categorise various human rights groups in Singapore, I decided to group them into these three conventional categories. Each chapter, however, discusses the multiple civil-political, socio-economic and solidarity aspects of their respective campaigns.

Emerging civil society on civil and political rights

Activism in civil and political rights has been meagre but has gradually grown over the past few years with the benefit of some members' solid legal backgrounds, youth, international connections and professionalism. Chapter 1 documents the history of anti-death penalty campaigns in Singapore. Once described as 'the Disneyland with the Death Penalty', Singapore's retention of the death penalty is justified by the ruling elites for keeping the society a safe and secure place. Against this line of argument, Priscilla Chia and Rachel Zeng, two prominent campaigners representing the new generation of human rights activists, introduce key individuals and organisations who have led the local discourses and advocacy, including David Marshall, J.B. Jeyaretnam (former Non-Constituency Member of Parliament from the Workers' Party) and the Think Centre (a NGO working broadly on human rights issues in Singapore) as well as their own organisations: We Believe in Second Chances (Chia's) and the Singapore Anti-Death Penalty Campaign (Zeng's). While the recent amendments to the death penalty regime seem to suggest the government's willingness to make progress, the authors argue that not only are these changes problematic from a human rights perspective; they could potentially build inertia towards making a fundamental shift in the death penalty regime. The continued vigour with which the government has defended the use of the death penalty under the banner of 'Singapore Exceptionalism' at international forums also suggests its reluctance to make further progress on this front.

In Chapter 2, Parveen Kaur and Yeo Si Yuan examine the limits and challenges of local activism against torture, which is almost non-existent. While local activists argue that the death penalty, arbitrary detention, caning and other forms of corporal punishment are grave and torturous human rights violations, the public sentiment is still largely tolerant of caning at home and in schools, believing in its efficacy. Based on my own classroom surveys (the size is capped at 45 students aged between 18 and 25, approximately 80 per cent female social science students) in 2011 to 2015, around 20 per cent support corporal punishment at home and in school, while 10 per cent strongly oppose it. The majority held "no opinion" on the matter. Furthermore, approximately 8 per cent, exclusively male students who completed national service, say they would inflict corporal punishment on their children in future because they believe in its disciplinary effects.

Gaining access to official figures on caning has not been available. This opens up broader issues relating to government accountability and transparency. Activists from the Think Centre argue that indefinite detention without trial under the ISA is a form of psychological torture. Police brutality is also a form of torture allegedly used in interrogations. Human rights activists have called for law enforcement authorities to implement video recordings of interrogations and this has been continually ignored. Acknowledging the difficulty in advocating the issues of torture and the challenges in the political environment, the authors seek to highlight instances of activism against torture as applied in Singapore, and to provide the local context as to why there are so few groups in Singapore calling for the abolishment of caning and other forms of inhumane treatment.

Chapter 3 examines the evolution of media activism for press freedom and right to information. Garry Rodan (1998, 2003) has covered the topic of media freedom extensively and has offered a critical perspective on the "vulnerabilities of Singaporeans to the wide range of sanctions embedded in the political economy of Singapore" and "the subtle but powerful reinforcement of the legislation hostile to civil society". Following up on Rodan's critical argument, Howard Lee from The Online Citizen (TOC) and Ana Ansari offer new evidence of online media practitioners in a dialectical manner. They argue that the state has attempted to add further regulatory restraints to the already tightly controlled conditions imposed upon the media. They offer a glimpse of action taken by online media practitioners as an organised movement in the FreeMyInternet campaign, followed by the attempts by the state to silence criticism online over recent years through legal action, which serves as the primary means of restricting freedom of expression. The battle for free speech in Singapore continues to evolve, with both the state and advocates becoming more sophisticated in the methods used to push their agenda.

International Press Freedom indices have persistently ranked Singapore in the region of 150th among nations, and this has been attributed to two main factors: strict media regulations and the use of punitive laws to penalise dissenting voices. The former includes the Newspaper and Printing Presses Act and the media pass system, while legal cases against Alan Shadrake and blogger Roy Ngerng typify the latter. However, with the gaining popularity of the Internet in Singapore, the resistance from online media – particularly organised socialpolitical websites like TOC as well as independent bloggers – has been increasing in tone and volume. This culminated in the FreeMyInternet protest in 2013 against the amendments to the Broadcasting Act, which sought to impose a firmer regulatory regime upon online media with rather ambiguous, catch-all parameters. In the meantime, the government continues to use defamation laws, the Sedition Act and even the Protection from Harassment Act (originally intended to prevent online victimisation of individuals) to silence its online critics.

In Chapter 4, Lim Li Ann, Connie Ong, Mohd Salihin Subhan and Benjamin Choy, together with Tan Tee Seng, a former leader of the student unions and himself a detainee under the 1987 Operation Spectrum, offer a truly collaborative work among students and activists to trace back the history of arbitrary detention and the activism against it. They interviewed former detainees, searched the archives and combined their findings with a secondary literature review, documenting activism against arbitrary detention since the 1950s. Singapore authorises arbitrary imprisonment under the ISA, which is designed to maintain public order and protect national security. This law, however, has been used against opposition party members, trade unionists, social workers, artists, journalists, professionals, and other activists who criticise government policies. They were accused of being "communists, euro communists, Chinese chauvinists, Marxists, terrorists and fundamentalists" who pose a threat to national security. Chia Thye Poh, for example, was imprisoned for 32 years for posing a threat to national security.

According to the government, 2,460 people have been imprisoned under the ISA between 1959 and 1990. Not all of the relevant figures have been published, which raises questions about the government's accountability and transparency. According to Tan Tee Seng, between 2001 and 2013 at least 78 Muslim Singaporeans were imprisoned, with 11 still in prison as of November 2015. None has attempted *habeas corpus* against the state. Tan shares his own and his contemporaries' struggles to survive after being released, and to live as human rights activists in Singapore.

Scholarly activism on socio-economic rights

As part of the SG50 celebration, David Chan (2015) edited *50 Years of Social Issues in Singapore*, which covers comprehensive social issues in Singapore. The volume is an effective reminder of Singapore's economic success, along with its potentially serious social issues such as rising inequality and the ageing population. There has been increasing pressure for the state to strengthen the existing social safety net. While the government has responded to such demands by introducing initiatives such as the Pioneer Generation Package in 2014, the state has nevertheless held the long-standing position that citizens should depend on the government only as a last resort. The state has traditionally emphasised self-reliance, family support and community help as a source of social security.

Singapore is not a signatory of the International Covenant on Economic, Social and Cultural Rights (ICESCR). Instead of referring to international legal standards, Chapter 5 seeks to examine what socio-economic rights mean in the context of Singapore, and the progress she has made since independence in the provision of social security. In particular, Catherine Smith, Kimberly Ang and Bryan Gan focus on the evolution of the four main pillars of social security in Singapore: retirement savings (CPF), home ownership (HDB), healthcare (Medisave, Medishield and Medifund), the minimum wage and trade unions. The authors trace the circumstances that demanded the creation of each of the five pillars, how each of these pillars has changed over the years, the controversies surrounding each of these pillars, as well as the extent to which they have catered to the needs of Singaporeans. The pressure for increased social security over the years is also explored, together with the emergence of sporadic calls for better provision of welfare.

Although no specific organisations have emerged to push for reform in the existing social security system, numerous academics and activists have voiced their concerns pertaining to the loopholes that exist in the current system and suggestions for how it could be improved. Prominent activists in this area include Roy Ngerng, who campaigned actively against the current CPF scheme. The authors predict that an increased focus will be given to CPF, as it appears to be one of the most controversial aspects of Singapore's social security system. Medisave is also equally controversial, as it hinges upon the same question as to whether the state can mandate individuals to contribute to their Medisave and CPF accounts. Chapter 5 examines these concerns and suggestions while evaluating the state's response to them over the years. As Singapore turns 50 in 2015, the authors provide a grounded review on how far Singapore has come in terms of the provision of a social safety net as socio-economic rights and the tensions that exist between citizens' demands and the state's response.

Established movements on group rights

Unlike the weak and much repressed activism on civil-political and socio-economic rights, civil society on group rights (those of migrant workers, women, sexual minorities, the disabled and, to some extent, racial minorities) has been growing in Singapore, especially since the beginning of the new millennium. Over the past 50 years, Singapore has been a destination for labour and marriage migrants and asylum seekers alike. As of June 2016, the entire population of Singapore was 5.6 million, of which 3.9 million are citizens and permanent residents.[3] Singapore's economy has been largely dependent on cheap foreign labour from other countries in the region such as Indonesia and the Philippines for domestic work, and Bangladesh and India for construction. Critics of existing labour laws argue that the current framework creates and perpetuates various employment-related problems faced by migrants, while rendering avenues of recourse somewhat inaccessible. Legal restrictions on job mobility and the absence of minimum labour standards for domestic workers, for instance, systematically disadvantage migrant workers.

In this context, Chapter 6 evaluates the origin and evolution of migrant rights activism in Singapore over the past 50 years. Several scholars (Yeoh and Huang 1999; Perera and Ng 2002; Lyons 2005; Yeoh and Annadhurai 2008) have extensively covered the NGOs working for migrant workers in the past. While Lyons' work (2005) focused on the ethnospace of activism and the critical assessment of Transient Workers Count Too (TWC2) in particular, later work by Yeoh and Annadhurai (2008) highlighted the role played by civil society in providing a 'transformative' space for transnational workers in Singapore. They also documented the three waves of women's and migrant workers' rights groups in Singapore and showed how they evolved throughout several decades. They divided the civil society actors working on migrant domestic workers into service-oriented and advocacy-oriented groups, although how their roles were divided was not very clear from the reading. Nicola Piper (2006) pointed out that labour activism in Singapore in general is circumscribed by legal constraints upon civil society organisations as well as "co-optive mechanisms to diffuse political challenges through state-led organs".

The decisive turn in migrant worker activism was in 2001 when the brutal death of an Indonesian domestic worker, Muawanatul Chasanah, sparked public outrage. The following years saw the emergence of civil society organisations focusing solely on migrant worker issues, and several more changes have occurred since 2010. A new requirement in 2012, for instance, now mandates a weekly day off for domestic workers. The SMRT bus drivers' strike of 2012 and the Little India riot in 2013, which underscore the ever-growing salience of safeguarding migrants' rights in Singapore, are discussed in Chapter 6. Evelyn Ang and Sheena Neo argue that what emerges from this history is a distinct sense of how local activism is circumscribed by shifting state–society relations. The dialectical interplay among the various parties that produced what little change there has been thus far serves to remind us that state–society interactions are often more complex than the dichotomy suggests. Negotiations concerning migrants' rights influence economic ideas, political culture as well as larger social imaginaries that bind both 'state' and 'society' – but are themselves also influenced by these contextual factors. In making their case, the authors supplement research from news media and other sources with a series of in-depth interviews with local activists. These individuals span a wide range of domestic and international organisations that have addressed migrant issues at some point: TWC2, HOME, Healthserve, UNWomen, Project X and AWARE, among others.

Together with HOME, AWARE has been leading one of the two most successful human rights activist organisations in Singapore that aims to advance women's rights. Celebrating its thirtieth anniversary in 2015, AWARE has contributed to a more gender-equitable Singapore. These successes include changes to the police handling of rape cases, revisions to the Women's Charter to provide more protection for victims of domestic violence and a constitutional amendment to accord citizenship rights to the children of Singapore women. AWARE has been able to speak to the government that has been more receptive to them than to the others. In Chapter 7, entitled 'Against a teleological reading of the advancement of women's rights in Singapore', Edwina Shaddick and Goh Li Sian from AWARE, along with Isabella Oh, critically evaluate the teleological and even celebratory narrative implicit in many accounts of women's history in Singapore. They argue that the benefits of advancement in women's rights over past decades have often been unevenly distributed. Although the government's abandonment of the Graduate Mothers Scheme in the 1980s (educational priority to the children of women who graduated from university) may be considered a victory for women's advocates, eugenicist tendencies persist in Singapore's social policies even today. For example, the Home Ownership Plus Education Scheme, introduced in 2004, provides comprehensive benefits for low-income families who have no more than two children.

Shaddick, Goh and Oh propose a reading of women's rights history that goes beyond the optimistic 'forward-march' narrative. The advancement of women's rights cannot be read as 'two steps forward, one step back' but rather is recognised as 'some steps forward, an unknown number of steps back, and an equally undisclosed number of steps sideways'. Issues such as polygamy, marital rape and domestic violence, of key concern to women in Singapore's post-independence era, have not disappeared, defying the teleological reading of women's rights history. Moreover, the authors emphasise the state–society relations seeing more gender-equitable policies as a result of negotiations between civil society and the state, and highlight the role of international laws such as the UN Convention on the Elimination of all Forms of Discrimination Against Women (CEDAW) that provide a measure of international scrutiny to Singapore's political legitimacy. Starting from the women trade unionists in the 1950s and 1960s, Saddick, Goh and Oh offer a unique interpretation of women's rights history in Singapore and reveal a more complicated picture than was previously envisioned. The authors conclude that the current outlook is ambivalent. The 2014 Protection from Harassment Act was applied against anti-government dissent, suggesting that what exists of Singapore's state feminism, already a concession to feminist advocates, also functions as a guise for state repression.

Moving on from women's rights activism, Chapter 8 looks at how the Singapore LGBTQ (Lesbian, Gay, Bisexual, Transgender and Queer) communities have organised themselves in a space where their interests lack cultural resonance and where their civil-political rights are curtailed as compared to their counterparts in Western liberal democracies. Jean Chong, a co-founder of

Sayoni, a local queer women's organisation, examines how the state has framed human rights in its culture of survival and economic development in the historical context, and how creatively the LGBTQ communities have organised their activities in a pragmatic manner. She argues that the community has focused on decriminalisation and legal reforms to achieve equality while avoiding questioning the interlocking nature between anti-discrimination and civil-political rights, and the unintended consequences as a result of such actions.

While many activists struggle with how to survive and negotiate with the government, the disabled community faces a dynamic paradigm shaped by the state ratification of the CRPD in 2013 that can empower individuals with disabilities as well as disabled people's organisations. Prior to 2013, declarations for persons with disabilities were articulated in government reports and blueprints such as the 1988 Advisory Council for the Disabled and the Enabling Masterplans (2007–2011 and 2012–2016), while specific disability rights were not explicitly articulated in any separate legislation. Instead, the rights of persons with disabilities are subsumed under the Constitution of Singapore where it guarantees the fundamental liberties of all citizens in Article 14 to include freedom of speech and expression; the right to assemble peacefully and without arms; and the right to form associations. Despite the guarantee to the fundamental constitutional rights and the declarations put forward by the government policies on disability issues, it is arguable that persons with disabilities are still denied their full protection of human rights.

In Chapter 9, Wong Meng Ee from the National Institute for Education, a specialist in special education, and Reuben Wong, a political scientist from the National University of Singapore, together with Ian Ng and Jean Lor, analyse the struggles of persons with disabilities in Singapore and examine broad issues including education, employment, accessibility and advocacy against the backdrop of civil society 'rules' where OB (out-of-bounds) markers exist and public opinion is a poor guide for formulating policy. The PAP has dominated Singapore's politics since independence and has been the architect of building Singapore's economic prosperity based on meritocratic principles. Given the political environment, it is arguable that the growth of a stronger rights-based *civil* society has not been conducive for bringing up disability issues, yet such constraints nevertheless continue to act as preconditions for *civic* participation. Exacerbating the elitism and pragmatism is the influence of the medical model where society has discounted persons with disabilities and regarded them as defective, and, therefore, in need of charity. The authors argue that there has been a dual track for able and disabled bodies in government policies where the mainstream track responds to fully functioning members of society while another track exists for persons with disabilities, who are viewed as needing welfare and rehabilitation in order to cope with functioning in society. Following this dual track, persons with disabilities are educated separately, have fewer employment opportunities, and have limited access to transportation and information.

Furthermore, given how voluntary welfare organisations (VWO) are run, agencies representing persons with disabilities are not inclined to take vigorous action in pursuing disability rights in practice. The authors argue that this is to avoid running against state actors, rather than to foster good relations in order to maintain a steady stream of funding. The study of disability issues as advocated by VWOs presents the opportunity to explain the conditions that have promoted or prevented the struggles of people with disabilities in Singapore.

Capacity and confidence of human rights society in Singapore

The following nine chapters provide readers with a better understanding of human rights society in Singapore in their respective fields. However, what we have planned here is an academic adventure for students to learn and document a lesser known part of their own society and a self-discovery of their own strengths and weaknesses for local activists. It was a mutual learning process between university students and local activists. For that, the project had its own meaning to make the year of 2015 more special for their own respective society. On top of weekly classes, I also formed a discussion group called the 'Thursday Club' and organised 12 monthly meetings to invite local activists to speak to the broader audience and discuss contemporary human rights issues in Singapore. It created a space where invited speakers from civil society interacted regularly with students. The membership had grown to 200 by the end of the year and it still grows to celebrate the book's publication.

As we will see in the following chapters, the capacity and confidence of human rights activists has been questioned. Activists constantly face serious funding and resource issues. Many act as *pro bono* and this condition limits their energy and commitment. Many do not or cannot receive government funding. Those who receive government funding have negotiated what they could and could not do. Local activists are rarely given opportunities to train themselves in documentation, research, updating their knowledge and skills on human rights campaigns, public presentation, litigation or journalism. For some activists, it was their first time engaging with the young and educated audience who objectively questioned their beliefs and confronted them with other national interests such as economic growth or national security. This project challenged them in many ways in this regard. It is the first of its kind and therefore incomplete in many aspects. Any missing gaps or errors are my own. It is hoped that more active discussions and new discoveries follow this meaningful project.

Notes

1 "China's actions 'raise chances of conflict significantly'", *TODAY*, 22 February 2016. Available at www.todayonline.com/world/americas/south-china-sea-area-genuine-tension-sino-us-ties-obama (last accessed 28 February 2016).
2 "GE2015: PAP vote share increases to 69.9%, party wins 83 of 89 seats including WP-held Punggol East", *The Straits Times*, 12 September 2015. Available at www.

straitstimes.com/politics/ge2015-pap-vote-share-increases-to-699-party-wins-83-of-89-seats-including-wp-held-punggol (last accessed 28 February 2016).

3 Department of Statistics Singapore. Available at www.singstat.gov.sg/statistics/latest-data#16 (last accessed 17 December 2016).

References

Chang, D. (2015). *50 Years of Social Issues in Singapore*. Singapore: World Scientific.

Chong, T. (2006). "Embodying society's best: Hegel and the Singapore state". *Journal of Contemporary Asia* **36**(3): 283–304.

Chua, B.H. (2000). "The relative autonomies of the state and civil society". In *State–Society Relations in Singapore*, edited by G. Goh and G.L. Ooi. Singapore: Oxford University Press, pp. 62–76.

Gellner, E. (1994). *Conditions of Liberty: Civil Society and Its Rivals*. New York: Allen Lane/Penguin Press.

Goh, G. and G.L. Ooi, Eds. (2000). *State–Society Relations in Singapore*. Oxford: Oxford University Press.

Gomez, J. (2005). "International NGOs: Filling the 'gap' in Singapore's civil society". *Sojourn: Journal of Social Issues in Southeast Asia* **20**(2): 177–207.

Hill, M. and K.F. Lian (1995). *The Politics of Nation Building and Citizenship in Singapore*. London: Routledge.

Huntington, S.P. (1993). *The Third Wave: Democratization in the Late Twentieth Century*. Oklahoma: University of Oklahoma Press.

Kah, S.L., E. Liao, T.L. Cheng and Q.S. Guo (2012). *The University Socialist Club and the Contest for Malay*. Amsterdam: Amsterdam University Press.

Keane, J. (1988). "Despotism and democracy: The origins and development of the distinction between civil society and the state 1750–1850". In *Civil Society and the State*, edited by J. Keane. London: Verso, pp. 35–72.

Kumar, K. (1993). "Civil society: An inquiry into the usefulness of an historical term". *The British Journal of Sociology* **44**(3): 375–395.

Lee, T. (2005). "Gestural politics: Civil society in 'New' Singapore". *Sojourn* **20**(2): 132–154.

Lyons, L. (2005). "Transient workers count too? The intersection of citizenship and gender in Singapore's civil society". *Sojourn: Journal of Social Issues in Southeast Asia* **20**(2): 208–248.

Mutalib, H. (2000). "Illiberal democracy and the future of opposition in Singapore". *Third World Quarterly* **21**(2): 313–342.

Mutalib, H. (2010). "Authoritarian democracy and the minority Muslim polity in Singapore". In *Islam and Politics in Southeast Asia*, edited by J. Saravanamuttu. London: Routledge, pp. 144–164.

Perera, L. and T. Ng (2002). "Foreign funding: Managing conflicting views". In *Building Social Space in Singapore: The Working Commitee's Initiative in Civil Society Activism*, edited by L. Parera. Singapore: Select Publishing, pp. 93–96.

Piper, N. (2006). "Migrant worker activism in Singapore and Malaysia: Freedom of association and the role of the state". *Asian and Pacific Migration Journal* **15**(3): 359–380.

Putnam, R.D., R. Leonardi and R.Y. Nanetti (1994). *Making Democracy Work: Civic Traditions in Modern Italy*. Princeton, NJ: Princeton University Press.

Rajah, J. (2012). *Authoritarian Rule of Law: Legislation, Discourse and Legitimacy in Singapore*. Cambridge: Cambridge University Press.

Rodan, G. (1998). "The Internet and political control in Singapore". *Political Science Quarterly* **113**(1): 63–89.

Rodan, G. (2003). "Embracing electronic media but suppressing civil society: Authoritarian consolidation in Singapore". *The Pacific Review* **16**(4): 503–524.

Seligman, A. (1992). *The Idea of Civil Society*. New York: Free Press.

Stillman, P.G. (1980). "Hegel's civil society: A locus of freedom". *Polity* **12**(4): 622–646.

Tanaka, Y. (2002). "Singapore: Subtle NGO control by a developmentalist welfare state". In *The State and NGOs: Perspective from Asia*, edited by S. Shigetomi. Singapore: ISEAS–Yusof Ishak Institute, pp. 200–221.

Tay, S. (1998). "Towards a Singaporean civil society". *Southeast Asian Affairs*: 244–261.

Whitehead, L. (1997). "Bowling in the Bronx: The uncivil interstics between civil and political society". In *Civil Society: Democratic Perspectives*, edited by R. Fine and S. Rai. London: Frank Cass.

Worthington, R. (2003). *Governance in Singapore*. London: RoutledgeCurzon.

Yeo, K.W. (1973). *Political Development In Singapore, 1945–1955*. Singapore: Singapore University Press.

Yeoh, B. and K. Annadhurai (2008). "Civil society action and the creation of 'transformative' spaces for migrant domestic workers in Singapore". *Women's Studies* **37**: 548–569.

Yeoh, B. and S. Huang (1999). "Spaces at the margins: Foreign domestic workers and the development of civil society in Singapore". *Environment and Planning A* **31**(7): 1149–1167.

1 Tracing the history of the Anti-Death Penalty Movements in Singapore

Priscilla Chia, Rachel Zeng, Audrey Tay and Koh Shi Min

Introduction: Disneyland with the death penalty

Singapore makes for an interesting case study on capital punishment. Despite the city's overwhelming success in the social and economic spheres on a par with the likes of many developed countries, it finds itself in an unlikely alliance of countries on the issue of the death penalty.

The death penalty is mainly imposed for murder and drug offences in Singapore.[1] Not only does Singapore have the death penalty; some offences such as intentional murder also attract the Mandatory Death Penalty. In the 1990s, Singapore was executing about 60 persons a year, earning herself the sobriquet of the "Disneyland with the Death Penalty". Since then, the number of executions has decreased dramatically. Based on available statistics, only about three to four executions per year have been carried out in recent times (Associated Press 2012; Singapore Prison Service 2013, 2015).

For a country that has consistently defended the necessity of the death penalty on the international stage, the amendments to the death penalty regime in 2012 came as a surprise to many observers (Wong *et al.* 2012). The amendments, which came into force in 2013, gave judges the discretion to determine the sentence of the offender for selected drug and murder offences that previously attracted the Mandatory Death Penalty.

For murder offences, the death penalty remains mandatory only for 'murder with an intention to kill'.[2] For drug offences, the judge has the discretion of not imposing the death sentence if the offender is able to show that his role was merely that of a mule, and that he was either suffering from an abnormality of mind at the time of the offence or that the Public Prosecutor had issued a certificate of substantive assistance to him. At the time of writing, it is estimated that around 23 individuals are currently on death row in Singapore and have exhausted all their legal appeals.[3]

Interestingly, despite Singapore's persistent relationship with the death penalty since the country's independence, a concerted movement pushing for the abolition of the death penalty only came about during the past decade.

In the early decades of independence, the Anti-Death Penalty Movement (ADPM) existed largely on the fringes of society but was led by prominent individuals such as David Marshall and Joshua Benjamin Jeyaretnam. The beginning of the twenty-first century consolidated the growth of the ADPM, a turning point in the history of activism on the death penalty front. This chapter is one such attempt to document the development of the local ADPM, less visible to an outside observer, but a growing presence in Singapore's civil society today.

Early activism before the new millennium

In the early days of Singapore, organisations and individuals who were perceived as threats to the state could be detained under the Internal Security Act (ISA), and mass security operations such as Operation Coldstore in 1963 resulted in the detention of over 100 trade unionists and left-wing politicians (*The Straits Times* 1963). As such, civil society activity was somewhat muted during this period. Against this backdrop, instances of activism regarding the death penalty were few and far in between, with the main protagonist being David Marshall. Unfortunately, owing to the rarity of such activism, these efforts went largely unnoticed by society.

David Marshall: the dawn of activism

David Saul Marshall served as Singapore's first elected Chief Minister in 1955. He was remembered for his many positions of prominence, including that of a diplomat, an award-winning criminal lawyer, head of the Labour Party and the founder of the Workers' Party (Ang n.d.; Arunasalam 2008). However, his efforts at campaigning for human rights in Singapore are less well known. An exhibition of his private papers at the Institute for Southeast Asian Studies (ISEAS) in Singapore provided ample historical evidence that he was passionate about the pursuit of human rights. One such paper revealed that, in 1966, he put an advertisement in the newspapers to form an apolitical council for human freedom in Singapore, with the aim of speaking out on constitutional issues, giving assistance to individuals who considered themselves to have been unfairly treated by the government and educating people on their constitutional rights (Marshall 1965, 1966).

Although Marshall was never officially regarded as an activist, he was "Singapore's best known opponent of the death penalty", frequently contesting the death penalty in public speeches, conferences and interviews. Marshall "abhorred the death penalty and believed strongly in equality, fairness and, above all, human dignity" (Tan 2008). He was one of the only individuals who opposed the death penalty as a matter of principle. His objection to the death penalty was formed on the grounds of its ineffectiveness in the deterrence of crimes, and the lack of humanity towards the incarcerated. In fact, it was the existence of the death penalty that drove him towards his career as a criminal lawyer.

The issue of the deterrence effect of the death penalty was one which Marshall was deeply concerned about. In an article published by *The Malay Mail* in 1960, Marshall argued:

> Killing (the convicted) is to cheapen life and when the state cheapens life, the people cannot be blamed for following suit. I know of no other deterrent to crime other than the certainty of detection and conviction.
>
> (Marshall 1960)

Interestingly, Marshall eventually conceded that the death penalty did deter crime, but maintained that it was not an effective deterrent (Marshall 1969). He maintained that the punishment was a result of bloodlust and brutalities, which would increase, rather than decrease, the commission of violent crimes (Marshall 1960; *The Sunday Times* 1974). Marshall was described as a believer in the value of every single person[4] – he believed that everyone is redeemable (Mosley 1994). He was therefore opposed to the concept of this irrevocable punishment for its lack of a chance for reformation (Tan 2008). He criticised the adoption of such draconian measures to eliminate crime, stating that it would not only result in a lack of respect for life but would also be the driving force behind the elimination of humanity (Mosley 1994). He asserted that:

> It is far more important to maintain a climate of humanity and decency as the context within which our people live and develop than to enforce brutal measures colouring the entire way of life, in order to eliminate a few aberrant elements.
>
> (Marshall 1960)

One of the key strategies Marshall employed was the humanisation of those convicted. On multiple platforms, Marshall emphasised that the convicted should not be treated as a separate class or species but fellow human beings, our brothers and sisters, our flesh and blood (Marshall 1960). Such efforts were aimed at generating empathy as opposed to bloodlust towards the incarcerated – an injection of humanity into the unyielding administration of justice. This is also one of the most successful strategies used by anti-death penalty campaigners today.

Marshall never stopped campaigning for the abolishment of the death penalty, raising this issue during one of his last public speeches at the Substation in 1994, before his death in 1995. This speech had, in fact, inspired greater discussion of the death penalty on newspaper forums, resulting in wider discussion and heightened awareness of the issue (*The Straits Times* 1994). Although his campaign against the death penalty was deemed unsuccessful in his time (Tan 2008), on hindsight his efforts marked the dawn of today's abolitionist movement.

Flor Contemplacion: the protest that never happened

In the 1990s, a rare case placed Singapore under an intense international spotlight: the conviction and eventual execution of Flor Contemplacion (*Contemplacion*). Contemplacion, a Filipino maid, was charged with the alleged murder of fellow maid Della Maga and the son of Maga's employer (Reuters 1991). She was executed in January 1993 (The Associated Press 1995). Especially with the new evidence that surfaced nearing her execution, not only did her case attract immense regional and international efforts to defer or retract her sentence; it also resulted in a diplomatic fall-out between the Philippines and Singapore.

In addition to the pleas of the then Philippines president Fidel Ramos (Reuters 1995b), government officials (Kyodo News 1995; Reuters 1995d) and Philippines-based organizations (Agence France-Presse 1995), international communities such as Amnesty International, the International Commission of Jurists and the Law Association for Asia and the Pacific collaborated with the Integrated Bar of the Philippines Committee on Human Rights (Reuters 1995b) to attempt to appeal for a suspension of her sentence.

Contemplacion's plight shaped her as the rallying point against the poor treatment of domestic workers in Singapore. In the early hours of 17 March 1995, the day of her execution, many Filipinos gathered in small groups across the island, holding silent vigils, before converging on Changi Prison where a final mass demonstration would be held to condemn Contemplacion's execution. However, the plan was leaked to the authorities. Roadblocks were erected on all the roads in Changi Village leading to the prison. Active troops and the installation of machine-gun nests on the rooftops near its main entrance revealed an unprecedented show of security at Changi Prison on that day (Reuters 1995a; The Associated Press 1995; Shadrake 2010).

A few days after Contemplacion's execution, the Philippines recalled its Singapore ambassador and downgraded its diplomatic representation to a charge d'affaires (*New York Times* 1995). Later, the Singapore government recalled its ambassador from Manila at the request of the Philippines government (*Los Angeles Times* 1995).

Contemplacion's case stands out in its rarity as an instance of activism led mainly by fellow Filipinos working in Singapore.

Development of activism after the new millennium

The rise of the Internet and social media in the early 2000s improved the public's access to information and provided a platform for individuals to share their thoughts, beliefs and opinions. These technological advancements created a spike in online discussions, some of which led to activism regarding the topic of the death penalty in Singapore. One such example is Alex Au, a prominent socio-political commentator who has been writing critically about the death penalty on his blog, The Yawning Bread.

Members of the law community in Singapore had also called for the revision of the death penalty on several occasions in their professional capacity. This issue was first raised in 2006 following the request from Australia's Bar Association to help in the clemency petition of Nguyen Tuong Van. Although the Law Society of Singapore did not intervene in this case, they set up a Review Committee on Capital Punishment to examine the issue of capital punishment as a sentencing policy (Jeyaretnam 2006). The following year, they contested the Mandatory Death Penalty in the council's report for proposed Penal Code Amendments that was submitted to the Ministry of Home Affairs (Singapore Law Society 2007). In the run-up leading towards the revision of the mandatory death penalty, the Association of Criminal Lawyers of Singapore had also repeatedly called for increased discretion in sentencing, "leaving the courts to administer justice by sentencing offenders to the gravity and circumstances of the case" (Raj 2010).

The following section of this chapter documents the contributions of individuals such as Joshua Benjamin Jeyaretnam and M. Ravi, as well as organisations such as the Think Centre, Open Singapore Centre, Singapore Anti-Death Penalty Campaign, We Believe in Second Chances, MARUAH and the arts community to the ADPM.

The first human rights NGO: activism outside and from within

Zulfikar bin Mustaffah was convicted and sentenced to death for drug trafficking in 2001. This was the earliest case in which collaborative activism against the death penalty was documented. It was also the first time the issue of the death penalty was brought into Parliament by then non-constituency MP Joshua Benjamin Jeyaretnam with the help of a local non-governmental organisation, the Think Centre.

The Think Centre was the first local organisation to focus on human rights issues in Singapore, including the use of the death penalty. Since its conception in 2000, it raised the issue of the death penalty on local, regional and international platforms across the years. As anti-death penalty activism increased, the Think Centre began to collaborate locally against the death penalty with groups such as the Singapore Anti-Death Penalty Committee (SADPC), We Believe in Second Chances and individuals such as Joshua Benjamin Jeyaretnam. In addition, it has assisted in providing information in order to raise the issue of the death penalty during parliamentary discussions (Hansard 2001). Beyond the local context, the Think Centre has worked with other regional and international human rights organisations such as Amnesty International. They recommended for Singapore to hold a moratorium on the death penalty in the human rights report that was submitted to the United Nations (UN) in 2002. In 2011, they used the Universal Periodic Review (UPR) as an avenue to push for the moratorium on the death penalty in Singapore (Think Centre 2011).

In Zulfikar's case, besides submitting a clemency petition to the President, the Think Centre worked with the late Joshua Benjamin Jeyaretnam, then a Non-Constituency Member of Parliament (NCMP), for his speech in

Parliament. Jeyaretnam was granted permission to speak in Parliament on 11 July 2001. He made it clear that the intention of tabling a Motion to speak was to make a plea which was not just on behalf of Zulfikar, "but a plea for all those who may find themselves in the situation in which this man found himself and has been convicted and sentenced to death" (Hansard 2001). Following that, he went on to present the facts of the case to the gallery consisting of Cabinet Ministers, elected Members of Parliament and Nominated Members of Parliament.

According to the parliamentary transcript (Hansard 2001), Jeyaretnam raised a total of three points relating to the case within the time he was allocated. His first point established the fact that Zulfikar had been a drug addict since the tender age of 14. He had been in and out of the drug rehabilitation centre (DRC) ever since. With that, it was highly possible that the long-term drug abuse had compromised his mental capabilities. Second, Jeyaretnam emphasised that Zulfikar was merely following the instructions he had been given. Since Zulfikar had not opened the bag, he could not have known what it contained. His third point emphasised that, based on the judgment of the Judicial Commission, he was doubtful that Zulfikar's background and mental faculties had been taken into consideration by the court. Therefore, he questioned whether it was beyond reasonable doubt that Zulfikar was indeed guilty of the crime for which he was sentenced to death. Jeyaretnam humanised Zulfikar, showing that he was not just another death row statistic but a fellow human being.

In his reply to Jeyaretnam, Ho Peng Kee, then Minister of State for Law and Home Affairs, stated that there were safeguards in the judicial system. He mentioned that in the case of Zulfikar, due process had taken its course as he had been represented by a legal counsel of his choosing, and the case had gone up to the apex court. Ho insisted that Parliament was not a place to discuss cases, since it is "a separate organ of the state" (Hansard 2001). He also reinforced that judges in Singapore were reputed for their integrity and competency, and refuted what he considered to be a false allegation made by Jeyaretnam that the court had been mistaken, which had led to more than one case of miscarriage of justice. He recommended that the law be followed in order for Singapore to enjoy a high standard of law and order.

Even though this had been the first time the subject of the death penalty had been raised in Parliament, the whole exchange, which lasted for 30 minutes, went largely neglected by the mainstream media. Touting the exchange as "a historical point", Sinapan Samydorai recognised the gap in public information, and the Think Centre filled it by publishing a report from the gallery seats in Parliament (Think Centre 2001). The entire episode brought attention to the issue of the death penalty in Singapore, not only in the government but also in the online community. Despite its limited reach, this was still one of the earliest displays of activism in Singapore, and it spurred many discussions online, albeit short-lived ones.

Despite the attempts made by the Think Centre to raise public awareness through letter-writing campaigns, the publication of articles and statements of the case on its website, as well as appeals made to local authorities, Zulfikar was executed on 28 September 2001.

The human rights lawyer, M. Ravi

In 2002, Vignes Mourthi, a Malaysian national, was sentenced to death for drug trafficking after his appeal had been thrown out by the apex court. Different actors came into play at various points in Mourthi's case. In November 2002, Mourthi's father approached J.B. Jeyaretnam for help. Jeyaretnam assisted the family in submitting a clemency petition to the President, which was eventually rejected. As eluded to in *Kampong Boy* penned by Ravi (2013), Jeyaretnam conceived a plan to overturn the original conviction on procedural or constitutional grounds which would have resulted in a new trial for Mourthi. To do so, Jeyaretnam, who was unable to take on the case due to his disbarment as a result of his undischarged bankruptcy, approached Ravi Madasamy, better known as M. Ravi, a fellow lawyer in Singapore, for help. Ravi was initially reluctant to take up the case due to his lack of experience in handling capital cases, as well as his doubts about the chances of obtaining a new trial. However, after meeting Mourthi's family, Ravi could not turn them down and decided to take up the challenge, despite the knowledge that Vignes could be executed the following week.

The appeal for a retrial was heard by then-Chief Justice Yong Pung How, and he ruled that "the case cannot be reopened, as it had already gone through the courts" (Shadrake 2011). Vignes and his co-accused, Moorthy Angappan, were executed at dawn the following day. Ravi's first attempt at activism in the realms of the death penalty, which had included going out of his way to assist the devastated family with the funeral arrangements, was heavily criticised by some members of the legal profession through mainstream media channels such as *The Straits Times*.

Despite the emotional episode following Mourthi's case, Ravi continued to work on other capital cases. He went beyond his role as a legal counsel, becoming an active campaigner against the death penalty. His efforts contributed greatly to the expansion of the ADPM in subsequent years, which resulted in heightened awareness and public debates on the use of the death penalty. For instance, he was the founder of an organisation that campaigns as part of the ADPM, which will be discussed further later in this chapter.

On 17 October 2003, the Think Centre and Jeyaretnam, who was no longer a NCMP, held a press briefing calling for a Criminal Case Review Commission. During this press briefing, the rejection of the application for a retrial on behalf of Vignes Mourthi was examined (Jeyaretnam 2003). The Think Centre also released a statement two days later that offered arguments against the use of death penalty, questioning whether a miscarriage of justice had occurred in the case of Vignes, and calling upon the government to hold a moratorium on all executions, as well as to consider shifting away from the use of the death penalty (Samydorai 2003).

Activism across borders

On 10 August 2010, civil society actors and Malaysian activists, including Lawyers for Liberty and the Civil Rights Committee of the Selangor Chinese Assembly Hall, submitted a memorandum to the Singapore High Commission's First Secretary in Kuala Lumpur. Among other things, they demanded an acknowledgement of the miscarriage of justice in Mourthi's case, and for the Singapore government to "make amends" to Mourthi's family (Lawyers for Liberty 2010). Once again, despite the throngs of reporters outside the Singapore High Commission, the event went unreported by Singapore's mainstream media outlets, but was instead reported by alternative news media such as The Online Citizen (2010c) and socio-political blogger Jacob69.[5]

Growing civil society

Shanmugam Murugesu was convicted of drug trafficking and was sentenced to the gallows in 2003. Since he was a sportsman who had represented Singapore in water sports events, his death sentence attracted more attention, especially from the arts community, which was unprecedented.

M. Ravi became involved in Shanmugam's case in 2005. As the case had already been heard by the High Court, Ravi tried unsuccessfully to get his client a reduced sentence through the courts. Thus, the last alternative, as Ravi identified in his book, was "to marshal public opinion against the execution and hope this might influence the President to grant clemency" (Ravi 2013).

J.B. Jeyaretnam and Dr Chee Soon Juan founded the Open Singapore Centre ("OSC"), as they wanted "to advocate and promote transparency and accountability in Singapore, principles and practices valued everywhere in the world" (Chee 2001). Although the OSC was founded in 2001, it only adopted an active role in campaigning against the death penalty in 2005. In collaboration with the Think Centre, the OSC organised a forum on the death penalty that took place on 16 April 2005 at Furama City Centre Hotel. The event was publicised via an article on the Singapore Democratic Party website (Singapore Democratic Party 2005). Panellists of the forum included Sinapan Samydorai from the Think Centre, the late Dr Anthony Yeo who was a pioneer of the counselling profession in Singapore, M. Ravi, Jeyaretnam and Chee, Chairperson and Director of OSC respectively, and Tim Parritt from Amnesty International. Unfortunately, Parritt's professional visitor's pass had not been granted by the Immigration and Checkpoint Authority prior to the event, thus barring him from speaking at the forum. According to a report on Agence France-Presse (2005), no reasons were given for the denial of the pass. Despite the setback, the forum went on as planned. The topic of the forum revolved around the upcoming execution of Shanmugam and called once more for a moratorium on the death penalty. Despite being a rare event, there was no mainstream coverage on the forum.

The involvement of the arts community came about after a few members of the arts community attended the forum. With the involvement of the arts community came a wider variety of events, such as a candlelight vigil held in solidarity with Shanmugam a week before his execution,[6] a music compilation called "Songs for Sam" released in the memory of Shanmugam (Think Centre 2006), and two concerts organised by the arts and punk rock community held at Substation's Guinness Theatre in his memory and to advocate against the death penalty about three months after his execution (Think Centre 2005). Despite granting the licence required to hold the concert, the police informed the organisers that no images of Shanmugam were allowed to be shown prior to and during the event, citing concerns that their use would result in the glorification of an "ex-convict" and "executed person" (TODAY 2005).

The unprecedented involvement of the arts community led to many creative and never-before-seen forms of campaigning. The utilization of concerts, songs and dance was very different from the usual demonstrations, forums and speeches. People who had been acquainted with Shanmugam, including certain academics, were among those who participated in the campaign.[7] The story of his circumstances as an unemployed person with twin sons and an elderly mother to support had allowed many people to relate to him.[8] Despite the intense campaigning, and the support which the campaign had garnered, the President denied the clemency petition and Shanmugam was hanged on Friday, 13 May 2005.

The beginnings of the Singapore Anti-Death Penalty Committee

Following Shanmugam's execution, Ravi founded the Singapore Anti-Death Penalty Committee (SADPC), together with nine other individuals, to run public campaigns against the death penalty. It is now known as the Singapore Anti-Death Penalty Campaign. In the early years of its founding, most members of the SADPC chose to remain anonymous (Masters 2005), and Yasmin Ibrahim (2006) attributed this to the "climate of persecution" in Singapore. The SADPC ran public campaigns on behalf of death row inmates Nguyen Van Tuong and Iwuchukwu Amara Tochi, often in collaboration with the Think Centre and the Open Singapore Centre. It took a break from public campaigning after the execution of Tochi in 2007, and regrouped spontaneously in 2009 to work on the campaign for a young Malaysian drug trafficker Yong Vui Kong, who was facing the gallows.

In what could be described as an initially "hopeless" case of Yong Vui Kong, Ravi, a forceful advocate, together with efforts from various abolitionist groups, would eventually turn this case into a pivotal point in the history of the death penalty in Singapore. Yong Vui Kong, a young Malaysian, was caught trafficking in more than 40 grams of diamorphine. At that time he was barely 19 years old.

He was convicted of the crime and was scheduled to be hanged on 4 December 2009 (The Online Citizen 2013).

The campaign for Yong Vui Kong was launched on 10 October 2009 by SADPC during a forum organised to commemorate the Seventh World Day against the Death Penalty. The most consistent strategy evident throughout the four-year campaign was to create a human story, revealing details from his poverty-stricken background, and the relations between him and his family members that the common person on the street could relate to. Details such as this are often lacking in media reports, which often results in the dehumanisation of and lack of empathy towards individuals who are incarcerated. For example, Yong's campaign was launched by his eldest brother Yong Yun Leong who was offered the opportunity of giving a brief summary of Yong's case towards the end of the forum.[9] To contribute to this strategy, Lianain Films released a video interview featuring Yong's eldest brother.[10]

Collaboration, new groups and the formalisation of the working group

SADPC's first collaboration with The Online Citizen (TOC), one of the largest independent alternative media websites in Singapore, occurred when Ravi received the news that his application for access to Yong had been denied by the Singapore Prison Service (SPS) on 18 November 2009 (The Online Citizen 2009a). The publication of SPS's denial of access helped generate curiosity and awareness about the case, which had led to the start of plenty of online discussions on the mandatory death penalty in relation to drug crimes. At the same time, TOC began its public advocacy, launching its campaign advocating for a moratorium on the death penalty (The Online Citizen 2010a).

The tight control of mainstream media in Singapore has led to views on the death penalty being largely limited to justifying the need for the death penalty in Singapore, and attempts by both David Marshall and the SADPC to write letters to the mainstream media were met with negative results. None of the letters was published. In a climate of tight control of the media, TOC also became an important partner of the ADPM groups to reach out to the public, especially with its wide viewership. In a dramatic twist of events, Ravi managed to obtain a stay of execution for Yong (Lui 2009).

Alongside these joint efforts, there were also notable efforts by various NGOs and individuals to highlight Vui Kong's case. Maruah, a local human rights organisation that deals with various issues of civil and political rights, initiated a campaign, "Not in Our Name: No to the Death Penalty", calling upon the government to grant a reprieve to Yong (The Online Citizen 2009b).

Around the same time of Vui Kong's case, M. Ravi was handling another case of a Malaysian drug trafficker, Cheong Chun Ying, another Malaysian national. Cheong was convicted of trafficking in heroin, and was sentenced to suffer the mandatory death penalty that was then in place. Cheong's father, Cheong Kah Pin, has, since his son's arrest, been tireless in his efforts to do all he can for his son and to speak to the media to highlight Cheong's case. Unlike the campaigning for Vui Kong, the advocacy for Cheong was largely conducted through social media (The Online Citizen 2011), and efforts by the various death penalty organisations were concentrated on highlighting Cheong's case through a series of videos and articles. Fortunately for both Yong and Cheong, they were given a chance to be resentenced under the new amendments and had their sentences commuted to life imprisonment and several strokes of the cane (BBC 2013; TODAY 2015).

Building on the momentum of The Online Citizen's campaign, one of the editors of TOC, Kirsten Han, fronted a separate non-governmental organisation to advocate against the death penalty. Together with a photographer from TOC, Damien Chng, We Believe in Second Chances (WBSC) was formed, with the specific aim of campaigning for Yong. Han and Chng, who are the founders of WBSC, were actively involved in TOC's efforts in raising public awareness about Yong.

Because WBSC had members who were legally trained, it was able to cast a different dimension to the whole issue by highlighting the problems with the laws pertaining to capital punishment. Among WBSC's most prominent reports is one on the government's proposed changes to the mandatory death penalty (The Associated Press 2012), which was distributed to Members of Parliament, as well as to Opposition members. It was also the first time that a Nominated Member of Parliament called for the complete abolishment of the death penalty, with reference to WBSC's report (Ong 2012).

The close collaboration that already existed among the various abolitionist groups eventually culminated in a decision to formalise such close working collaboration. The Singapore Working Group on the Death Penalty, which consists of the Think Centre, SADPC and WBSC, was formed. The alliance was also formed as a signal of solidarity and strength. Since the formalisation of the Singapore Working Group on the Death Penalty, joint statements have been published on their website, highlighting the consolidation of activism against the death penalty in Singapore. Statements against executions in the case of Tang Hai Liang and Foong Chee Peng (Zeng 2014), and statements to commemorate events in the case of the Tenth World Day Against the Death Penalty (Zeng 2012) have been made. In addition, the group publishes open letters to the Singapore Parliament (Zeng 2015).

Activism becomes personal

In 2015, SADPC and We Believe in Second Chances took on the case of Kho Jabing, a Sarawakian of Iban and Chinese ethnicity, who was on death row for a robbery that had resulted in the death of his victim. He was convicted and sentenced to the mandatory death penalty in 2011. Because of the amendments to the death penalty, Jabing was given the opportunity to be resentenced. In 2013, he came before the High Court to be resentenced, and was given life imprisonment and caning. However, the Prosecution appealed his sentence, and his life sentence was reversed by a majority decision in the Court of Appeal, with two other judges dissenting. This is the first time that both groups have had the opportunity to work on a campaign for an inmate who has been incarcerated for a murder offence.

The campaign began with a fundraiser in April 2015, after SADPC received the green light from Jabing through his legal team to campaign with the purpose of funding his family's trip to Singapore so that they could visit him in prison. With the help and donations of personal friends, both organisations managed to fly the Jabing family to Singapore in May 2015. The purpose of the visit was to submit a personal clemency letter to the President and to spare the life of Jabing, who had exhausted all his legal avenues.

Jabing's clemency was eventually rejected in October. His family was immediately flown to Singapore and informed, on 2 November, that his execution would take place on 6 November 2015. Due to a stroke of luck, Chandra Mohan, a senior lawyer, filed a criminal motion on 4 November, asking the court for a stay of execution on the grounds that the majority of the Court of Appeal that sentenced Jabing had made an error of law and fact in its judgment. At the time of this writing, a stay of execution had been granted by the Court on 5 November 2015, pending the hearing on the substantive ground of the Criminal Motion filed on behalf of Jabing.

Regional and international collaboration

Where possible, members of the ADPM in Singapore have also collaborated with regional and international organisations. For instance, during the period when M. Ravi was campaigning for Yong Vui Kong, he had also sought collaboration with Malaysian NGOs and had gone to Kuala Lumpur personally to lobby Malaysian parliamentarians (The Online Citizen 2010b). Malaysian activists then set up a website, 2ndChancesforYong, together with the Save Vui Kong campaign, in support of Yong's case (Save Vui Kong 2010). About a month later, then Malaysian Foreign Minister Anifah Aman wrote a clemency plea for Yong addressed to the President of Singapore (*The Star* 2010). A joint forum entitled "Drugs and the Death Penalty" was held in Singapore by both local and Malaysian NGOs.[11] Particularly striking were the collaborative efforts among local abolitionist groups throughout the campaign for Yong. Apart from the use of social media, other collaborative events included, celebrating Yong's birthday in the park.[12]

In light of the impending execution of Jabing, SADPC and We Believe in Second Chances intensified their collaboration with international groups and especially regional groups to heighten the focus on Jabing's case. On the international front, collaborations with Amnesty International led to a global call for letters to be written to the President, as well as to the Cabinet (Amnesty USA 2015). Simultaneously, working together with the Think Centre in the Singapore Working Group on the Death Penalty, a letter-writing campaign was launched after Kho's clemency petition was rejected by the President upon the advice of the Cabinet in October 2015 (Zeng 2015).

The assistance of Malaysian NGOs was crucial in raising regional awareness. Kirsten Han coordinated and facilitated the family's meetings with NGOs such as Amnesty International Malaysia, the Civil Rights Committee from the Kuala Lumpur Selangor Chinese Assembly Hall (KLSCAH) and SUARAM, as well as parliamentarians in Kuala Lumpur. With the help of Malaysian NGOs and the Malaysian Bar, the family were invited to a parliamentary roundtable in Kuala Lumpur, where they were given the opportunity to raise Jabing's case in front of Malaysian ministers and parliamentarians.

Significantly, the Bar Council of Malaysia published a press release urging the Malaysian government to intercede with the Singapore authorities on Jabing's case (Thiru *et al.* 2015). At the time of writing, Jabing is awaiting a judgment from the Court of Appeal as to the merits of the Criminal Motion that was heard on 23 November 2015.

Challenges for the death penalty movements in Singapore

Recognising the interconnectedness of the death penalty with other social and political forces

The discourse on the death penalty and its progress must be located in the context of the philosophy and groundings of the criminal justice system of Singapore. Fundamentally, Singapore's criminal justice system adopts the characteristics of a crime-control model. According to the former Chief Justice of Singapore, a crime-control model is one that reflects conservative values and gives priority to secure the protection and order of society as opposed to a 'due-process' model that secures liberal values and gives the accused maximum protection of his or her rights (Chan 2006). Not surprisingly, penal sentences are relatively harsh, and include long incarceration periods, corporal punishment (which is mandatory in some instances) and capital punishment. Inevitably, substantive progress on the death penalty front is dependent on reforms and shifts in values in the criminal justice system as a whole in Singapore.

By implication, the ADPM here may be critiqued with being too singularly focused on the death penalty, without canvassing other related issues that have a profound connection with and impact upon the death penalty. Such issues include, for instance, the rights of prisoners, questions of justice and the morality of the penal system that prioritises deterrence and just retribution over rehabilitation and restorative justice. Thus, the ability to understand the interconnectedness of issues pertaining to criminal justice and a greater willingness to engage in those issues is necessary for further traction and development on this front.

Likewise, the ADPM cannot ignore the interplay between the death penalty and social, economic and political forces. The ADPM in America is a case in point showing the importance of recognising how interwoven the death penalty is with other social and political realities. The success of the ADPM in America reached its peak in the 1960s. This was possible largely because the anti-death penalty organisation made a tactical move to align itself with other progressive social movements, especially with the Civil Rights Movement. Death penalty activists in America, for instance, found themselves advocating against slavery, racism and prison reform. Professor Herbert Haines, a leading scholar on the issue of capital punishment in America, has observed that it was precisely because anti-death activists understood the deep connection between the death penalty and such social issues and problems.

The subject of the death penalty implicates much broader issues of political, economic and social realities. One cannot, for instance, speak about the death penalty without considering the impact of inequality, poverty and social class. How the issue of drug consumption has been framed as a crime issue rather than a health and social issue also affects the legitimacy of the death penalty as a solution to this problem. It is probably unrealistic for the ADPM in Singapore to be fronting all the related causes, but the ADPM may consider engaging with and supporting such causes whenever possible. When there is a flourishing of civil and political movements, the effect would be to loosen the political control exercised by the state and to create conditions in which the state may possibly be more receptive to the demands of changes, including those of death penalty advocates and of other advocates as well.

Bridging the gap between the ADPM and related stakeholders

Another challenge for the ADPM in Singapore is how to conceive of its role in relation to other related stakeholders. In order to make substantive and meaningful progress, the ADPM can no longer afford to stand by itself. It needs to build coalitions, both internationally and locally.

The progress card in relation to building coalitions with regional and international organisations looks relatively promising. Local ADPM organisations are members of the Anti-Death Penalty Network in Asia, an independent cross-regional organisation made up of NGOs, lawyers and individual members. We Believe in Second Chances and SADPC also work closely with its Asian counterparts such as Amnesty International Malaysia, and such close collaboration is important because death row inmates in each respective country comprise Singaporeans and Malaysians. Equally, there is a degree of collaboration between local ADPM organisations and international organisations working on the death penalty, such as Amnesty International and the World Coalition Against the Death Penalty. While the effectiveness of international pressure cannot be directly observed, its importance cannot be understated. On this front, continued close collaboration with regional and international organisations is desirable.

However, the picture is less rosy when it comes to a working relationship with local stakeholders. The absence of a working relationship between local ADPMs and the government is a missed opportunity. History has consistently demonstrated that the abolishment of the death penalty is usually led by elite political and policy leaders – and Singapore is unlikely to be an exception to this historical trend. For instance, the 2012 amendments were one such development which was led from above. For substantive changes to take place on the death penalty front, the ADPM needs to realise the importance of engaging with the relevant ministries.

Other stakeholders with which the ADPM needs to be more actively engaged are lawyers. In recent years, the partnership between the ADPM and human rights lawyer M. Ravi has brought about several notable developments. By challenging the constitutionality of the death penalty, it has allowed the issue of the death penalty to come under public scrutiny. This has also been the launch pad of the subsequent public advocacy for Yong Vui Kong, who eventually managed to escape the death penalty under the amendments. If one were to look at successful abolitions movements around the world, lawyers are not only often at the forefront of such advocacy, but close collaboration between advocacy groups and lawyers are commonly found.

Aside from the partnership with M. Ravi, such close collaborations in the local context are almost non-existent. Local ADMPs should take this opportunity to reflect why this is so and how they can start building bridges. Both civil activists and lawyers are important stakeholders when it comes to the death penalty, and solidarity between both parties can provide the cause for a potential push forward and enhance its legitimacy.

Conclusion

As the global trends tend towards the abolishment of the death penalty to respect basic human rights, it is high time to re-evaluate Singapore's attitude towards the death penalty. The growing activism in Singapore has pushed us one step closer to upholding the human rights to which individuals are entitled. The anti-death penalty campaign has been fighting hard battles to protect the lives and rights of individuals on a case-by-case basis. However, we need to do more for the grander scheme of things, namely to address the legislation of the death penalty, since that is the only route towards the protection of and respect for all lives. It is high time for us to temper justice with humanity in the pursuit of a more progressive society. After all, "there is no place for the death penalty in the 21st century" (UN News Centre 2014).

Notes

1 Penal Code (Cap 224, 2008 rev. edn), Section 300.
2 Ibid.
3 We Believe in Second Chances, "Universal periodic review: Singapore, individual stakeholder submission to the United Nations" (June 2015).
4 Personal interview, Jean Marshall, 29 September 2015, Singapore.

5. J. George (2010). "Malaysian activists cry murder over Singapore government's hanging of Vignes Mourthi". Available at https://jacob69.wordpress.com/2010/08/10/malaysian-activists-cry-murder-over-singapore-governments-hanging-of-vignes-mourthi/ (accessed 13 October 2015).
6. Personal interview, founders of SADPC (anonymous), 13 October 2015, Singapore.
7. Personal interview, Sinapan Samydorai, 2015, Singapore.
8. Ibid.
9. Singapore Anti-Death Penalty Campaign (2009). "7th World Day Against The Death Penalty (Singapore) – videos". Available at https://singaporeantideathpenaltycampaign.wordpress.com/2009/10/25/hello-world/ (accessed 13 October 2015).
10. Lianain Films (2009). *Vui Kong's Story*. Singapore.
11. K. Han (2011, 24 April). "Drugs and the death penalty – 'What can we do'". Available at https://webelieveinsecondchances.wordpress.com/2011/04/24/thoughts-on-drugs-and-the-death-penalty/ (accessed 13 October 2015).
12. We Believe in Second Chances. (2012, 15 January). "Dear Vui Kong, Happy Birthday". Available at https://webelieveinsecondchances.wordpress.com/2012/01/15/dear-vui-kong-happy-birthday/ (accessed 13 October 2015).

References

Agence France-Presse (1995). "Militant groups ask Singapore to stay hanging of Filipina maid. Manila," Singapore: *Agence France-Presse*: 2.

Agence France-Presse (2005). "Singapore bars Amnesty activist from speaking at forum: Opposition group". Singapore: *Agence France-Presse*.

Amnesty USA (2015). "Urgent action: Execution looming if appeals rejected".

Ang, S.L. (n.d.). "Icon of justice: Highlights of the life of David Saul Marshall". *Biblioasia*. Singapore: Lee Kong Chian Reference Library, National Library: 6.

Arunasalam, S. (2008). "David Saul Marshall". Available at http://eresources.nlb.gov.sg/infopedia/articles/SIP_283_2005-01-13.html (accessed 14 October 2015).

BBC (2013). "Singapore lifts death sentence for drug trafficker".

Chan, S.K. (2006). "From Justice Model to Crime-Control Model". Address by Chief Justice Chan Sek Keong of Singapore for Golden Jubilee Celebrations 2006, International Conference on Criminal Justice under Stress: Transnational Perspectives. New Delhi, India, 24 November.

Chee, S.J. (2001). "Open Singapore Centre". Media Release.

George, J. (2010). "Malaysian activists cry murder over Singapore government's hanging of Vignes Mourthi". Available at https://jacob69.wordpress.com/2010/08/10/malaysian-activists-cry-murder-over-singapore-governments-hanging-of-vignes-mourthi/ (accessed 14 October 2015).

Han, K. (2011, 24 April). "Drugs and the death penalty – 'What can we do'". Available at https://webelieveinsecondchances.wordpress.com/2011/04/24/thoughts-on-drugs-and-the-death-penalty/ (accessed 13 October 2015).

Hansard (2001). "A case of drug trafficking". *Zulfikar Bin Mustaffah* 73.

Ibrahim, Y. (2006). "Capital punishment and virtual protest: A case study of Singapore". *First Monday* 11(10).

Jeyaretnam, J.B. (2003). "J.B. Jeyaretnam calls for a Criminal Cases Review Commission". Available at www.thinkcentre.org/article.cfm?ArticleID=2207 (accessed 21 November 2015).

Jeyaretnam, P.S. (2006). "Ring out the old, ring in the new". *Law Gazette*. Available at www.lawgazette.com.sg/2006-1/Jan06-president.htm (accessed 21 November 2015.

Kyodo News (1995). "Manila to ask Singapore to defer hanging of Filipina". *Kyodo News*. Japan: Kyodo News International Inc.: 1.
Lawyers for Liberty (2010). "Memorandum of Protest: Wrongful execution of M'sian Vignes Mourthi and malicious prosecution of Alan Shadrake".
Lianain Films (2009). *Vui Kong's Story*. Singapore.
Los Angeles Times (1995). "Singapore agrees to recall Its Manila envoy". *Los Angeles Times*.
Lui, T.Y. (2009). "Speech by RADM (NS) Lui Tuck Yew at the Singapore Press Club". Eminent Speakers Series. Singapore.
Marshall, D. (1960). "The death penalty: A deterrent but not an effective one". *The Malay Mail*. Singapore.
Marshall, D. (1965). "N.S.P. Manager of Advertising Department for Straits Times, Sin Chew Jit Poh, Utusan Melayu, Tamil Malar". ISEAS: 1.
Marshall, D. (1966). "I.S.S.M. Hussain". ISEAS: 1.
Marshall, D. (1969). "The death penalty: A deterrent but not an effective one". *The Malay Mail*: 1.
Masters, C. (2005). "Nguyen hangman sacked". *Sunday Telegraph*.
Mosley, J. (1994). "Hail to the Chief". *Personality*: 4.
New York Times (1995). "Singapore puts off Prime Minister's trip to Manila". *New York Times*.
Ong, A. (2012). "Abolish death penalty, urge 3 MPs". *The Straits Times*: 1.
Raj, C. (2010). "Singapore criminal lawyers call for the abolition of mandatory death penalty". Available at http://sgdeathpenalty.blogspot.sg/2010/11/singapore-criminal-lawyers-calls-for.html (accessed 21 November 2015).
Ravi, M. (2013). *Kampong Boy*. Singapore: Ethos Books.
Reuters (1991). "Singapore Court charge Filipina maid with murder". *Reuters News*: 1.
Reuters (1995a). "Singapore security tight as fate of maid awaited". *Reuters News*: 1.
Reuters (1995b). "Ramos seeks clemency for Filipina in Singapore". *Reuters News*: 1.
Reuters (1995c). "Support for Filipina maid in Singapore snowballs". *Reuters News*: 2.
Reuters (1995d). "Boycott urged in Philippines over maid's execution". *Reuters News*: 2.
Samydorai, S. (2003). "Think Centre calls for a moratorium on death penalty". *Forum Asia*, 2 June 2010. Available at www.forum-asia.org/?p=6697 (accessed 28 December 2016).
Save Vui Kong (2010, 28 August). "Yong Vui Kong's journey". Available at http://savevuikong.blogspot.sg/p/yong-vui-kongs-journey.html (accessed 13 October 2015).
Shadrake, A. (2010). *Once a Jolly Hangman: Singapore Justice in the Dock*. Malaysia: Strategic Information and Research Development Centre.
Shadrake, A. (2011). *Once a Jolly Hangman: Singapore Justice in the Dock*. Pier 9.
Singapore Anti-Death Penalty Campaign (2009). "7th World Day Against The Death Penalty (Singapore) – Videos". Available at https://singaporeantideathpenaltycampaign.wordpress.com/2009/10/25/hello-world/ (accessed 13 October 2015).
Singapore Democratic Party (2005). "Forum on death penalty and the rule of law".
Singapore Law Society (2007). "Executive summary of Council's Report on the Proposed Amendments to the Penal Code". Available at www.lawsociety.org.sg/forMembers/ResourceCentre/FeedbackinPublicConsultations/2007/ExecutiveSummaryProposedAmendmentstothePenal.aspx (accessed 21 November 2015).
Singapore Prison Service (2013). "Greater community involvement contributes to lower re-offending rates". S.P. Service. Singapore: Singapore Prison Service, p. 11.
Singapore Prison Service (2015). "Strong community efforts essential in preventing re-offending". S.P. Service. Singapore: Singapore Prison Service, pp. 1–10.

Tan, K. (2008). *Marshall of Singapore: A Biography*. Singapore: ISEAS Publishing.
The Associated Press (1995). "Filipino maid hanged in Singapore". *The Associated Press*.
The Associated Press (2012). "Police summon citizens' group members over forum". *Associated Press*.
The Online Citizen (2009a, 19 November). "Lawyer for death-row inmate denied access to client". Available at www.theonlinecitizen.com/2009/11/lawyer-for-death-row-inmate-denied-access-to-client/ (accessed 13 October 2015).
The Online Citizen (2009b, 7 December 2009). "Calling for end to the mandatory death penalty". Available at www.theonlinecitizen.com/2009/12/calling-for-an-end-to-the-mandatory-death-penalty/ (accessed 13 October 2015).
The Online Citizen (2010a, 23 March). "The moratorium on the Mandatory Death Penalty Campaign". Available at www.theonlinecitizen.com/2010/03/the-mandatory-death-penalty-campaign/ (accessed 13 October 2015).
The Online Citizen (2010b, 6 July 2010). "Malaysian FM: 'If I save one life, it will give me great satisfaction'". Available at www.theonlinecitizen.com/2010/07/malaysian-fm-%E2%80%9Cif-i-save-one-life-it-will-give-me-great-satisfaction%E2%80%9D/ (accessed 13 October 2015).
The Online Citizen (2010c). "'I want my son's name back'". *The Online Citizen*.
The Online Citizen (2011, 30 April). "Please do not execute Cheong Chun Yin". Retrieved Available at www.theonlinecitizen.com/2010/07/malaysian-fm-%E2%80%9Cif-i-save-one-life-it-will-give-me-great-satisfaction%E2%80%9D/ (accessed 14 October 2015).
The Online Citizen (2013, 24 September 2013). "Yong Vui Kong happy for 2nd chance: M Ravi". Available at www.theonlinecitizen.com/2013/09/yong-vui-kong-happy-for-2nd-chance-m-ravi/ (accessed 13 October 2015).
The Star (2010). "Wisma Putra pleads for Sabahan on Singapore death row". *The Star*. The Star Online.
The Straits Times (1963). "107 held in Singapore dawn drive". *The Straits Times*.
The Straits Times (1994). "Mandatory death penalty deters many from crime". *The Straits Times*.
The Sunday Times (1974). "Concluding a two-part discussion: Caning and the death penalty". Singapore.
Think Centre. (2001). "Death penalty case gets an airing in Parliament". Available at www.thinkcentre.org/article.cfm?ArticleID=973.
Think Centre (2005). "Hung at dawn: Concert against death penalty".
Think Centre (2006). "Death penalty: *Songs for Sam*".
Think Centre (2011). S.f.D., Singapore Anti Death Penalty Campaign, Humanitarian Organisation for Migration Economics. Universal Periodic Review on Singapore for the 11th Session of UPR.
Thiru, S., L. Shim and B. Soh (2015). Joint Press Release, "Abolish the mandatory death penalty and restore judicial discretion in sentencing". The Malaysian Bar.
TODAY (2005). "Withdrawn at dawn – those concert posters," 5 August, p. 6. Available at http://eresources.nlb.gov.sg/newspapers/Digitised/Article/today20050805-1.2.13.2.
TODAY (2015). "Two convicted drug traffickers escape gallows, imprisoned for life". *TODAY*. Singapore.
UN News Centre (2014). "'Death penalty has no place in 21st century,' declares UN chief".
We Believe in Second Chances (2012, 15 January). "Dear Vui Kong, Happy Birthday". Available at https://webelieveinsecondchances.wordpress.com/2012/01/15/dear-vui-kong-happy-birthday/ (accessed 13 October 2015).

Wong, W.K., M.A. Kadir and M. Faizal (2012). "Changes to the mandatory death penalty regime – An overview of the changes and some preliminary reflections". *Law Gazette*.

Zeng, R. (2012). "Commemorating the 10th World Day Against the Death Penalty".

Zeng, R. (2014). "Joint statement on the executions carried out on 18 July 2014".

Zeng, R. (2015). "Mercy for Kho Jabing: An open letter to the Cabinet".

2 Inhuman punishment and human rights activism in the little red dot

Parveen Kaur and Yeo Si Yuan[1]

Introduction

This chapter highlights the activism in Singapore against torture and inhumane punishment in the country's recent history. We first examine the legal compliance of the definition of torture and inhuman punishment in Singapore with international standards, and elaborate on the effects of such treatment upon those who receive it. We then survey specific instances of torture under the state, and the resultant activism found against it. In examining the interaction between the acts of the state and activism, this chapter focuses on three alleged victim groups: (1) political prisoners who were detained under Operations Coldstore and Spectrum; (2) migrant workers, and (3) judicial caning in Singapore.

Notwithstanding the specific instances of activism here, our findings also show that there has been a general lack of activism against such forms of torture and inhuman punishment. While this may be a limitation in chronicling the history of activism, this chapter further examines the reasons for this pronounced dearth. Thus, the trammelling forces of culture, victim psychology, state-induced structural constrains, as well as the inherent limitations within, and between, non-governmental organisations (NGOs) in Singapore, will be examined.

Definitional challenges: Singapore vs. International Standards

Torture and caning violate Article 5 of the Universal Declaration of Human Rights (UDHR), which declares, "no one shall be subjected to torture or to cruel, inhuman or degrading treatment or punishment",[2] as well as Article 7 of the International Covenant on Civil and Political Rights (ICCPR).[3] Such violations are also enshrined in Articles 1, 2, 4, 10, 11, 12, 13 and 15 of the Convention Against Torture (CAT).[4] Most states in the world accept that torture is contradictory to international law: as of October 2016 there were 160 state parties to the CAT.

The Singapore Constitution, however, does not include any express prohibition of torture or other cruel, inhuman or degrading punishment. The prohibition listed in Article 5 of the UDHR is noticeably omitted from the Singapore Constitution, despite the recommendation by the Constitutional Commission of 1966 to include such a clause on the basis that it is a fundamental human right included in most modern constitutions (Chan 1993). Singapore has also not ratified the CAT, although ministers speaking in Parliament have endorsed the view that torture is wrong and that no one should be subjected to it (Jayakumar 1987).

It is also worth noting that the ASEAN Human Rights Declaration, which was unanimously adopted by ASEAN states in 2012, contains an explicit clause which states that human rights may be limited to preserve "national security" or "public morality".[5] Thus, while Article 14 does prohibit torture,[6] the Declaration is characteristic of a favourite argument among Asian nations in the area of human rights: that of cultural relativity or "Asian values". Therefore, even as the Declaration reaffirms the observance of the UDHR, it equally stresses that human rights have two mutually balancing aspects: the rights of individuals and the obligations to society (or the state). Thus, this in turn legitimises certain state violations in ASEAN countries.

Singapore subscribes to the 'dualist' view of international and domestic law, essentially regarding the two as separate legal systems. This ensures that international law would not form part of domestic law unless expressly adopted by the legislative branch of the state. Hence, it may be argued that even the ratification of conventions is not enough to ensure proper enforcement unless the laws have been transplanted into domestic legislation, as was argued by the Supreme Court in the case of Yong Vui Kong.[7]

Penal legislation, which introduced sentences of caning and whipping into Singapore, has its historical roots in the archaic criminal law systems of India and England. Whipping was abolished in England in 1948[8] and in India in 1955.[9] Singapore has, however, retained caning as one of the primary penal sanctions. Caning was initially reserved for violent crimes, but its use has since expanded to non-violent crimes such as vandalism and drug abuse.

Official Judicial Corporal Punishment is currently practiced in 33 countries (World Corporal Punishment Research 2011). In Singapore, judicial caning is ordered for over 35 offences; it is a mandatory punishment for rape, drug trafficking, illegal money lending and overstaying by visiting foreigners. Caning in Singapore only applies to males between the ages of 18 and 50. According to the Singapore Director of Prisons, Quek Shi Lei, the warder "uses the whole of his body weight, and not just the strength of his arms, to strike" (Raman 1974). The skin at the point of contact is "usually split open" (Raman 1974); it "disintegrates" and leaves a "white line and then a flow of blood" (World Corporal Punishment Research 2012). The buttocks are usually covered in blood following three strokes, after which recipients are usually in a "state of shock", with many collapsing upon release.

In 1979, in one of the few public discussions on caning in Singapore, David Marshall expressed his objection towards judicial caning. He said: "I think very few of us have any real understanding of what actually occurs. There is a lack of understanding of basic principles and the options open to the authorities". Marshall claimed that caning "degrades the concept of the sanctity of the individual" (The Sunday Times 1974). In a powerful letter to the Malayan Law Journal (Marshall 1993), he asked:

> Have any of our judges, any of our Magistrates, witnessed a caning in our prisons? It may be salutary for all concerned if those empowered to order the infliction of this brutal punishment were to have visual experience of what it means?

Marshall also criticised the Singaporean government over the caning of American teenager Michael Fay who had pleaded guilty to vandalism, describing the sentence as "grossly excessive" (Shenon 1995). To date, he represents one of the very few Singaporeans who have publicly and actively criticised the use of caning in the country.

Efforts to campaign against judicial caning have been sparse and unconsolidated. Rachel Zeng, a prominent anti-death penalty activist from the Singapore Anti-Death Penalty Campaign, attempted to start a campaign against judicial caning, but was unable to overcome the many obstacles she faced.[10] The most notable example of an attempt to challenge judicial caning was the constitutional appeal filed by lawyer M. Ravi in August 2014. He was, however, unsuccessful in establishing that judicial caning was unconstitutional, or that it constituted torture.[11]

The government has no qualms about describing caning as particularly demeaning. Former Prime Minister Lee Kuan Yew described caning as a "rather humiliating experience" when proposing caning as punishment for vandalism (Parliament of Singapore 1966). Former Director of Prisons Mr Quek Shi Lei once described how prisoners feared the pain of caning and the humiliation they experienced when it caused them to lose control and cry out. Furthermore, he added, the "indelible" scars from the caning would be a source of humiliation for them for the remainder of their lives.[12]

Yet, Singapore also denies that caning is "unusual" or "cruel". Lee defended this when confronted with Michael Fay's caning controversy: "The punishment is not fatal. It is not painless. It does what it is supposed to do, to remind the wrongdoer that he should never do it again. And it does work" (*The Straits Times* 1994).

The judiciary did not respond favourably to M. Ravi's constitutional challenge against judicial caning either. Ravi argued that judicial caning was unconstitutional and constituted torture. However, this was dismissed on the basis that "there is, as yet, no international consensus that the use of caning as part of a regulated regime of punishment with appropriate medical safeguards constitutes torture".[13]

Periodic cycles of public security, detention, degrading treatments and activism

1950s to 1960s: the PPSO, torture and David Marshall

Individuals detained under the Preservation of Public Security Ordinance (PPSO) in the 1950s and 1960s often recall the unimaginable conditions they were made to live in, as well as the mistreatment and violence they suffered at the hands of their interrogators.[14] The most notable detainees were members of Barisan Sosialis, the now-defunct political party that broke away from the People's Action Party in 1961. An interview with Dr Poh Soo Kai, detained during Operation Coldstore under the PPSO, revealed the various abuses that he and his fellow inmates were put through. As he recalled, "people were beaten up, or asked to exercise – squat up and down".[15] Often, detainees were forced to "squat up and down" for more than 100 times at one go. Other forms of physical torture included being kept in a very cold room for long periods of time (dressed in a singlet, while the interrogators dressed up "like it was winter"), having cold water poured over them, being stripped naked, slapped, beaten up and punched. "They all got bashed up", recounts Poh. One detainee was beaten up so badly that there was "blood all over; he kept his [bloody] shirt to show me". This was done in order to "break them", or to "get something from them", often in the hope that detainees would "spill on [their] friends".

In addition to physical abuses, detainees were often psychologically tormented by means of solitary confinement and simply not knowing when they would be released. Poh was himself kept in solitary confinement for up to six months at a time, and was allowed no more than ten minutes a day out of his cell to clear his bowels. Locked in cells with bright fluorescent lights that were permanently switched on, detainees often lost track of time, suffered from sensory deprivation and found it impossible to sleep. Some were kept in ice-cold cells, while others were in "small cells that were very hot because there was no window – only one small outlet at the top". According to Poh, the PPSO allowed detention without trial for "only" a period of one month. To circumvent this rule, many detainees were "brought out in a police car, told to put one foot on the ground, and promptly told, 'Now, I'm re-arresting you'". This illustrates what Poh describes as the worst form of torture: the prolonged, indefinite length of detention. "Even convicted criminals have a better time because they know when they will be released," he mused. "In this case, we [had] no idea".

In 1980, Amnesty International released a report detailing a 1978 mission to Singapore. The report corroborates Poh's accounts of torture and mistreatment, further alleging that one detainee was assaulted and forced to pour his own urine over himself (Amnesty International 1980). The report also details the various medical conditions detainees suffered as a result of their mistreatment, and how many went on hunger strikes in protest of their conditions. Poh describes in vivid detail how hunger strikes led to force-feeding, and "when

[one] victim vomited, the prison guards used her as a mop to clean up the vomit". The government dismissed these allegations as "baseless", stating that Amnesty International was "merely repeating misleading reports" by detainees (*The Straits Times* 1980).[16] Back in the 1960s, the public knew little of these horrible abuses. Detainees, during rarely allowed family visits, were strictly banned from talking about conditions in prison, said Poh. Doing so would bring an immediate end to such visits.

David Marshall brings matters into the public sphere

Sometime after Operation Coldstore, hints of the abuse of PPSO detainees surfaced after lawyers were finally allowed to meet their detained clients. Learning of this, Singapore's first Chief Minister and then-Member of Parliament for Anson, David Marshall, took it upon himself to investigate the situation. On 11 March 1963, David Marshall wrote to the Minister of Home Affairs, Ong Pang Boon, about the "number of citizens deeply perturbed by rumours as to the conditions of detention of detainees". Marshall (1963a) sought verification of these rumours by requesting Ong to inform him about the actual conditions in prison. In his letter, Marshall expressed his astonishment that detainees were denied access to their lawyers for more than a month after being detained. Three days later, Marshall wrote to the Solicitor-General of the State-Advocate-General's Chambers to address the "inhumane conditions existing in respect of detainees" (Marshall 1963f). Marshall implored the Solicitor-General to "take urgent steps to ascertain the truth [...] to make such representations as your humanity and sense of decency call for".

Days later, Marshall wrote once again to Ong to express his unhappiness, claiming that he had received confirmation that the rumours of torture were true. "I believe that you are perhaps not conscious that the horrors of cold-blooded cruelty directed towards human beings have long-term repercussions," wrote Marshall (1963b), warning that he (Marshall) would be "forced to make a major political issue out of the inhuman treatment of detainees" should conditions not be improved. Marshall (1963c) later made a formal request to the Commissioner of Prisons to visit Outram Road Prison to personally meet and examine the condition of detainees.

Upon inspecting Outram Road Prison, Marshall (1963d) produced a Report on Conditions of Detention of PPSO Detainees. Among the various violations and abuses, Marshall reported how "the heat in each cell was oppressive [...] this is particularly so when the cell door is locked and remains locked for 23 hours and 15 minutes in every day". Moreover, detainees were denied their rights to talk, to sing and to any belongings. Marshall concluded that the conditions for detention were radically worse than any conditions imposed by previous governments. Outraged at this predicament, Marshall seemed to take it upon himself to alleviate the plight of the detainees. Two days after his visit, he wrote to the Commissioner of Prisons to request permission to forward books, dictionaries, chess sets and puzzles to the detainees – paid for with his own money (Marshall 1963e). David Marshall's visit to Outram Road Prison, as well as his report on the inhuman conditions that detainees were under, made it into *The Straits Times* (1963a) on 25 March, finally bringing matters into the public sphere.

Public outrage was, however, largely restricted to the Barisan Sosialis and relatives of the detainees. Apart from these two groups of people, no record or evidence of responses against the mistreatment of detainees can be found. Dr Lee Siew Choh, then-Chairman of the Barisan Sosialis, expressed his shock at the treatment of detainees. Lee dismissed the government's claim that solitary confinement was a necessity as "nonsense", and compared their predicament to criminals – concluding that criminals were better treated (*The Straits Times* 1963b). Barisan's activism against the inhumane conditions culminated in the April 22 procession of relatives and party members, a march from Barisan headquarters in Victoria Street to City Hall dubbed the "City Hall Battle". The aim of the march was to persuade the government to bring about changes to the conditions of detainees (*The Straits Times* 1963c). The procession, deemed a protest by the government and hence illegal, was put down with seven party members arrested (*The Straits Times* 1963b). Such activism, incorporating the work done by David Marshall, is rare and ultimately demonstrates precious instances of non-detainees speaking out against the terrible conditions detainees suffered while imprisoned under the PPSO in the 1960s.

The government responds to international pressure

In 1963, when David Marshall first raised the issue of the abuse of detainees, the Singapore government responded in a manner described by Marshall (1963g) as a "not unexpected reply combining abuse, slimy innuendo and falsehood". In its initial response, the government effectively dismissed Marshall's claims of torture as "fanciful". It concluded that Marshall had "got his facts wrong" and argued that "had Mr. Marshall, when he was Chief Minister, manifested the same passionate concern he now shows […] detainees could today be accommodated in more congenial cells" (Singapore Government 1963).

The government only properly responded to the allegations when the Honorary Secretary of Amnesty International, Peter Benenson, wrote to then-Prime Minister of Singapore Lee Kuan Yew, demanding answers for the systemic abuse of detainees. Benenson (1963a) asked that the government allow a delegate of the International Committee of the Red Cross (ICRC) to inspect prisons in Singapore. Benenson (1963b) later wrote to Marshall that failure of the Singapore government to respond would prompt Amnesty International to release a copy of their letter to the London office of *The Straits Times*. Facing the prospect of international condemnation, the Singapore government agreed to allow the ICRC access to inspect local prisons. The delegation visited Singapore on 15 May 1963. With this visit, Marshall (1963e) observed that "there has been some amelioration […] detainees are allowed to receive books" and that in the next few months, "conditions would be immeasurably improved".

In the face of such international scrutiny and pressure, then-Prime Minister Lee Kuan Yew made the decision to end solitary confinement, stating, "it will end as soon as possible" (*The Malay Mail* 1963). He gave this assurance to the British Colonial and Commonwealth Secretary, Duncan Sands. Managing to elicit such a response from the Singapore government was a milestone in human rights activism. That external, international parties were allowed into local prisons to investigate the conditions and detainees, coupled with the fact that conditions had indeed improved, is testament to the efforts and activism of David Marshall.

1970s to 1980s: Operation Spectrum and the activism of victims

Teo Soh Lung's *Beyond The Blue Gate* (2011) describes how detainees of the ISA in the 1987 Operation Spectrum suffered under similar conditions as their predecessors of the 1960s. A detainee herself, Teo (2011) was subjected to "harsh and intensive interrogation, deprived of sleep and rest [...] for as long as 70 hours inside freezing cold rooms". Detainees were slapped, taunted, doused repeatedly with cold water, and were made to stand continuously for over 20 hours. In an interview with Teo, she recounted how, when finally allowed to sit, she was provided with "three-legged chairs".[17] This was done as a form of psychological torture, which made it impossible for detainees to sit comfortably, fall asleep or even rest.[18] At this time, however, there was no individual like David Marshall to fight for their rights; the victims had to become their own advocates.

Victims-turned-activists

On 18 April 1988, nine ex-detainees released a joint statement denouncing government accusations against them and detailing the abuses they had suffered (*The Straits Times* 1988a). Similar to the governmental response to the Barisan march of 1963, these individuals were promptly re-arrested the following day, putting an end to their short-lived act of activism. Nonetheless, this succeeded in providing the public with a glimpse into state brutality, prompting some debate among Singaporeans on the need to protect the rights of detainees (*The Straits Times* 1988b).

Dismissed by the government

Responding to the 1987 joint statement released by the ex-detainees of Operation Spectrum, then-Member of Parliament Dr Ow Chin Hock expressed his disappointment at Singaporeans who wished to discuss the need to protect detainees' rights. He claimed that such individuals "had benefited from the system, yet do not value the prosperity and stability that we have achieved" and had "undermined the credibility of the government, misled the people and weakened Singapore's defence" (*The Straits Times* 1988b). In her book, Teo Soh Lung (2011) recounts that when asked about the "serious allegations" of ill-treatment of detainees, then-Minister for Trade and Industry Lee Hsien Loong replied, "It is not true that we ill-treat people [...] where is the evidence? There can be none". Similar to the government's response to the work of David Marshall in the 1960s and to the Amnesty International report in 1980, a trend of governmental dismissiveness may be observed. In fact, one feature of the government was found to be its frequent refusal to engage advocates and victims in dialogues and discussions. Moreover, the government was quick to counter not only allegations and statements, but also the credibility of individuals.

It was only in 2012 that a public event was finally held (and allowed by the government) to shed light on Operation Spectrum. Human rights organisations MARUAH and Function 8 (founded by former ISA detainees) organised an event at Hong Lim Park to commemorate the twenty-fifth anniversary of Operation Spectrum. The event attracted more than 400 people, and featured exhibits of detention cells, interrogation rooms, as well as vivid descriptions of the conditions detainees were put through (Boey 2012). The event was educational in nature, and was targeted at the youth of Singapore. After the first cases of state brutality some 50 years past, it was the first of its kind.

1980s to the present: state violence against migrant workers

SMRT bus drivers' strike

On 26 November 2012, 171 SMRT bus drivers went on strike to protest against mistreatment by their employers. It was classified as an "illegal strike" by then-Acting Minister for Manpower Tan Chuan-Jin, and five drivers were subsequently charged under the Criminal Law (Temporary Provisions) Act (Xinlin 2013).[19] Lynn Lee, a local filmmaker, interviewed the workers who were arrested and published their interviews on her website. Two of the workers arrested alleged that they were abused by the police (Xinlin 2013). One worker alleged that he was punched in the stomach, interrogated for eight hours and locked in a small room. Moreover, he witnessed his colleague being slapped many times and stated that his colleague suffered more than him. Another worker alleged that the police hit him so hard that others "could hear the sound". He claimed that the officer interrogating him said, "Do you know I can dig a hole and bury you? No one will be able to find you. I have ways to make you talk. I have ways to make you confess".[20]

Little India riots

On 8 December 2013, angry mobs attacked a bus and emergency vehicles in Little India. This was Singapore's first riot in over 40 years. As a result of the riot, measures such as increased police presence and alcohol restrictions were implemented in Little India to prevent a repeat of such unrest (Sim 2015). A four-member Commission of Inquiry led by former Supreme Court Judge

Govinda Pannir Selvam was appointed by Deputy Prime Minister and then-Minister for Home Affairs Teo Chee Hean (Sim 2015). Twenty-five people were charged in relation to the riots while another 57 were deported (Committee of Inquiry 2014). Three workers later alleged that the police had assaulted them during interrogations.

The only known and prominent activism came from Madasamy Ravi (M. Ravi), a human rights lawyer. He filed a complaint on behalf of the three workers, detailing the abuses that they were put through, and attempted to fight their case (Ravi 2014). According to the complaint, one worker claimed that "he was forcefully grabbed by the neck" and "continuously called derogatory names by Tamil-speaking police officers". Further, an officer threatened to lock him up for 48 hours without any valid reason. He was denied use of the washroom and was forced to wait an entire hour before he could relieve himself. Numerous police officers punched and slapped him during and after his interrogation.

In the same complaint, another worker alleged that he was forced to remove his shirt and undershirt, following which he was made to kneel on the floor and forced to admit his involvement in the riots. The officer "then poured a bottle of cold water over him and lowered the temperature in the room" and "used the bottle to whack him on the head" (Ravi 2014). The third worker stated that he was slapped four to five times, even before the police started interrogating him. All three were threatened that they would be "sent home in body bags" (Ravi 2014).

Government responses

Lynn Lee was investigated for contempt of court after publishing interviews with the SMRT workers. She spent a total of 13 hours under interrogation, during which time the police took apart her laptop, mobile and hard disk. She said:

> I started wondering seriously if I, rather than the alleged perpetrators, was the one being investigated. Were they trying to establish if I had somehow manufactured the allegations? Or that I had worked with He and Liu's lawyers and various NGOs to fabricate things?[21]

According to Lee, the officer sent to confiscate her electronic devices was not from the Internal Affairs Office (IAO) (which is supposed to work independently), but from the Bedok Police Station. Furthermore, she was told that the IAO was investigating the claims made by ex-SMRT drivers but she says she was asked many irrelevant questions.

In contrast, Jolovan Wham experiences the lack of interest and attention given by the government to reported cases of torture. His NGO, the Humanitarian Organisation for Migration Economics (HOME), which advocates for the rights of migrant workers, has received about eight or ten complaints of mistreatment by Immigration and Checkpoints Authority (ICA) officers in the past five years. Usually anecdotal, he claims that the abuse generally consists of slapping and punching carried out during interrogation or questioning, although these attacks are not severe enough to leave visible injuries.[22] Officers from the Ministry of Manpower are also known to use verbal abuse, as he highlights one known case of a shoe that was thrown at a migrant worker. However, when he raises these cases to the authorities, Wham says that they are sometimes confronted by "disinterested officers", and "while there are state mechanisms to address this, these mechanisms are usually unreliable and not credible because they are not independent".[23]

Constraints, external

Human rights activists and NGOs in Singapore face many obstacles in their bid to speak out against torture and inhuman treatment in Singapore. Every activist we have spoken to highlights the actions of the government and socio-cultural norms in Singapore as impediments. These, coupled with the psychology of victims, make it extremely difficult to initiate comprehensive activism against such violations. This chapter considers such factors as being beyond the direct control of activists, and representative of factors limiting the human rights movement in Singapore. Within civil society, many considerations also make it challenging for activists. These factors are constituted of various inter- and intra-NGO constraints.

Caning as an 'essential feature' of the justice system

In places like England, the recommendation to abolish corporal punishment was strongly backed by the lack of evidence that caning constituted a unique deterrent (Departmental Committee on Corporal Punishment 1938). However, in Singapore, the converse seems to be happening. The government insists adamantly that caning plays a unique, irreplaceable role in Singapore's criminal justice system as a more effective deterrent than other sanctions like imprisonment. For example, in arguing for the imposition of caning for the offence of vandalism, former Prime Minister Lee Kuan Yew opined,

> the offender is quite prepared to make a martyr of himself and go to the goal. [...] But if he knows he is going to get three of the best, I think he will lose a great deal of enthusiasm.
> (Parliament of Singapore 1966)

Similar sentiments evolved in arguing for the imposition of caning to alleviate the problem of illegal workers in Singapore. Then-Minister for Trade and Industry, Lee Hsien Loong, asserted that imprisonment was not a viable sanction as the illegal workers enjoyed staying in jail where they were clothed, fed and looked after in comfort. He believed in the solution of caning (Parliament of Singapore 1989a). By arguing for caning as such, the state has generated a strong public consensus that specific offences and offenders deserve the harsh punishment of caning. This consensus was clearly illustrated by the overwhelming public support to cane rash motorists (*The Straits Times* 1992).

However, it should be noted that the reasoning the legislature traditionally relies on is superficial and often ignores the underlying root causes of crime. The incidence of crime is a complex sociological problem caused by many factors, including economic hardship, unemployment and minority disenfranchisement. Simply instilling harsher punishments is ineffective in sustainably resolving social issues. At the start of 2015, *The Straits Times* (2015) reported that the recidivism rate in Singapore had reached a nine-year high. This suggests that simply implementing unforgiving punishments is not enough to tackle crime in the long run.

Furthermore, the legislature has, at times, generalised statistics and data to support its claims. For example, after the Immigration (Amendment) Bill was passed, making caning mandatory for undocumented immigrants and over-stayers, more than 10,000 undocumented workers voluntarily surrendered to the authorities before the sanctions came into effect (Parliament of Singapore 1989b). This statistic was then used in Parliament by then-Minister for Home Affairs Dr Shunmugam Jayakumar to enhance the Immigration (Amendment) Bill to include mandatory caning for more groups of people (Parliament of Singapore 1989b).

The state, culture and victims

Activists see the state as the main actor responsible for torture in Singapore. According to activists, four main effects of the state impede activism in this field: (1) strict legislation and interpretation of the Constitution; (2) a sense of fear induced by various methods, including the Internal Security Act; (3) secrecy over evidence and documents, and (4) inadequate attention towards claims.

Strict legislation and interpretation of the Constitution

Singapore's constitutional rights – specifically Article 14(1) – allow Singaporeans the right to freedom of speech and expression, the right to assemble peaceably and without arms, and the right to form associations – subject to Parliament's imposition of restrictions as necessary for the interests of the security of Singapore, its relations with other countries, public order or morality.[24]

However, activists find themselves limited by the Miscellaneous Offences Rules which state that a permit must be granted for "any assembly or procession of five or more persons in any public road, public place or place of public resort intended –

a to demonstrate support for or opposition to the views or actions of any person;

b   to publicise a cause or campaign; or
c   to mark or commemorate any event".[25]

Along with this, the Public Entertainments and Meetings Act clearly states that no public entertainment shall be provided except –

a   in an approved place; and
b   in accordance with a licence issued by the appropriate Licensing Officer.[26]

Thus, activists are limited to campaigning at the Speakers' Corner, before which they are required to register their intentions with the police.

Fear and secrecy

The risk of arbitrary detention continues to deter activists today; many cite Operation Coldstore and Operation Spectrum as sources of a real sense of fear. Further, activist and socio-political blogger Martyn See also suggests that there is "unseen pressure from the government to not let civil society unite".[27] This is done through "warnings [given] to leaders to cut funding", and "whispering campaigns".

Activist Sinapan Samydorai from the human rights organisation Think Centre held that in the past, "[the government] didn't want people to mention human rights", "they will take you in".[28] Ex-political detainee Dr Poh Soo Kai also mentions that additional fears stem from bankruptcy due to governmental lawsuits.[29]

Activists are also faced with the challenge of obtaining and examining evidence. According to Wham, it is difficult to "challenge the establishment [when it is] shrouded in secrecy – documents classified under the premises of 'national security', or under the Official Secrets Act [makes things difficult to prove]".[30]

Inadequate attention towards claims

As revealed in the specific contexts above, the attitude of dismissiveness by the government underscores ignorance, apathy, or even approval of such treatment in Singapore. It is an obstacle that activists have to regularly navigate through, and a fundamental reason for the lack of activism in Singapore.

Normalisation

Another issue commonly raised is that of the general public's 'normalisation' towards torture and caning, especially caning. Because caning is familiar to Asian culture and households, and is carried out early in institutions of primary education, many in Singapore are not opposed to the idea of caning. Instead, many are desensitised to the brutality behind caning, viewing state-sanctioned caning as a natural progression from the less traumatic versions conducted in schools or homes.

Samydorai asserts that "the community itself doesn't campaign against it", and because Singapore has its roots as a migrant country, violent practices, including those of corporal punishment, were brought in from various ethnic cultures and assimilated into our current society.[31] See concurs that regarding torture and caning, there is "not a rampant feeling amongst the public", and that there is "little noise" because the public probably think that "they deserve it".[32] Zeng also attributes this "docile society" to the "internalisation of moral norms".[33]

Psychology of victims

Activists also mention that activism is hindered by the perspectives of victims towards the treatment. In the case of migrant workers, victims themselves sometimes "don't want the hassle", offers Wham. This leads inadvertently to a "personal normalisation" which stems from an erroneous belief that "it is the same, or even worse, in my own country", and that "if my employer can do anything to me, what more the state?" Eventually, this develops into a vicious cycle, resulting in a permanent "culture of disempowerment".[34]

Moreover, when asked about the difficulties former PPSO or ISA detainees faced in speaking out against their mistreatment, Poh offers a compelling reason: the fear of facing their peers. Due to the harsh methods of interrogation, detainees often caved in to forced confessions that implicated others. "They want you to say things about your friends that are not true. That is where they have a hold over you", said Poh. He continued:

> And when they come out, they feel bad. They can't talk to their friends [...] and that is one of the worst things that most detainees suffer from [...] they keep quiet, they dare not talk [...] not that they have told anything wrong, but they have said something about their friends which is not true and they feel it.[35]

Finally, victims of torture sometimes fail to see themselves as having been abused. Poh, for one, did not initially consider solitary confinement a form of torture as, in his own words, "I can take it".[36]

Constraints, internal

Intra-NGO constraints

Within NGOs, activists point to several limitations that inhibit advocacy against torture and caning. These include a lack of resources within civil society itself, as well as the priority of other 'more pressing' human rights issues to tackle. Already, NGOs and activists operate with limited budgets, manpower and support. Martyn See reasons that many activists have "bigger fish to fry".[37] In other words, they have to tackle issues that are deemed 'more important', issues that resonate more with the public. As such, activists have to be strategic in choosing their battles, as "it doesn't make sense to spend a disproportionate amount of time on things that will gain less traction". This appears to be a direct response of activists to the culture in Singapore under which they operate.

This is a stand with which Wham concurs. He claims the need to "prioritise time and resources", and that it was fundamentally "an issue of resources".[38] Wham claims that HOME would support and contribute to a campaign against caning, but would be unable to lead it due to the strain on its resources, as it has its own campaigns and everyday dealings in migrant workers' rights with which to contend. Rachel Zeng, who attempted a campaign against judicial caning in recent years, further conceded that torture is presently "not on the agenda at all – [and] instead subsumed as a small point under more major points".[39]

Inter-NGO constraints

Individuals we spoke to were also keen to point out that being "an activist does not equate to being a *human rights* activist", nor does being one equate to being a democracy activist, or one who campaigns for transparency.[40] To illustrate this point, Zeng and Wham discussed the clashing interests and goals within civil society. They offered that animal rights activists, for instance, would wish to see animal abusers caned for their transgressions. As a result, it was often difficult to gather traction from within the community of NGOs and activists, much less from the general population. Wham explains:

> Not everyone is rights-based […]. A lot of people are pro-caning. Animal welfare groups, when they hear of animal abusers, they will say "Cane them!" We hear it all the time.[41]

Conclusion: the way forward

Fundamentally, there has been a strong consensus among activists that education and knowledge of human and constitutional rights are a large part of the solution. Activists believe that there is a lack of education on the basic constitutional rights accorded to each Singaporean citizen,[42] which leads to a "blind submission to authority".[43] Martyn See sees this as a problem, since "[the] government doesn't pay attention to [international] human rights norms".[44] Currently, only students at the tertiary level have the opportunity to learn about and discuss constitutional rights. Activists believe that this is too late a stage, and that education should be given from as early as primary school level. One act of resistance by the state is labelling organisations as 'political associations'. NGOs labelled as such are reportedly limited in their avenues to conduct public education. According to Samydorai, "you can't even talk about it in public – not on the radio, television, newspaper, etc".[45] Activists believe that there should be more freedom in according such education, and consequently instilling a greater public knowledge of the matter.

Furthermore, activists also feel that an effective route for change in Singapore lies in that of applying external pressure. Samydorai suggests that the key to evoke change would be for human rights activists in Singapore to work with international actors. Pressure from the international community has also worked as an effective method for a country that is particularly concerned with maintaining its image and relations with the rest of the world. One such way would be through the submission of shadow reports for international reports like the Universal Periodic Review (UPR). This is no longer counted by the state as 'subversive', and has evidently worked as a method of persuasion on controversial issues in the past.

Notwithstanding these challenges, activists also recognise the process of change that is occurring with time. There are now more spaces, and leeway granted, to opposing voices. For example, a recent Detention–Writing–Healing forum held in 2006 saw the sharing of prison experiences by two ex-political detainees Michael Fernandez and Tan Jing Quee, openly presented by the theatre company The Necessary Stage (S/PORES 2009). Thus, while activists continue to dispute current realities in Singapore, it is certain that the future does hold significant promise for a nation that is admittedly young, and only just beginning to see itself in the mirror.

Notes

1 The authors would like to thank Ted Tan, Soe Min Than and Nicholas Harrigan for providing useful comments on primary sources for interviews, government documents and NGO reports.
2 UN General Assembly (1948). Universal Declaration of Human Rights, 10 December 1948, 217 A (III). Available at www.un.org/en/universal-declaration-human-rights/index.html.
3 UN General Assembly (1966). International Covenant on Civil and Political Rights, 16 December 1966, United Nations, Treaty Series, vol. 999, p. 171. Available at www.ohchr.org/en/professionalinterest/pages/ccpr.aspx.
4 UN General Assembly (1984). Convention Against Torture and Other Cruel, Inhuman or Degrading Treatment or Punishment, 10 December 1984, United Nations, Treaty Series, vol. 1465, p. 85. Available at www.ohchr.org/EN/Professional Interest/Pages/CAT.aspx.
5 Association of Southeast Asian Nations, ASEAN Human Rights Declaration, 12 November 2012, 8.
6 Association of Southeast Asian Nations, ASEAN Human Rights Declaration, 12 November 2012, 14.
7 Yong Vui Kong vs. Public Prosecutor (2015) 2 SLR 1129 (Court of Appeal, 4 March 2015).
8 Criminal Justice Act (Cap 58, 1948) s 2 (United Kingdom).
9 Abolition of Whipping Act 1955 (No. 44 of 1955) (India).
10 Personal interview, Rachel Zeng, 21 September 2015, Singapore.
11 Yong Vui Kong vs. Public Prosecutor (2015) 2 SLR 1129 (Court of Appeal, 4 March 2015).

12 "Caning – What it means when a court orders" (1974) 2 MLJ: xxiv.
13 *Yong Vui Kong* v. *Public Prosecutor* (2015) 2 SLR 1129 (Court of Appeal, 4 March 2015).
14 The Preservation of Public Security Ordinance allows for individual detentions without trials. Having expired in 1963, it has been succeeded by the Internal Security Act.
15 Personal interview, Poh Soo Kai, 9 September 2015, Singapore.
16 As this chapter will go on to show, such responses were hardly atypical of the government, and it was not the first time that the government had acted in this manner – even individuals such as David Marshall were subjected to harsh dismissals.
17 Personal interview, Teo Soh Lung, 1 October 2015, Singapore.
18 Personal interview, Teo Soh Lung, 1 October 2015, Singapore.
19 The Criminal Law (Temporary Provisions) Act allows for suspected criminals to be detained without trial for any period not exceeding one year.
20 L. Lee (2013). "I have ways to make you confess". Lianain Films. Available at www.lianainfilms.com/2013/01/i-have-ways-to-make-you-confess/.
21 L. Lee (2013). "In which Lim makes me Kopi at the Internal Affairs Office". Lianain Films. Available at www.lianainfilms.com/2013/02/in-which-lim-makes-me-kopi-at-the-internal-affairs-office/.
22 Personal interview, Jolovan Wham, 25 September 2015, Singapore.
23 Ibid.
24 Constitution of the Republic of Singapore (1999 Reprint) Article 14(1).
25 Miscellaneous Offences (Public Order and Nuisance) Act (Cap 184, 2000 rev. edn) s 2(1).
26 Public Entertainments and Meetings Act (Cap 257, 2001 rev. edn) s 3(b).
27 Personal interview, Martyn See, 2 October 2015, Singapore.
28 Personal interview, Sinapan Samydorai, 28 September 2015, Singapore.
29 Personal interview, Poh Soo Kai, 9 September 2015, Singapore.
30 Personal interview, Jolovan Wham, 25 September 2015, Singapore.
31 Personal interview, Sinapan Samydorai, 28 September 2015, Singapore.
32 Personal interview, Martyn See, 2 October 2015, Singapore.
33 Personal interview, Rachel Zeng, 21 September 2015, Singapore.
34 Personal interview, Jolovan Wham, 25 September 2015, Singapore.
35 Personal interview, Poh Soo Kai, 9 September 2015, Singapore.
36 Ibid.
37 Personal interview, Martyn See Tong Ming, 2 October 2015, Singapore.
38 Personal interview, Jolovan Wham, 25 September 2015, Singapore.
39 Personal interview, Rachel Zeng, 21 September 2015, Singapore.
40 Personal interview, Jolovan Wham, 25 September 2015, Singapore.
41 Personal interview, Rachel Zeng, 21 September 2015, Singapore.
42 Personal interview, Sinapan Samydorai, 28 September 2015, Singapore.
43 Personal interview, Rachel Zeng, 21 September 2015, Singapore.
44 Personal interview, Martyn See Tong Ming, 2 October 2015, Singapore.
45 Personal interview, Sinapan Samydorai, 28 September 2015, Singapore.

References

Amnesty International (1980). *Report Of An Amnesty International Mission To Singapore 1978*. Amnesty International.

Benenson, P. (1963a). Personal letter to the Prime Minister of Singapore, regarding systemic ill-treatment of detainees, 12 March.

Benenson, P. (1963b). Personal letter to David Marshall, regarding AI's letter to Singapore Government, 1 April.

Boey, E. (2012). "Over 400 people mark 25th anniversary of ISA arrests". *Yahoo! News*.
Chan, W.C. (1993). "Fundamental liberties in Singapore". *Commentary* 11(2): 25–32.
Committee of Inquiry (2014). Report of the Committee of Inquiry into the Little India riot on 8 December 2013. Ministry of Home Affairs, Committee of Inquiry: 57.
Departmental Committee on Corporal Punishment (1938). Report of the Departmental Committee on Corporal Punishment, England (1938): 68.
Jayakumar, S. (1987). Singapore Parliamentary Debates, Official Report (29 July 1987), vol. 49 at cols 1491–1492 (Professor S. Jayakumar, Minister for Home Affairs).
Marshall, D. (1963a). Personal letter to the Minister of Home Affairs of Singapore, in response to rumours as to the conditions of detention of detainees. Ministry of Home Affairs, ISEAS, 11 March.
Marshall, D. (1963b). Personal letter to the Minister of Home Affairs of Singapore, expressing his unhappiness and warning of political action. Ministry of Home Affairs, 15 March.
Marshall, D. (1963c). Personal letter to the Commissioner of Prisons, requesting a visit to Outram Road Prison. Commissioner of Prisons, 16 March.
Marshall, D. (1963d). *Report on Conditions of Detention of PPSO Detainees in Outram Prison*.
Marshall, D. (1963e). Personal letter to the Commissioner of Prisons to forward items to detainees. Commissioner of Prisons, 25 March.
Marshall, D. (1963f). Personal letter to Peter Benenson, regarding ICRC access and improved conditions. P. Benenson, 9 April.
Marshall, D. (1963g). Personal letter to the Editor of *The Straits Times* in response to government press release, 26 March.
Marshall, D. (1993). Personal letter to the Editor of the Malayan Law Journal, regarding caning, 4 November.
Parliament of Singapore (1966). "Punishment for Vandalism Bill". Parliamentary Debates of Singapore, 26 August.
Parliament of Singapore (1989a). "Immigration (Amendment) Bill". Parliamentary Debates of Singapore, 26 January, at col. 618.
Parliament of Singapore (1989b). "Immigration (Amendment No. 2) Bill". Parliamentary Debates of Singapore, 31 August, at col. 512.
Raman, P. (1974). "Branding the bad hats for life". *The Straits Times*.
Ravi, M. (2014). "Allegations of assault by members of the police force". S.P.F. Internal Affairs Office.
S/PORES (2009). *A Public Oral History of the Singapore Left in 2006*.
Shenon, P. (1995). "David Marshall, 87, opponent of Singapore authoritarianism". *New York Times*.
Sim, C. (2015). Little India riot. *Singapore Infopedia*.
Singapore Government (1963). Statement by The Singapore government on conditions of political detainees in Outram Road Prison.
Teo, S.L. (2011). *Beyond The Blue Gate. Recollections of a Political Prisoner*. Singapore: Function 8.
The Malay Mail (1963). "Discussions on solitary confinement – Assurance by Lee". *The Malay Mail*, 1 May.
The Straits Times (1963a). "Marshall hits at detainee conditions". *The Straits Times*.
The Straits Times (1963b). "Shocking, says Barisan leader". *The Straits Times*.
The Straits Times (1963c). "Unlawful exercise of power against detainees' claims QC". *The Straits Times*.

The Straits Times (1974). "Caning and the death penalty". *The Straits Times*.
The Straits Times (1980). "Amnesty's torture, assault charges 'baseless'". *The Straits Times*.
The Straits Times (1988a). "9 ex-detainees deny being involved in Marxist plot". *The Straits Times*.
The Straits Times (1988b). "Some still harping on need to protect rights of detainees". *The Straits Times*.
The Straits Times (1992). "All approve of jail and cane: 'It will deter rash motorists'". *The Straits Times*.
*The Straits Times*s (1994). "Fay's caning 'not a human rights issue'". *The Straits Times*.
The Straits Times (2015). "Prison service sees highest recidivism rate in nine years". *The Straits Times*.
World Corporal Punishment Research (2011). "Singapore: Judical and prison caning; Table of offences for which caning is available". World Corporal Punishment Research. Available at www.corpun.com/sgjur2.htm.
World Corporal Punishment Research (2012). "Judicial caning In Singapore, Malaysia and Brunei. Corporal Punishment Research. Available at www.corpun.com/singfeat.htm.
Xinlin (2013). "SMRT drivers' strike – A stand for dignity". Available at https://twc2.org.sg/2013/03/31/smrt-drivers-strike-a-stand-for-dignity/.

3 Singapore's press for freedom
Between media regulation and activism

Howard Lee and Ana Ansari[1]

Introduction

In 2015, Reporters San Frontieres' World Press Freedom Index[2] ranked Singapore 153rd among 180 countries and regions, below countries like Myanmar, the Philippines, the Russian Federation and Afghanistan (Reporters Without Borders 2015). On the surface, it seems curious that Singapore would rank below countries where incarceration and death are among journalists' occupational hazards. However, journalists' safety is just one of the components of the index; countries are also evaluated on media pluralism, independence, self-censorship and legislative frameworks, among other things (Reporters Without Borders 2015) – it is likely that Singapore's performance on these factors has earned it this abysmal ranking in the index.

From the outset, it would be hard to fault Singapore for any direct infringement of international standards. Article 14 of Singapore's Constitution,[3] governing freedom of speech, assembly and association, is congruent with both Article 9 of the Universal Declaration of Human Rights (UDHR)[4] and Article 19 of the International Convention for Civil and Political Rights (ICCPR).[5] The provisions for freedom of speech specify restrictions in the interest of the "security of Singapore or any part thereof, friendly relations with other countries, public order or morality and restrictions designed to protect the privileges of Parliament or to provide against contempt of court, defamation or incitement to any offence".[6]

However, these provisions have long been used to justify action against dissenting voices. The suppression of the press has been exercised in different forms: (1) the tightening of media regulations; (2) the imposition of direct punitive measures, and (3) direct interference by the government. The result of this is Singapore's press environment today – monopolistic, controlled and highly self-censored.

Under the Newspaper and Printing Presses Act (NPPA) and the Broadcasting Act, the ownership, funding, sales and distribution of all media outlets are regulated. As a result of media crackdowns over the years, just two media organisations own all of the local newspapers and local broadcast stations. There are no independent print publications – all of Singapore's alternative news media exists online, and even these outlets are subject to strict regulation.

Journalists, bloggers and other individuals or organisations critical of the government and its policies face the threat of punitive measures, either in the form of monetary fines or jail terms. An arsenal of legislative tools such as the country's strict defamation, sedition and contempt of the court laws are all actively enforced.

The struggle for the control of the press has long preceded Singapore's status as an autonomous state, and is an important aspect of its political history. Over the past 50 years, many journalists and concerned citizens – media freedom activists – have fought against these laws and regulations. Activism has taken place in various ways and forms – through bold editorials, union strikes and demonstrations, organised rallies, and through the defence and support of those persecuted for expressing themselves.

This chapter details the history of press freedom activism in Singapore, and how this activism has evolved with the changing media landscape and regulations over the past 50 years. The chapter begins with an introduction to Singapore's press, pre-independence. It then goes on to explore the government's crackdown on and shaping of the media between the 1970s and the 1990s and the resultant lack of activism by members of the press. Finally, it examines the rise of new media – and how it influenced a new brand of activism, which has been challenged by new regulations by a government struggling to adapt. We conclude with a look at the future of media freedom activism in Singapore – and the reality that this future may not be so bright.

Pre-independence activism

The press environment in Singapore was starkly different during the post-war British rule compared to what it is today. It was vibrant and competitive, made up of multiple student journals, union publications and newspapers in the nation's official languages[7] (Seow 1998). One could pick up newspapers such as *Utusan Melayu* (published in Malay), *Nanyang Siang Pau* and *Sin Chew Jit Poh* (both published in Chinese), or the *Singapore Herald* (published in English). There were more independent and politically minded student-run journals like *Fajar* by the Socialist Club at the University of Malaya.

But the government was wary of the press. In 1959, prior to Singapore's independence, the People's Action Party (PAP), led by Lee Kuan Yew, warned journalists and editors through rally speeches against trying to "sour up or strain relations with the Federation [of Malaya] and Singapore" (*The Straits Times* 2015a). The PAP could take action against any guilty person under the Preservation of Public Security Ordinance (PPSO) (Hoffman 1959c).[8]

On 20 May 1959, then editor-in-chief of *The Strait Times*, Leslie Hoffman (1959c), responded to Lee's statement with a front-page editorial entitled "Think again, Mr Lee". That editorial was just one in a series of rebuttals published by Hoffman (Hoffman 1959a, 1959b),[9] a Eurasian journalist who would be editor-in-chief of *The Straits Times* for 14 years. He drew a parallel between the PAP's approach to the press and that of the Japanese during the

Occupation, pointing out the hypocrisy of Lee's threat to invoke the PPSO when he himself had opposed it in Parliament, and urging Lee to "choose between democracy and totalitarianism" (Hoffman 1959c).[10] Eventually, Hoffman reached out to the International Press Institute (IPI) for support.

In response, the IPI made the PAP's threats against *The Straits Times* a part of the discussion agenda at their general assembly (*The Straits Times* 1959a) and sent an "impartial observer" to Singapore to investigate the situation. Armand Gaspard, a Swiss journalist, spoke alongside Leslie Hoffman at the University of Malaya Socialist Club's forum on press freedom, warning that a loss of press freedom would be the "start of totalitarianism" (*The Straits Times* 1959b).

The intervention was the first of a few attempts by the IPI over the years to address press freedom in Singapore. This attempt concluded when the IPI determined that both parties – Hoffman and the PAP – were "overreacting" (*The Straits Times* 2015a). Later, Hoffman moved *The Straits Times* head offices to Kuala Lumpur, out of the reach of the PAP after their victory at the 1959 General Elections (*The Straits Times* 2015c). Hoffman, who had championed the free press in Singapore since the Japanese Occupation,[11] would not return for the remainder of his career.

During his career as a journalist in Singapore, Hoffman was one of the foremost advocates of press freedom in Malaya, alongside others such as David Marshall and Said Zahari. Marshall, Singapore's first Chief Minister and a lawyer, would defend journalists in court against charges from the government and engaged international human rights organisations such as Amnesty International over Singapore's press freedom standards. Zahari, a former editor of *Utusan Melayu*, once led a 91-day strike for editorial independence, protesting UMNO's takeover of the newspaper (The Straits Times 1961). When Operation Coldstore took place in 1963, Zahari was one of the journalists among the 113 detainees accused of communist activity.[12] He would spend 17 years behind bars under the Internal Security Act.

Post-independence, early activism and the anti-communist movement: 1965 to 1971

The crackdown on publications and members of the press continued after Singapore gained independence. In 1965, the Malay-language publication *Utusan Melayu* came under fire when Lee Kuan Yew accused it of "poisoning the minds" of its readers with communist and "anti-Malay" sentiments (*The Straits Times* 1965). Later, in 1967, *Utusan*, like *The Straits Times*, moved its operations from Singapore to Kuala Lumpur, after further accusations that it was knowingly creating political tensions between Singapore and Malaysia. By 1970, the government no longer granted *Utusan* the necessary permits for operation and it ceased distribution in Singapore altogether (History SG 2014).

Utusan was just one of the many newspapers that would find itself removed from the media landscape. The year 1971 was particularly tumultuous for the press, as the government clamped down on foreign funding, "communism" and dissent. Publications were being merged or had their yearly newspaper licences revoked. *The Eastern Sun*, an English-language publication, was quickly shut down when Lee Kuan Yew charged the newspaper with committing "black ops" and receiving "red money", although the publication had a clear anti-communist editorial line (*The Straits Times* 1971d). The tabloid *The Singapore Herald* would also have its licence revoked (Ministry of Culture 1971b). In the midst of a series of debates about the future of the *Herald* and the sources of its funding, the Ministry of Culture (1971a) issued the following statement:

> The real issue is not the freedom of the press. It is whether foreigners, including an ex-chief minister of a foreign government and currently a high-ranking diplomat in its employ should occupy a commanding position from which they can manipulate public opinion in the Republic. No government can allow this.

The theme of foreign manipulation of public opinion is one that the government constantly addresses, even in present-day Singapore.

The closure of the *Herald* in May 1971 invoked a vocal response from the public and other members of the press. The Singapore National Union of Journalists (SNUJ) launched a "Save the Herald" campaign, and its own members donated to the Herald in an effort to help (*The Straits Times* 1971b). The student union at the University of Singapore issued a statement supporting the *Herald* (Tamney 1972) and went about selling the newspaper in an effort to raise funds for the *Herald*, hoping to replace its Hong Kong investor's funds with local money. Nevertheless, the support was not enough; all efforts failed and the *Herald* was closed. The two editors of the *Herald*, Australian Bob Reece and his Malaysian wife Adele Koh, were ordered to leave Singapore (*The Straits Times* 1971a). Although the *Herald's* finances had been in the spotlight and was the purported cause of the closure, Cheong Yip Seng, former editor-in-chief of Singapore Press Holdings, would later reveal in his memoir that the *Herald's* constant defiance of government directives issued to the press had gotten itself banned from press conferences and marred its relationship with the government, contributing to its ultimate demise (Cheong 2013).

That same year, four editors from the *Nanyang Siang Pau (Nanyang)*, a Chinese-language newspaper, were detained under the Internal Security Act for using their newspaper to 'glorify' communism. The four were Lee Mau Seng, the General Manager of *Nanyang*, editor-in-chief Shamsuddin Tung, senior editorial writer Ly Singko and Public Relations manager Kerk Loong Seng (*The Straits Times* 1971a). The detention order was for two years. The four were legally represented by David Marshall and Amarjit Singh (*The Straits Times* 1971f) who petitioned the court for an open trial on their behalf. Lee Eu Seng, chairman of *Nanyang* and brother of Lee Mau Seng, also protested strongly on behalf of the four, all the while denying the charges against them. He printed numerous editorials in *Nanyang* decrying the use of the Internal Security Act (ISA) in their detention. In May that year, *Nanyang* printed a blank editorial entitled "Our Protest" (*The Straits Times* 1971c) – a silent protest in the name of the detained.

The arrests of the *Nanyang* four had also sparked international outrage. Human rights group Amnesty International wrote a letter to Lee Kuan Yew, requesting the release of the *Nanyang* four (Ennals 1971). Amnesty also raised the issue of *Utusan* editor Said Zahari's eight-year detention without trial in a press statement regarding the arrests (Amnesty International 1971). Then-president of the IPI, Ernest Meyer, released a statement declaring that the IPI was considering practical intervention in the situation in Singapore (*The Straits Times* 1971e).

The year 1971 also saw the "last great strike" by the Singapore National Union of Journalists (SNUJ), which took place over poor working conditions for journalists (Mesenas 2013); there would be no public demonstrations by members of the local press ever again.

Lawful repression and 'OB markers': 1974 to 1994

In the years that followed there were fewer instances of activism. Nevertheless, the government remained diligent in its shaping of the press. Francis Seow, a lawyer and political dissident who lived in exile in the USA, detailed this 'master plan' to control the press in *The Media Enthralled*. He argued that sophisticated tools to suppress the media were used in the country's legal boundary (Seow 1998).

One of these tools, the Newspaper and Printing Presses Act (NPPA),[13] was enacted in 1974. The key tenants of this act are summarised below:

1 Newspapers cannot be published without a permit and licence; licences must be renewed annually, and can be revoked by the minister.
2 Newspaper companies must be public companies. No individual is allowed to hold more than 3 per cent of ordinary shares. Management shares, which give shareholders 200 times the voting power of ordinary shareholders, have to be approved by the government.
3 There is to be no more foreign ownership of newspapers.
4 The sale and distribution of foreign publications will be regulated.[14]

Twenty years later, the Broadcasting Act was enacted to license and regulate broadcasting services such as television and radio.[15] Both Acts were aimed specifically at establishing a "nation building" media (Bokhorst-Heng 2002). The media were no longer encouraged to play a watchdog role; instead, mainly to transmit the state's agendas in line with the positive development and security of the nation.

In his book *OB Markers*, Cheong Yip Seng (2013), former editor-in-chief of *The Straits Times*, explains that the government used to dictate what 'out-of-bounds' markers are that the press should not cover. He recalled incidents where the first Prime Minister Lee Kuan Yew would approach him to raise concerns about articles published in his newspaper. Lee would then elucidate the government's positions on policies. Lee's concerns involved a range of issues, from serious matters such as the media's framing housing policies, to trivialities such as overly critical reviews of local television programmes.

Efforts were also made to reduce the level of competition among newspapers. In 1984, Singapore Press Holdings (SPH) was formed by means of a merger between *The Straits Times* Press, Times Publishing Berhad, and Singapore News and Publications Ltd (*The Straits Times* 1984) in a move that would define Singapore's press for decades to come. The merger resulted in competing newspapers – *The Straits Times* and *The Singapore Monitor* – being held by the same company. The *Monitor* would shut down due to a loss of advertisers later in 1985. Readers, journalists, and even members of the PAP, reacted to the closure of the *Monitor* with shock and concern (*The Straits Times* 1985). *The Straits Times* was the only English-language newspaper left standing. Today, Singapore Press Holdings Limited owns nine of the nation's ten daily newspapers, published in the four national languages, and has a 40 per cent stake in the eleventh and final paper, *TODAY*, owned by Mediacorp Press (*Financial Times* 2004).

By the time the *Monitor* had shut down, all the press unions had merged and been subsumed under the National Trades Union Congress (NTUC) (Seow 1998). The creation of the two Acts of Parliament that govern the ownership and very existence of media outlets, coupled with the merging of media houses and the removal of unions, has the effect of stifling the diversity of voices in Singapore's media industry and are the main sources of today's lack of media freedom.

Catherine Lim, mrbrown and online media: 1994 to 2006

A new medium emerged in Singapore in 1994. Tan Chong Kee launched *Sintercom*, an Internet community with the objective of providing a platform for free-flowing discussion on various national issues. However, as a result of attempts by the government to regulate the website under the Singapore Broadcasting Authority (SBA), Tan eventually decided to close down the website as it became increasingly difficult to continue publishing with integrity, given the onerous and ambiguous content restrictions imposed upon the website (*Computer Times* 2001). Sintercom officially shut down in 2001.

However, this was not the demise of online media – on the contrary, it was just the beginning. At the time, many other platforms were created and continue to operate today. Human rights groups, the Think Centre and MARUAH were founded in 1999 and 2007, respectively. Both have persistently put media freedom in the top ranks of their advocacy agendas. *The Online Citizen*, a socialpolitical website in Singapore, has been surviving since 2006. Other websites, such as the *Independent, The Middle Ground* and *Mothership.sg*, also emerged to fill the socio-political space online.

It is worth noting that some of these sites are headed or staffed by former mainstream media journalists and editors. It is not surprising, considering that when journalists tried to break with newsroom control and implement a streak of 'contentious journalism' they were fired or cold-shelved for attempting to break the mould (Cheong 2013). Editors and writers seeking greater freedom of expression were pushed into the online format, where there is a greater democratisation of information and which is perceived as not being bound by the "OB markers" that limit the mainstream media.[16]

Catherine Lim, a novelist, political commentator and well-known critic of Lee Kuan Yew, penned a column in *The Straits Times* and was embroiled in an exchange of words with Lee's succeeding Prime Minister, Goh Chok Tong. In her critique of the Lee–Goh leadership transition (Lim 1994a, 1994b), Lim pointed out the emotional estrangement between the government and the people. Then-Prime Minister Goh responded to her articles, saying she should have entered partisan politics if she wished to criticise the government (*The Straits Times* 1994), implying that she should not criticise government through the media. Lim's column was suspended as a result of the affair. She continued to write for *The Straits Times*, but was discouraged by heavy editing and the newspaper's general reluctance to publish her work. In 2007, she began blogging instead.[17]

Another blogger, Lee Kin Mun (a.k.a. mrbrown), wrote a satire on the ruling party's progress narrative "Singaporeans are fed, up with progress!" for Mediacorp's free tabloid *TODAY* on 30 June 2006 (Lee 2006). *TODAY* subsequently suspended the column and mrbrown eventually withdrew his participation from mainstream media, although he continued blogging.

The case of mrbrown remains a classic example of how the Singapore government has attempted to "talk online compliance into being". Following his "Singaporeans are fed, up with progress!" article (Lee 2006), *TODAY* published a response from the Press Secretary to the Minister for Information, Communications and the Arts entitled "Distorting the truth, mr brown?" (Bhavani 2006). The response criticised mrbrown's views as "polemics dressed up as analysis", suggesting that he offer "constructive criticism" and to emerge from behind his online persona and pseudonym. Various information and communications ministers have echoed similar views down the years. One such minister was Lui Tuck Yew (2009), who talked about the new media in an address to the Singapore Press Club, saying:

> Tempting though it might be, the solution is not to import new media technology into print or into the mainstream media. Not their approach, not their practices, not their standards. Because this, in my view, would be subtraction by addition.

Nevertheless, 2006, which was a general election year, was a watershed year for political blogging, and GE2006 became known as the 'Internet election'. The government had pledged to adopt a lighter approach to the regulation of the Internet, although they issued many warnings again political posts, and still required 'political' blogs to register with the MDA (Lee and Kan 2009).

Nevertheless, blogging as a medium for political discussion was slowly gaining greater volume, exposure and legitimacy (Lee and Kan 2009). Bloggers like Alex Au of YawningBread pushed the boundaries, posting political content despite a ban on "explicitly political content" during the election period (The Online Citizen 2006). They offered readers an alternative look at the election from what the mainstream media was presenting, giving greater coverage of opposition news and expressing anti-PAP sentiments (The Online Citizen 2006).

New Media, Bloggers 13, #FreeMyInternet: 2007 to 2013

Following the 2006 general elections (Lee 2010), the government recognised the strength and importance of online media, and began to adopt a more serious approach towards the institutionalisation of "new principles of responsible use and self-regulation for blogs and other user-generated websites" (Kenyon *et al.* 2013).

In 2007, the government appointed the Advisory Council on the Impact of New Media on Society (AIMS) to study the social, ethical, legal and regulatory implications of a rapidly growing new media sector, and how the Singapore government should engage with citizens, regulate the Internet, and protect minors from harmful online content.

In April the following year, a group of bloggers, known as Bloggers 13, submitted a paper, entitled *Proposals for Internet Freedom in Singapore*, to the then-Ministry of Information, Communication and the Arts (MICA)[18] outlining their views (The Online Citizen 2008). One of the key proposals was to allow the online community to regulate itself rather than provide for government enforcement. The eventual consultation paper published by AIMS in September 2008, entitled *Engaging New Media – Challenging Old Assumptions*, included proposals that were mostly in line with what Bloggers 13 recommended.

However, with regard to regulation, Bloggers 13 (2008) noted that there had been no consultation on the matter of new media and that there should have been a discussion on the removal of "administrative discretion". The proposals and recommendations crafted by AIMS were submitted to the government. Although 17 out of the 26 recommendations made by AIMS were adopted (Ibrahim 2013), there was no indication thereafter as to whether those proposed by Bloggers 13 were ever implemented.

However, the government subsequently proposed to implement an "online code of conduct" (Siew 2012) through the MDA, in which it suggested measures to prevent hate speech online due to what it claimed to be a "lack of sheltered online space for moderate views". At the forum during which this suggestion was made, the Chief Executive of MDA, Aubeck Kam, was met with stiff opposition from those bloggers present.

In June 2013, the MDA proposed to amend the existing Broadcasting Act to bring "greater parity" in regulations between traditional media outlets operating online platforms and larger independent news websites (Gov.sg 2013). The amendments included a requirement for websites classified as requiring an individual licence to post a S$50,000 performance bond and to be subject to a take-down notice within 24 hours should it publish "articles or pictures against the public interest". Websites that fall under this ambit include those that report an average of at least one article per week on Singapore over a period of two months, and reach at least 50,000 unique viewers a month over a period of two months (MDA 2013).

Although the initial list of ten sites that would be affected by the new ruling included nine websites owned by the two existing traditional media houses, namely Singapore Press Holdings and Mediacorp, the proposal sparked outrage among the online community. The two media houses and a business as established as Yahoo! would certainly be able to easily afford the bond. However, for independent websites who fulfilled the criteria it would be a make-or-break matter to fork out the S$50,000 performance bond and to be subject to administrative requirements for declaring funds. Thus far, only *Mothership.sg* has been added to the list (*The Straits Times* 2015d), and it is widely believed that with their financial backing they would be more than able to support the costs associated with the individual licensing regime.

The outrage over the new scheme gave rise to what may be considered the most significant events in the history of media freedom activism since the 1960s. Roy Ngerng, whose blog is read by thousands,[19] wrote an impassioned post about the implications of the MDA ruling on Singaporeans' rights,[20] noting the hypocrisy of the content take-down aspect of the ruling, given Singapore's adherence to the ASEAN Human Rights Declaration.[21] Unlike the UDHR or ICCPR, the ASEAN Human Rights Declaration does not advocate for a person's right to freedom of opinion through any medium.

The #FreeMyInternet movement was started by more than 20 bloggers and activists, including some of the most popular names in the blogosphere, including civil society activists such as Ngerng, Ravi Philemon, Andrew Loh, Kirsten Han, Rachel Zeng and activist filmmakers like Martyn See and Lynn Lee (Free My Internet 2013). The media freedom advocates were joined by some 3,000 people in their protest at Hong Lim Park on 8 June 2013 (Soh 2013). The movement also included an online blackout and a petition to the Ministry of Communication and Information to recall the licensing scheme completely (Xu 2013).

The movement's widespread reach online and the massive turnout (the third largest at Hong Lim Park that year) succeeded in raising awareness about media freedom – at least within the context of the Internet. The government, however, stood firmly by the ruling.

Furthermore, the MDA has continued to add additional layers to the amended Broadcasting Act to keep any influential website not listed among the 11 within its fold. An additional registration regime was imposed on *The Online Citizen, The Independent, The Middle Ground* and *Inconvenient Questions* to ensure that any funding for these websites is declared to the MDA. This additional declaration of funds to MDA was in parallel with restrictions on the mainstream media brought about by the NPPA, justified by the government as a means to "prevent the site from being controlled by, or coming under the influence of, foreign entities or funding, thus ensuring that Singapore politics remain a matter for Singaporeans alone" (*The Straits Times* 2013).

Instruments of fear: 2013 to 2015

In spite of these regulations, the growth of online media has continued and so has the dissent. While the Internal Security Act (ISA) has not been invoked against any member of the press since Operation Coldstore, the government has resorted to litigation via the sedition act, contempt of court charges and defamation suits to suppress these voices.

The first-ever use of the Sedition Act against an individual took place in 2005 (*The Straits Times* 2005). Since that first instance, approximately eight individuals have been investigated or charged under the Act (*The Straits Times* 2012). However, two of the more high-profile litigations against individuals have taken place over the past three years. These are cases which have incited the greatest international attention and reactions from the local public, although these responses pale in comparison to the public reaction that the #FreeMyInternet movement provoked.

The first incident took place in 2014 when blogger Roy Ngerng was served with a defamation suit by Prime Minister Lee Hsien Loong. Ngerng was found guilty of defaming Lee through various blog posts on Singapore's national mandatory savings fund, the Central Provident Fund (CPF). Ngerng was accused of falsely alleging that Lee was guilty of criminally misappropriating funds through the CPF (MyPaper 2014). After a lengthy legal procedure, Ngerng was ordered to pay S$150,000 in damages to Lee (*The Straits Times* 2016).

In May 2014, Ngerng published a personal plea on his website for donations to the fund.[22] By June, he had received contributions from over 1,000 donors and exceeded his target amount by over $10,000 (*The Straits Times* 2014). Although some of these contributions came from overseas, it was still a great show of support from the Singaporean public for Ngerng's right to freedom of expression.

The second incident took place in 2015 in the form of the arrest of 16-year-old Amos Yee, a blogger and YouTube personality. Since his arrest and trial, Yee has been charged and found guilty of making wounding remarks against Christianity and for circulating an obscene image of Lee Kuan Yew and former British Prime Minister Margaret Thatcher in a sexual position (Channel NewsAsia 2015a).

Following Yee's arrest, a small group of "individuals and activists concerned about freedom of expression in Singapore"[23] formed the Community Action Network ("CAN!").[24] CAN! launched a campaign on Yee's behalf. They petitioned the government for his release, gathering some 6,800 signatures.[25] They also organised an event at Hong Lim Park on 5 July, urging Singaporeans to join them and "Call on the Singaporean government to free Amos Yee".[26] About 200 Singaporeans attended.[27]

The cases of Ngerng and Yee shared certain similarities. Both were legal cases that advocates have highlighted to be detrimental to freedom of speech (MARUAH 2015a, 2015b; The Community Action Network 2015). Both cases also involved the reputation of the country's political leadership.

Beyond individuals, legal action was also mounted by the government against news websites. The year 2015 also saw the use of the Sedition Act against the editors of the socio-political site *The Real Singapore* (TRS) for articles posted between October 2013 and February 2015. One of these charges included inciting "ill-will and hostility" between ethnic Indians and the Filipino community in Singapore (Channel NewsAsia 2015b). Although the site was indeed responsible for publishing misleading and falsely reported content (TODAY 2015), it was the regulatory over-reach of MDA that was flagged by free speech advocates as an area of greater concern (Au 2015),

The use of these legislative tools – or "instruments of fear", as they have been termed by activist Catherine Lim[28] – have been consistently justified by the government as necessary for the preservation of Singapore's status quo. In a blog post following the speech he delivered at the Singapore Advocacy Awards Lecture, Cherian George (2015) acknowledged that no human rights organisation would see freedom of expression as a universal right, but also lamented how often freedom of speech and Singapore's status quo were always presented as a mutually exclusive dichotomy in an argument that generally lends weight to proponents of "responsible speech" – chiefly the Singapore government – to advocate a broad-based clamp-down of free expression.

Conclusion

As illustrated in this chapter, the tools for the management of the local media have only become more sophisticated in the decades since the state's independence. The implementation of the NPPA and the Broadcasting Act, the consolidation of media houses, the eradication of media unions, the enforcement of invisible "OB markers" and the aggressive litigation against dissenting individuals and organisations have all been lawful and constitutional – and therefore hard to dispute.

There are multiple other complex factors that explain the lack of media freedom activism in Singapore. Among them are the country's strict freedom of speech and assembly laws, as well as the "instruments of fear" described within the chapter, which have led to a "culture of fear"[29] among society in general and within human rights society in particular. Activists, students and researchers who are genuinely interested in human rights issues and fundamental freedoms have practical concerns about the repercussions of angering the government, such as the loss of their professional reputation and exorbitant legal fees.

The second is the deep culture of self-censorship within the mainstream media. Combined with the weakening of union power, and the lack of editorial independence as famously documented by Cheong Yip Seng's *OB Markers*, this explains the dearth of activism from members of the mainstream media

– whether through organised demonstrations Singapore witnessed through the 1970s, or even through editorials like those by Leslie Hoffman or the editors of *Nanyang Siang Pau*.

What remains is a small group of activists fighting this battle, with most of their activism taking place through online media. A handful of these activists have also formed ad hoc coalitions such as the Roundtable, Bloggers 13 and #FreeMyInternet. Other human rights groups like the Think Centre and MARUAH have also joined the cause for media freedom in Singapore. Meanwhile, the remainder of the public express their support for the cause through attendance at rallies such as #FreeMyInternet and #FreeAmosYee, and through the support that was shown to Ngerng as he faced defamation charges.

However, few successful campaigns have been launched. Attempts at engaging international organisations such as Reporters Without Borders, the United Nations and Amnesty International in an attempt to convince the Singapore government to loosen their regulations through forums such as the Universal Periodic Review (UPR)[30] have also not been fruitful.

While the prevalence of activism online shows that there is some space available for media freedom advocacy, regulations over online media have only intensified in recent years. These regulations are coupled with a conscious effort to undermine the credibility of online media and activists, describing them as the "lunatic fringe" (The Online Citizen 2011) against the nation's progress. Some are accused of being funded – and influenced – by foreign sources. Legal action against news websites such as *The Online Citizen* and the *Independent* has continued to take place.

The challenges for media freedom activists are likely to persist. Unless the political climate changes, which is hard to predict given the fluctuating results of the past few general elections in Singapore, it is likely that the government will continue its current methods of governing the media, which do not include collaboration or consultation with media practitioners and civil society.

However, activists should persevere with their efforts to legitimise alternative news online – and with their engagement of international human rights organisations. There is a hope that as the UPR as a mechanism for improving states' human rights compliance progresses, Singapore, which in the past two cycles has received feedback from various countries regarding its media freedom laws (Amnesty International 2016), may succumb to international pressure to loosen regulations, and perhaps eventually, reform its strict media laws.

Notes

1 The authors would like to thank Nathan Bullock for providing a wealth of secondary sources for this chapter.
2 The World Press Freedom Index is a measure of media pluralism, independence, quality of legislative framework and the safety of journalists in 180 countries.
3 Constitution of the Republic of Singapore, Part IV, Article 14 (1965).
4 Universal Declaration of Human Rights, Article 19 (1948).

5 International Covenant for Civil and Political Rights, Article 19 (1966).
6 Constitution of the Republic of Singapore, Part IV, Article 14 (1965).
7 English, Malay, Tamil and Chinese.
8 The Preservation of Public Security Ordinance allows for individual detentions without trial. It expired in 1963 and was succeeded by the Internal Security Act.
9 See also *Threat to Freedom*, published 21 April 1959 and *Fancy and Fact*, published 30 April 1959.
10 The Japanese Occupation of Singapore took place from 1942 to 1945. During the Occupation, *The Straits Times* was renamed *The Syonan Simbun* and was used as a vehicle for Japanese propaganda.
11 During the Japanese Occupation, Leslie Hoffman endured torture for daring to express anti-Japanese sentiment in his writing in *The Straits Times* (2015b).
12 Operation Coldstore was a security operation in 1963 which led to the arrest and detention of 107 individuals under the Internal Security Act. Among the detained were journalists, student activists and trade unionists.
13 NPPA was an adaptation of the colonial Printing Presses Ordinance at the time of its conception (Seow 1998).
14 Newspaper and Printing Presses Act, rev. edn (2002).
15 Broadcasting Act 1994 (No. 15 of 1994).
16 Personal interview, P.N. Balji, 17 September 2015, Singapore.
17 Personal interview, Catherine Lim, 23 September 2015, Singapore.
18 Now known as the Ministry of Communications and Information (MCI).
19 Figure derived from http://thehearttruths.com/.
20 R. Ngerng (2013). "MDA's licensing requirement: Your rights and Singapore's future at stake". *The Heart Truths to Keep Singaporeans Thinking*. Available at http://thehearttruths.com/2013/05/31/mdas-licensing-requirement-your-rights-and-singapores-future-at-stake/.
21 ASEAN Human Rights Declaration, Article 22–23 (2012).
22 Available at https://thehearttruths.com/2014/05/29/please-support-roy-ngerngs-defamation-legal-defense-fund/.
23 Available at www.facebook.com/Freeamosyee-415160402019588/.
24 It is important to note that Yee's case was also significant, as he was tried as an adult rather than as a juvenile, despite his status as a minor at the time of the incident – in violation of the Convention for the Rights of the Child (CRC). Available at https://singaporecan.wordpress.com/2015/06/.
25 Available at www.change.org/p/the-singapore-government-drop-the-charges-against-amos-yee?lang=en-GB.
26 Available at www.facebook.com/events/1463527953947239/.
27 Community Action Network (2016). "Letter on Amos Yee not published because of concerns over sub-judice". The Community Action Network. Available at https://singaporecan.wordpress.com/2016/08/26/letter-on-amos-yee-not-published-because-of-concerns-over-sub-judice/.
28 Personal interview, Catherine Lim, 23 September 2015, Singapore.
29 See Gomez (2000) and George (2012).
30 See Reporters Without Borders (2014).

References

Amnesty International (1971). Press statement from Amnesty International. In *Journalists Detained in Singapore*, edited by M. Ennals. London: Amnesty International.

Amnesty International (2016). "Singapore: Contempt of the court bill is a threat to freedom of expression". London: Amnesty International.

Au, A. (2015). "In the real Singapore, MDA is the greater evil". *The Online Citizen.* Available at www.theonlinecitizen.com/2015/05/in-the-real-singapore-mda-is-the-greater-evil/.

Bhavani, K. (2006). "Distorting the truth, mr brown?" *TODAY.* Singapore.

Bloggers 13 (2008). "Statement for the media".

Bokhorst-Heng, W. (2002). "Newspapers in Singapore: A mass ceremony in the imagining of the nation". *Media, Culture and Society* **24**(4): 559–569.

Channel NewsAsia (2015a). "Teen blogger Amos Yee found guilty of two charges". *Channel NewsAsia.* Singapore.

Channel NewsAsia (2015b). "The real Singapore duo slapped with 7 charges under Sedition Act". *Channel NewsAsia.* Singapore.

Cheong, Y.S. (2013). *OB Markers: My Straits Times Story.* Singapore: Straits Times Press.

Computer Times (2001). "Speaking your mind online without fear". *Computer Times.* Singapore.

Ennals, M. (1971). Letter sent by Amnesty International to His Excellency Mr Lee Kuan Yew, Prime Minister of Singapore. K.Y. Lee: 1.

Financial Times (2004). "Singapore abandons bid to create media competition". *Financial Times.* Hong Kong.

Free My Internet (2013). "#FreeMyInternet – Movement against new licensing requirements for online media". Free My Internet.

George, C. (2012). *Freedom from the Press: Journalism and State Power in Singapore.* Singapore: National University of Singapore Press.

George, C. (2015). "Free speech: A selfish and irresponsible right?" *Freedom From the Press.* Available at http://blog.freedomfromthepress.info/2015/07/05/free-speech-a-selfish-and-irresponsible-right/.

Gomez, J. (2000). *Self Censorship: Singapore's Shame.* The Think Centre.

Gov.sg. (2013). "What is the licensing framework for online news sites all about?" *Factually.* Available at www.gov.sg/factually/content/what-is-the-licensing-framework-for-online-news-sites-all-about.

History SG (2014). "First issue of Utusan Melayu (1939–1970) is published". *History SG: An Online Resource Guide.* Available at http://eresources.nlb.gov.sg/history/events/cbef1b4b-65a2-40c0-aef6-65ea034f7974.

Hoffman, L.C. (1959a). "Threat to freedom". *The Straits Times.* Singapore.

Hoffman, L.C. (1959b). "Fancy and fact". *The Straits Times.* Singapore.

Hoffman, L.C. (1959c). "Think again Mr Lee". *The Straits Times.* Singapore.

Ibrahim, Y. (2013). *Media Development Authority's Licensing Framework for News Websites in Singapore.* Singapore: Singapore Parliament.

Kenyon, A.T., T. Marjoribanks and A. Whiting (2013). *Democracy, Media and Law in Malaysia and Singapore: A Space for Speech.* Abingdon: Routledge.

Lee, K.M. (2006). "TODAY: Singaporeans are fed, up with progress!" *MRBROWN.COM.* Available at www.mrbrown.com/blog/2006/07/today_sporeans_.html (accessed 15 December 2015).

Lee, K.Y. (1998). *The Singapore Story: Memoirs of Lee Kuan Yew.* London: Prentice-Hall.

Lee, T. (2010). *The Media, Cultural Control, and Government in Singapore.* Abingdon: Routledge.

Lee, T. and C. Kan (2009). "Blogospheric pressures in Singapore: Internet discourses and the 2006 general election". *Continuum* **23**(6): 871–886.

Lim, C. (1994a). "The PAP and the people — A great affective divide". *catherinelim.sg: Political Commentaries on Singapore*. Available at http://catherinelim.sg/1994/09/03/the-pap-and-the-people-a-great-affective-divide/ (accessed 15 December 2015).

Lim, C. (1994b). "One government, two styles". *catherinelim.sg: Political Commentaries on Singapore*. Available at http://catherinelim.sg/1994/11/20/one-government-two-styles/ (accessed 15 December 2015).

Lui, T.Y. (2009). Speech by RADM (NS) Lui Tuck Yew at the Singapore Press Club. Eminent Speakers Series. Singapore.

MARUAH (2015a). MARUAH's statement at #FreeAmosYee event. Singapore.

MARUAH (2015b). MARUAH's statement on defamation law and the case against Roy Ngerng. Singapore.

MDA (2013). Fact sheet – Online news sites to be placed on a more consistent licensing framework as traditional news platforms.

Mesenas, C. (2013). *The Last Great Strike*. Singapore: Marshall Cavendish.

Ministry of Culture (1971a). Government Statement on the Singapore Herald.

Ministry of Culture (1971b). Government Statement on the Singapore Herald.

MyPaper (2014). "Blogger accused of defaming PM Lee". *MyPaper*. Singapore.

Reporters Without Borders (2014). "Reporters Without Borders calls for support for blogger Roy Ngerng".

Reporters Without Borders (2015). World Press Freedom Index.

Seow, F.T. (1998). *The Media Enthralled: Singapore Revisited*. Boulder, CO: Lynne Rienner.

Siew, K.H. (2012). "Show us you mean business". *The Online Citizen*.

Soh, E. (2013). "Over 1,500 Singaporeans protest at rally against new online rules". *Yahoo! Newsroom*. Singapore.

Tamney, J.B. (1972). "The Singapore Herald affair". *Asian Studies Review*.

The Community Action Network (2015). "Amos Yee, Roy Ngerng, and freedom of expression in Singapore". The Online Citizen.

The Online Citizen (2006). "Review – GE 2006 and the Internet". *The Online Citizen*. Singapore.

The Online Citizen (2008). "Bloggers send 20-page proposal to minister". Available at https://theonlinecitizen.wordpress.com/2008/04/21/proposals-for-internet-freedom-in-singapore/.

The Online Citizen (2011). "Listening to lunatics". *The Online Citizen*. Singapore.

The Straits Times (1959a). "IPI to discuss PAP threat against *The Straits Times*". *The Straits Times*. Singapore.

The Straits Times (1959b). Forum on freedom of press. *The Straits Times*. Singapore.

The Straits Times (1961). "Utusan Melayu staff on strike". *The Straits Times*. Singapore.

The Straits Times (1965). "Utusan a danger to Malaysia, says Lee". *The Straits Times*. Singapore.

The Straits Times (1971a). "Herald husband and wife team ordered to quit Singapore". *The Straits Times*. Singapore.

The Straits Times (1971b). "'Save the paper' fundraising drive by SNUJ". *The Straits Times*. Singapore.

The Straits Times (1971c). "Silent protest of blank column by paper". *The Straits Times*. Singapore.

The Straits Times (1971d). "Herald affair". *The Straits Times*. Singapore.

The Straits Times (1971e). "IPI to act?" *The Straits Times*. Singapore.

The Straits Times (1971f). "Marshall: Grounds for ordering detention 'too vague'". *The Straits Times*. Singapore.

The Straits Times (1984). "Who's who in the new press holding company". *The Straits Times*. Singapore.

The Straits Times (1985). "Shock, sorrow and dismay". *The Straits Times*. Singapore.

The Straits Times (1994). "PM: No erosion of my authority allowed". *The Straits Times*. Singapore.

The Straits Times (2005). "Two charged with making racist remarks on Net". *The Straits Times*. Singapore.

The Straits Times (2012). "3 possible outcomes to Amy Cheong's case". *The Straits Times*. Singapore.

The Straits Times (2013). "The Breakfast Network website to register, undertake not to receive foreign funds". *The Straits Times*. Singapore.

The Straits Times (2014). "Blogger Roy Ngerng sued by PM raises $81,000". *The Straits Times*. Singapore.

The Straits Times (2015a). "Death & taxes". *The Straits Times*. Singapore.

The Straits Times (2015b). "Thin and grim". *The Straits Times*. Singapore.

The Straits Times (2015c). "Taking risks". *The Straits Times*. Singapore.

The Straits Times (2015d). "Mothership.sg told to comply with licensing requirements in place for online news sites". *The Straits Times*. Singapore.

The Straits Times (2016). "Blogger Roy Ngerng to pay $150,000 in damages to PM Lee in instalments". *The Straits Times*. Singapore.

TODAY (2006). "Singaporeans are fed, up with progress!" *TODAY*. Singapore.

TODAY (2015). "Govt orders shutdown of The Real Singapore". *TODAY*. Singapore.

Xu, T. (2013). "#FreeMyInternet – Movement against new licensing requirements for online media". *The Online Citizen*. Singapore.

4 Activism on arbitrary detention, the suspension of law

Lim Li Ann, Connie Ong, Mohd Salihin Subhan, Benjamin Choy and Tan Tee Seng

Introduction: rights or privileges?

Article 9 of the United Nations Universal Declaration of Human Rights (UDHR) asserts that "[n]o one shall be subjected to arbitrary arrest, detention or exile".[1] Despite this, Singapore has a protracted history of arbitrary detention – originating from the Emergency Regulations, introduced under British imperialism in 1948 (NLB n.d.), before the Preservation of Public Security Ordinance (PPSO) was legislated under the first Chief Minister David Marshall's governance in 1955 (Poh 2015a). The current incarnation – the Internal Security Act (ISA) – was adopted during the 1963 Singapore–Malaya merger and amended in 1989 following a landmark lawsuit.

This chapter defines arbitrary detention according to the three criteria established by the United Nations Commission on Human Rights, Resolution No. 1997/50.[2] First, what constitutes as 'arbitrary' includes the lack of legal basis to justify detention, thereby keeping an individual in detention as opposed to charging him or her in court. Second, arbitrary detention entails "deprivation of liberty".[3] Third, detention is arbitrary when detainees are unable to exercise "the right to a fair trial".[4] Arbitrary detention in Singapore, therefore, is not confined to the ISA. Under the Criminal Law (Temporary Provisions) Act (CLTPA), the Minister of Home Affairs may direct a "person [to] be detained for any period not exceeding one year" in the "interests of public safety, peace and good order".[5] The Misuse of Drugs Act (MoDA) specifies that a person can be detained if he or she is "reasonably suspect[ed] to be a drug addict",[6] and further provides for "presumption" of liability until proven the contrary.[7]

Concluding from the relevant statutes, arbitrary detention provides the Executive with unchecked powers of detention, without the need for public accountability, and with the Judiciary ironically relegated by law. Left without viable legal recourse, citizens opposing arbitrary detention resort to activism in an effort to influence its abolition.

Activism is perceived as social movements aimed to change incumbent policies and practices, conducted outside the conventional political processes and official institutions (Martin 2007). As such, although anti-ISA activism is often "crosswired with politics"[8] – which involves "institutional activists" (Pettinicchio 2012)

Activism on arbitrary detention 71

such as politicians also campaigning for the same cause – this chapter will not include such actors when referring to activists. We focus only on the role of extra-institutional actors – civil society – in anti-ISA activism. Anti-ISA activism in Singapore is driven by certain motivations, including abolition of the ISA, public education on past detentions, petitions for a Commission for Inquiry and socio-emotional support for ex-detainees through reflective discussions.

This chapter details the historical record of arbitrary detentions in Singapore, and highlight efforts of activism targeting the removal of the ISA in chronological order. While we focus on the history of activism following independence, what happened between 1954 and 1965 laid the foundation for Singapore's long tradition of activism against arbitrary detention, and is therefore worth mentioning briefly.

Giving power to the people: before 1963

The people's pledge

On 1 March 1954, the National Service Ordinance 1953 took effect (*The Straits Times* 1954a) – but not without dissent. Two months later, eight student representatives petitioned the Governor of Singapore for an exemption from National Service. In solidarity, some 500 Chinese middle school students assembled – unplanned – en route to Government House (Poh 2014). *The Straits Times* (1954b) reported this as a "demonstration", also known as the May 13 incident. Although the students were orderly, their refusal to disperse resulted in the police who confronted them wielding "guns [...] riot shields and batons" (*The Straits Times* 1954c; Poh 2014). Even then, 2,000 students insisted on occupying Chung Cheng School "until a settlement is reached between [their] delegation and authority" (*The Singapore Free Press* 1954).

In 1956, Lim Yew Hock became Singapore's second Chief Minister and banned the Chinese Middle School Students' Union (*The Straits Times* 1956a). In response, students occupied Chung Cheng School in the thousands and

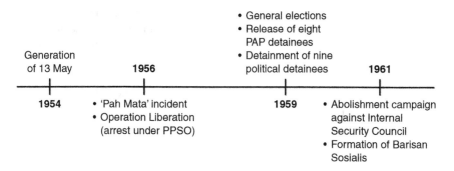

Figure 4.1 Timeline (before 1963).
Source: timeline created by authors.

threatened to persist until the Union was reinstated (*The Straits Times* 1956a). This lasted until 25 October 1956. On that day, then-assemblyman Lim Chin Siong spoke out against the arrests of the students and civil society members (Thum 2014) at a People's Action Party (PAP) rally, during which Lim stated:

> A lot of people don't want to shout Merdeka! [T]hey want to shout "pak mata" [beat the police]. This is wrong.
>
> (Singapore Special Branch 1956)

Whether causal or not, a riot followed, starting first from the Chinese middle schools before spreading. Confrontations with the police resulted in a death-toll of 15 (*The Sunday Times* 1956).

The government then commenced 'Operation Liberation' (*The Straits Times* 1956b). Alleged by Lim Yew Hock to have "work[ed] up violence, with a violence of words which could only lead to violence of action", Lim Chin Siong was arrested under the PPSO (*The Sunday Times* 1956). Between 25 to 31 October 1956, 911 others were arrested under the PPSO (Parliament of Singapore 1956), which permits the police to detain a person who "has acted or is about to act in any manner prejudicial to the public safety or the maintenance of public order" (*The Straits Times* 1956c).

In 1961, the PAP ran for the Anson by-elections. Trade Union Congress leaders including Lim Chin Siong expressed their support and called for the abolition of the Internal Security Council (*The Straits Times* 1961). Back then, the Council was represented by three British, three Singaporeans and one representative from the Federation of Malaya (Her Majesty's Stationery Office 1958; Chin and Hack 2004). Their rationale towards abolishing the Council was because "[a] popularly-elected government must exercise all the rights over matters of internal security" (Ministry of Culture 1962). Notably, there was no demand for the abolishment of the ISA (1960) itself, but only for the law to be transferred to a locally elected, fully democratic government.[9]

Activism against legislation of arbitrary detention was led by left-wing parties and trade unions. Poh Soo Kai, a founding member of the PAP, identifies himself first as an activist, second as a politician. He asserted that such movements that rejected colonial governance were important to "ask for self-determination so that we (Singaporeans) can decide for ourselves" and thus "people who believed in human rights were also anti-colonial". In the 1950s, the pursuit of independence was fundamentally also a pursuit of human rights. Lim Chin Siong and Poh later left the PAP and founded the Barisan Sosialis, a left-wing opposition political party (Poh 2015a).

Return our sons and daughters: 1963 to 1977

The Coldstore crackdown

On 2 February 1963, a group of 113 leaders of political parties, trade unions and mass organisations were detained under PPSO during Operation Coldstore (Poh 2015b). The state attributes the arrests of prominent Barisan Sosialis members to their alleged involvement in communist activities to overthrow the government (NLB 2014). Then-Prime Minister Lee Kuan Yew explains the security threat the opposition posed, as the "Communist leaders of the Barisan Sosialis [were] [...] organisers behind the scenes of anti-Government activity" and notes that "their propaganda" echoes "the foreign Communists in Moscow, Djakarta and elsewhere" (Internal Security Council 1963).

Academics have noted that both the British administration and Lee were reluctant to be perceived as responsible for the ISA detention of the Barisan Sosialis members, for fear of having to answer to the British Parliament and the dissatisfaction of the Singaporean public (Hong 2015). In addition, when Singapore was negotiating independence from the British through a merger with Malaysia between 1962 to 1965, students from different institutions often banded together to launch boycotts and hunger strikes to protest against dissolutions of student unions and government arrests (Huang 2006). Active student movements and the hesitance of key leaders to admit accountability for ISA arrests suggest that society was relatively politicised during the Operation Coldstore period.

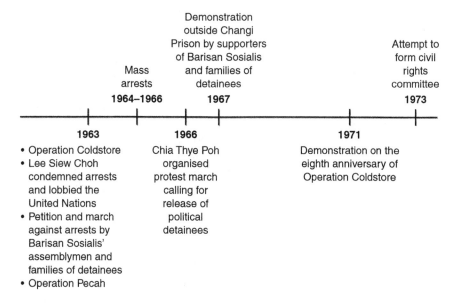

Figure 4.2 Timeline (1963–1977).

Source: timeline created by authors.

Several mass arrests followed the 1963 elections post-Operation Coldstore. In October 1963, more Barisan Sosialis leaders and trade unionists were arrested under Operation Pecah (Loh et al. 2012). According to Tan Jing Quee at the 2006 Detention-Writing-Healing Forum, "that night, 30 persons, mainly trade union leaders, and some candidates in the September elections, were taken" (S/PORES 2009). Nanyang University students, Barisan Sosialis members and trade unionists were continually arrested in 1964, 1965 and 1966 (Poh et al. 2013). In the 1970s, many highly educated professionals were also detained for participating in alleged terrorist activities (Poh et al. 2013).

The march for freedom

About a week after Operation Coldstore, Barisan Sosialis chairman Lee Siew Choh condemned the arrests and lobbied the United Nations to protest against the detention of Barisan Sosialis members and activists. He highlighted that such arbitrary detention was a "blatant denial of basic human rights by the British Government" (*The Straits Times* 1963).

On 22 April 1963, Lee and approximately 100 people marched to City Hall to present a petition against the arrest of members of the Barisan Sosialis under Operation Coldstore (*The Straits Times* 1963). Placards with messages such as "Return our sons and daughters" were carried. In an interview with Melanie Chew, Lee denied his involvement in the demonstration and clarified that the so-called City Hall Riot was actually a peaceful demonstration held by some of Barisan Sosialis' assemblymen as well as families of the detainees to ask for better treatment and the release of the Operation Coldstore detainees (Chew 1996).

Subsequently, on 8 October 1966, Chia Thye Poh organised a protest march, leading a group of supporters to march to Parliament House. He demanded the release of all political detainees and for "undemocratic" laws to be revised (Sam 1966). Another event showcasing anti-ISA activism was the 1967 demonstration outside Changi Prison. Hundreds of supporters of the Barisan Sosialis and some detainees' families were involved in this demonstration (Poh et al. 2013). Although these demonstrations did not influence the state's position on the ISA, anti-ISA activism persisted. On the eighth anniversary of Operation Coldstore in 1971, a group comprising mainly relatives of detainees demonstrated outside City Hall. They demanded the release of all political detainees by shouting slogans and distributing leaflets (Poh et al. 2013).

Poh was released ten years later in 1973. Upon his release, he tried to form a civil rights committee together with Gopalan Raman, Michael Fernandez and Ong Bok Chuan (Poh 2015c). The establishment of the National Human Rights Commission was "to ensure that every country abides by the norms of the Universal Declaration of Human Rights of 1948 as well as the other treaties and declarations assuring basic social and economic rights",[10] among which include speaking "against the internal security act and also to ask for [the] release of detainees".[11] However, the group only managed to have a preliminary meeting before the committee was "nipped in the bud"[12] when all four founders were detained.

A man on a mission: David Marshall

Among other prominent anti-ISA activists is David Marshall. In 1963, Marshall resigned as Singapore's Chief Minister and returned to practising law. He maintained close correspondence with Amnesty International (AI), liaised with the government, while also communicating with families of detainees. Peter Benenson, founder of AI, wrote to Marshall frequently to maintain efforts "to persuade the Internal Security Council to release all those detainees" (Benenson 1963). AI's goal was to release "Prisoners of Conscience" – those detained under the pretext of political and religious beliefs. Benenson (1963) stated that "If you [Marshall] have any influence with them [the Council], I do hope that you will exert it. We shall certainly do what we can from this end".

Coincidentally, Marshall's personal stance towards arbitrary detention is a cynical one; he once stated that "[t]he powers of detention of the Government under emergency laws are very extensive and comparable to the Lettres de Cachet of pre-revolution France" (Marshall 1971), which entails the King's authorisation of any one person's imprisonment without trial that is immune against appeal procedures (Duhaime n.d.). Thus, Marshall conveyed many of AI's requests and his own to the government – sometimes in his personal capacity. Considering trade unionist S. Woodhull's impending release, Marshall (1963) wrote to the Internal Security Department for permission to "assist [Woodhull] by taking him into [Marshall's] office as a clerk", confident that this "would develop [Woodhull] into a stalwart of the democratic system". Marshall held high regard for AI and followed up on their work regularly. In his request to the Barisan Sosialis for information on detainees, he remarked: "I find it particularly touching that strangers [AI] should take a greater interest in our detainees than our own people" (Marshall 1964).

However, one notable difference between the activism of David Marshall and that of Barisan Sosialis members and families of detainees is that the former campaigns for the release of detainees by engaging both international civil society and local governments, while the latter largely concentrates its efforts on local demonstrations.

The uphill struggle

However, aside from the activism from families of detainees, Barisan Sosialis members and David Marshall, there was a lack of anti-ISA activism among the rest of society. This could be due to Lee's 12 radio talks which warned the people that Barisan Sosialis members were tools used by the Communist Party of Malaysia (Lee 2014). Following Operation Coldstore, *The Straits Times* justified the use of PPSO to detain those involved in a "giant communist conspiracy to launch supporting action in the event of armed intervention by Indonesia in British Borneo" (Ali *et al.* 1963). The use of state media to explain PPSO detentions against alleged communists could have validated the arrests in the eyes of the masses.

Second, anti-ISA activism was hindered due to the prompt arrests of key leaders who demonstrated for the release of political prisoners. Following the demonstration outside City Hall in 1963, nine Barisan assemblymen were accused of being part of an unlawful assembly and assaulting police officers, and arrested for their attempt to "overawe the Government by criminal force" (Poh *et al.* 2013). The arrests meant that people involved in anti-ISA activism were left without their leaders to continue regular and sustained demonstrations for the release of political prisoners.

Anti-ISA activism back then was unable to change either the government's stance on the use of ISA or the release of political detainees. The demonstrations to campaign for the release of political prisoners were held at approximately three-year intervals (1963, 1966, 1967 and 1971), which may not have been frequent enough to pressure the government to amend or repeal the ISA, or even to release the prisoners.

Moreover, the Societies Act was revised in 1966 to give the Registrar of Societies high discretionary powers to refuse the registration of societies (Alagappa 2004). Under the Act, organisations that engage in social welfare are conferred automatic registration while groups advocating for civil and political rights are not (Thio 2009). Alleged links with communists could lead to the arrests of civil society members and the dissolution of their organisations, as observed in the fate of the Students National Action Front (Poh *et al.* 2013). The act hindered people from creating organised movements to campaign effectively for the release of detainees.

Another challenge faced by anti-ISA activists would be the fear of detention. Poh stresses that during Operation Coldstore,

> the detainees suffer inside but the families suffer outside. The family finds it difficult to make a living [...]. [The detainees'] brothers and sisters were teaching Chinese as private tuition to make a living. They [the public] were told "don't employ them", they tell their families it's dangerous to have this tutor and so they lose their jobs.[13]

This dissuaded people from joining anti-ISA movements for fear of being arrested, losing their source of livelihood and even implicating family members.

A dangerous idea: 1977 to 1987

The Euro-Communist arrests

On 10 February 1977, the Internal Security Department detained lawyer Gopalan Raman under the ISA (New Nation 1977c) on suspicion of pro-communist

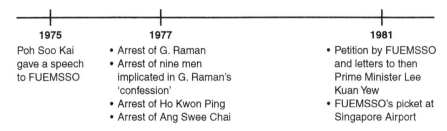

Figure 4.3 Timeline (1977–1987).
Source: timeline created by authors.

activities (Ministry of Home Affairs 1977). The following week, nine more men were also detained following an alleged confession by Raman regarding his supposedly pro-communist activities which implicated them (*The Straits Times* 1977a). Leading up to what was later known as the 'Euro-communist' arrests, the Ministry of Culture published a 26-page handwritten confession by Raman which detailed his alleged introduction to communist ideology, associations with communists in Europe and his plans to form a communist discussion group in Singapore and Malaysia (Raman 1977a). Raman himself denies the accusations laid down by the government, especially their claim that he was trying to free "hardcore" communists.[14]

Among the nine men implicated were lawyer Tan Jing Quee and former journalist A. Mahadeva, detained for the second time since Operation Coldstore (*The Straits Times* 1977a). P. Govindasamy and Michael Fernandez were also detained in 1964 after participating in alleged pro-communist trade union activities (*The Straits Times* 1977a).

Arun Senkuttuvan, a former correspondent for the Far East Economic Review (FEER), was "detained in connection with the communist plot to topple the government" (de Silva 1977). He appeared together with Raman in a televised press conference, during which he stated that the articles he wrote for FEER were critical of the government (*The Straits Times* 1977b). However, in *The Media Enthralled*, Francis Seow (1998) describes the press conference as a "theatrical flop" "carefully staged" by the government to implicate Senkuttuvan in a communist plot to "undermine" the government.

While Raman and Senkuttuvan were giving their press conference on 12 March 1977, Ho Kwon Ping was detained under the ISA on suspicion of carrying out anti-government activities as a journalist writing for the FEER (Kutty and Jansen 1977). Allegedly, he was questioned regarding Senkunttuvan's claims that the FEER was publishing a biased political narrative (New Nation 1977a).

Francis Khoo, another lawyer who was also pursued by the ISD for his connection with Raman, fled Singapore for London. Raman and Khoo were the counsel for the defendants in the trial of student activist Tan Wah Piow and two other workers, Ng Wah Ling and Tan Kim Hong who were accused of rioting in 1974 (Salient 1975). Instead, Khoo's wife Ang Swee Chai was detained under the ISA on 15 March 1977 and questioned about her husband's activities and political leanings (New Nation 1977b).

In his alleged confession, Raman also cited Poh as the leader of the Eurocommunists in Singapore (Raman 1977b). Poh had already been re-arrested in 1976 following his involvement in founding a civil rights committee (Function 8 2011).[15]

Of the nine men arrested, only two – Sekunttuvan included – were released unconditionally. The rest were released under certain conditions:

1. They could not leave the country or change address without prior approval.
2. They were not allowed to associate with or take part in communist activities.
3. They were restricted from all forms of association with former political detainees (including each other) with the exception of those who were members of the Singapore Ex-Political Detainees Association (SEPDA) (New Nation 1977b).

Voices from afar

Formed in 1966, SEPDA was the brainchild of then-Finance Minister Goh Keng Swee (Wong 1996). The organisation aimed to reintegrate ex-detainees back into society. Although helping many ex-detainees acquire gainful employment following their release, SEPDA also restricted the ex-detainees' actions. The aforementioned conditions were in place even as late as 1997 (Blackburn 2007). Gopalan Raman noted that the restrictions placed on his release remained in effect "for about 5–6 years".[16] Not being able to associate with each other without government approval meant that ex-detainees could not form a strong, collective resistance against the Euro-communist arrests.

Facing huge political pressure in Singapore, anti-ISA activism instead flourished overseas. The Federation of United Kingdom and Eire Malaysian and Singaporean Students Organisations (FUEMSSO) was a collection of students' unions formed in 1963. Comprised of Singaporean and Malaysian students based in the UK, FUEMSSO aimed to "promote awareness of issues and problems" (Florida State University 1983). FUEMSSO invited Poh to give a speech in 1975, during which he called for the "release of all political prisoners in Malaya and Singapore" (Poh 1975).

In 1976, Tan Wah Piow, who moved to London to seek political asylum, became the leader of the Singaporean students within FUEMSSO (*The Straits Times* 1987a). Five years later, FUEMSSO organised a series of events in Singapore, including a petition and protest letters calling for the release of the ISA detainees to then-Prime Minister Lee Kuan Yew. Later in the year they also organised a picket to show support for Poh who was at that time re-detained under the ISA (Ooi 2010).

Civil society underground: 1987 to 2001

The spectrum sting

On 21 May 1987, the police apprehended several households on the pretext of searching for illegal migrants (Teo 2010a).[17] Sixteen individuals were detained under the ISA that day (*The Straits Times* 1987b). Five days later, the Ministry of Home Affairs (MHA) justified the arrests as efforts "to contend with new hybrid pro-communist types who draw their ideological inspiration not only from Maoism and Marxism-Leninism, but also from the ideas of contemporary militant leftists in the West" (*The Straits Times* 1987c). The MHA claimed that the detainees leveraged their ties in religious organisations to "subvert the existing system of government and to seize power in Singapore" (*The Straits Times* 1987c). Their detentions were thus warranted because "they have to be rehabilitated to ensure that they do not revert to their old activities" (Ministry of Home Affairs 1987). On 20 June 1987, an additional six were detained.[18] All 22 arrests were conducted under "Operation Spectrum", also known as the "Marxist Conspiracy".

Religious solidarity

With ten of the first 16 detainees being volunteers and former volunteers at the Geylang Catholic Church, these arrests elicited an immediate response from religious organisations. Singapore's East Coast Church of Our Lady of Perpetual Successor held a special Mass just six days later, with more than 2,500 people attending. By that time, other religious organisations such as the Young

1987	1988	1989
• Operation Spectrum • Mass by Singapore's East Coast Church of Our Lady of Perpetual Successor • Religious and voluntary organisations wrote letters and public statements to government and general public • Activism from international civil society including *Report of the International Mission of Jurists to Singapore* • Cable messages from Australia and New Zealand to protest against arrests	• Spectrum detainees released and published joint statement denying their role as Marxist conspirators • Rearrest of eight out of nine signatories of joint statement • General Elections, opposition parties canvassed for repeal of ISA	Amendment of ISA preventing detainees from access to judicial reviews

Figure 4.4 Timeline (1987–2001).

Source: timeline created by authors.

Christian Workers Movement and the Catholic Students Society of the Singapore Polytechnic had written letters to the government appealing for the detainees' release (*The Catholic News* 1987).

International intervention

In Teo Soh Lung's (Teo 2010a) memoir on her detention experience, she expresses her thanks towards civil society groups that have shown her support.

> I thank the Emergency Committee for Human Rights in Singapore (NZ), European Committee for Human Rights in Malaysia and Singapore (KEHMA-S), Law Association for Asia and the Western Pacific (LAWASIA), The International Commission of Jurists (ICJ), the International Federation of Human Rights (FIDH) and the Asian Human Rights Commission (AHRC), The Association of the Bar of the City of New York, International Bar Association (IBA), Lawyers' Committee for Human Rights (New York), American Bar Association (ABA), Amnesty International (AI), Asia-Watch, Suara Rakyat Malaysia (SUARAM), Aliran Kepercayaan (ALIRAN), International Young Christian Workers, HK and other human rights organisations [...] for championing my cause. I owe my freedom to their hard work.

Similar to the religious organisations, most of these voluntary organisations sent letters to the Singapore government or wrote public statements to the general public. The Emergency Committee for Human Rights in Singapore (1987) writes of its "wish to inform people of conscience around the world who object to the use of the Internal Security Act to silence democratic dissent" (Rerceretnam 2006).

Among the most prominent gesture of activism from international civil society is the *Report of the International Mission of Jurists to Singapore*, dated July 1987. This is a joint report by the International Commission of Jurists, the International Federation of Human Rights and the Asian Human Rights Commission. What is unique is that besides criticising the legal basis of the ISA and reports of ill-treatment, the Mission (1987) also expresses its discomfort towards the government's position that "there is something inherently unlawful about sympathising with Marxist beliefs".

Then Senior Minister S. Rajaratnam stated that Western countries – Australia and New Zealand – had sent the Singapore government in excess of 400 cable messages to protest against the Marxist Conspiracy arrests (*The Straits Times* 1987d).

Local passivity

Local response, however, was negligible. Out of the aforementioned 14 voluntary organisations, only the Emergency Committee for Human Rights in

Singapore (1987) is exclusive to Singapore, and another – the European Committee for Human Rights in Malaysia and Singapore – has a concentration in Singapore issues. Even the former is only possible because it is managed remotely in New Zealand by a former partner of Teo's law firm, Lai Maylene (Ministry of Home Affairs 1988; Teo 2010a). Teo muses that many civil society organisations went underground during the late 1970s.[19] Constance Singam corroborated Teo's view in a separate discussion.[20] The Marxist Conspiracy had a significant quelling effect upon Singapore's civil society, with the Association of Women for Action and Research (AWARE) being a prominent example. With some of the arrested social workers from the Geylang Catholic Centre being AWARE members themselves, the threat of de-registration was palpable to AWARE (Lyons 2008). Such civil society organisations, having internalised state rhetoric, self-regulated their activities, resulting in a subdued level of activism in the 1980s through the late 1990s.

The spectrum re-arrests

The 22 "Marxist Conspirator" detainees were released between June and December 1987 (Loh 2015). On 18 April 1988, nine of them issued a joint statement asserting that they were never Marxist conspirators, denying the government's allegation. Instead, "[they] were rather community and Church workers, legal reformers, amateur dramatists, helpers of the Workers' Party, professionals and ordinary citizens exercising [their] constitutional rights to freedom of expression and association in Singapore" (Teo 2010a). Notably, the statement was "not intend[ed] to challenge the Government" but simply "to clear [their] names".

Releasing the statement was not an easy decision. Former detainees noted that the words in the statement were changed even up until their last meeting; there were times when they considered retracting the statement and times when some hesitated to pen their signatures (Teo 2010a). There was a sense of foreboding of a re-arrest. Indeed, on the day after the release, eight out of the nine signatories were re-detained under the same law[21] (*The Straits Times* 1988a) – and their worries proved to be legitimate. Refuting the detainees' intentions, the Ministry of Home Affairs (1988) asserts that those re-detained "were not aggrieved parties seeking redress, but were protagonists seeking to discredit the government".

Closely following the re-arrests were the 1988 General Elections on 3 September. The opposition campaigned against the ISA, with the Workers' Party demanding a repeal of the law while the Singapore Democratic Party demanded a restriction in application (Teo 2010a). Candidates discussed the detainees of Operation Spectrum, even holding one-minute silences at rallies.

For detainees, hunger strike is a common protest method – albeit not always carried through. In December 1988, ex-detainees had considered going on a hunger strike to protest against the "[p]roposed amendments to the ISA" and against "[s]olitary confinement and inequality of treatment" (Teo 2010a). However, disincentives that prevented a follow-through on the intentions included the implicit understanding that the government would not yield and that the physical separation between detainees rendered launching an organised movement impossible. "Without their support, nothing would change except that my health would deteriorate and that would do no one any good" (Teo 2010a).

Hunger strike or not, the government amended the ISA in the run-up to *Chng Suan Tze* v. *Ministry for Home Affairs* (Singapore Law Report 1988), preventing detainees from access to judicial reviews. The law in its current form remains identical to what it was 26 years ago.

The climate of fear

Evidently, local activism was uncommon. The ISA arrests had led to a "climate of fear" in civil society. In 1977, at least three local senior lawyers, G. Raman included, were detained under ISA and branded as Euro-communists. Francis Khoo left for Singapore and avoided the round of ISD arrests. Another decade later, lawyers Francis Seow and Patrick Seong were also arrested and detained in the midst of their efforts to release ex-ISA prisoner Teo Soh Lung (*The Straits Times* 1988b). With this, few local lawyers were willing to act as counsel for detainees, much less so activists who would campaign for their release.

Together with the fear of going against the government was the stigmatisation against ex-detainees. A documentary by the Singapore Broadcasting Corporation (1987) entitled *Tracing the Conspiracy* portrays ex-detainees as Marxist conspirators and enemies of the state. The widespread government narrative of communist subversion creates a social stigma against ex-detainees.

Civil society voices reclaimed: after 2001

Detaining a different crowd

Following the attacks on 11 September 2001 and the global rise of radical Islamist threats, the ISD departed from its conventional trend of arresting political dissidents to arresting radicalised Islamists, recasting the ISA as a vital tool to combat terrorism. It is noteworthy that the government still maintains that past political arrests have been necessary to quell "communist threats" (Ministry of Home Affairs 2002).

Relative to the ISA arrests in 1963 and 1987, arrests between December 2001 and May 2015, with at least 74 known incidents – all of whom were male and Muslim (Function 8 2011) – have not evoked comparable levels of public interest. Contrarily, Singaporeans express strong support towards the government under this "new security climate" (Cheong 2006).

This is pertinent following the 2003 arrests of Jemaah Islamiyah (JI) members in Singapore. The Singapore cell of the JI network was allegedly tasked to coordinate attacks on Western targets, namely the US Embassy and international schools, as well as local targets including the Ministry of Defence

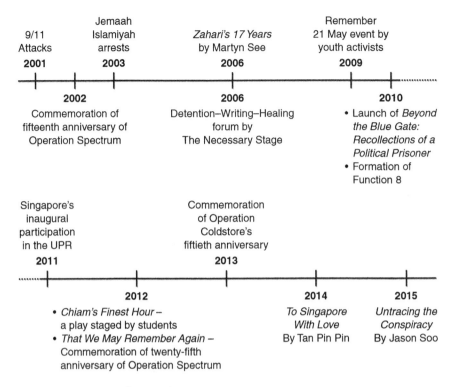

Figure 4.5 Timeline (after 2001).
Source: timeline created by authors.

and the Singapore–Malaysia Water pipeline (Ministry of Home Affairs 2003). Although the attacks on Singapore were prevented, JI's publicised attacks in Indonesia caused immense loss of life. Then-Minister for Home Affairs Wong Kang Seng (Wong 2003) argued that although the ISA did have its critics, "most Singaporeans" understood its value, and the role that the ISA and ISD played in affording them safety and security.

The security environment following the 11 September attacks and the rise of regional Islamic fundamentalism has allowed the government to recast the ISA as a vital tool to combat terrorism, and seemingly to obtain domestic legitimacy through the exclusive use of the ISA on "self-radicalised Singaporeans" (Ministry of Home Affairs 2015).

More than five decades after Operation Coldstore, the MHA persists with the traditional narrative of the communist threat. The Ministry maintains a contemporary-looking website entitled "The CPM Threat" (www.thecpm-threat.sg), detailing the violence of "Communist Killer Squads" while also citing Operation Coldstore, the Euro-communist arrests and Operation Spectrum in its timeline of events. In the wake of the 11 September attacks, the Ministry also published a booklet entitled *A Singapore Safe for All*, arguing that Singapore was under siege by communists in the 1950s and lists "[f]oreign subversion, terrorism and spying" as three security threats to Singapore that should be investigated through the ISA (Ministry of Home Affairs 2002). Today's anti-ISA activism faces an uphill battle.

Contemporary activism

Today's narrative of anti-ISA activism focuses largely on the past arrests of political detainees. This is especially prominent through commemorative events of landmark incidences. In 2002, the fifteenth anniversary of Operation Spectrum was commemorated by a small group of 52 people at a private restaurant in Singapore, among whom 11 were alleged "Marxist Conspirators" (Think Centre 2002). The dinner setting was casual – detainees sang songs they had sung during detention, messages from exiled detainees were read, and a minute of silence was observed for those who had passed away. Fast forward ten years: the twenty-fifth anniversary was commemorated, marking also a significant tenfold increase in attendance. During the decade in between, much had happened.

In 2006, The Necessary Stage (TNS) organised a Detention–Writing–Healing forum during the Singapore Fringe Festival. Held at the Esplanade, this forum marked the first time ex-political detainees, including Tan Jing Quee and Michael Fernandez, discussed their experience publicly at a mainstream venue. Previous discussions pertaining to ex-detainees were "tucked into academic institutions".[22] Notably, the forum did not demand the abolition of the ISA, but simply wanted "to hear the personal reflections of the players themselves on what we have learnt from our immediate past" (S/PORES 2009). Alvin Tan, founder of TNS, remarked that by "not being political", the government will also not react negatively by politicising the event.[23]

That same year, Martyn See released a film entitled *Zahari's 17 Years*, documenting the first political prisoner who would share his experience on camera following detention. See first drew inspiration from reading Said Zahari's book, *The Long Nightmare: My 17 Years as a Political Prisoner*. In creating the documentary, his intention was:

> to bring to light – first of all the issue of ISA, the issue that PAP came to power through very dubious means of arresting their political opponents, and that there's this whole generation of leaders that we lost because of detention without trial.[24]

The Ministry of Information, Communication and the Arts (2007) disagreed with the "distorted and misleading portrayal" and instituted a ban under Section 35(1) of the Films Act (2007),[25] deeming the film "contrary to the public interest" and disallowing any "possession or distribution" of the film (The Online Citizen 2009a). In 2013, See (2013)[26] wrote to the Minister for Communications and Information Yaacob Ibrahim to lift the ban, while also informing the Minister that he had – irrespective of the circumstance – made the film accessible online.

On 21 May 2009 a group of five youth activists organised the "Remember May 21st" event at Hong Lim Park. They read their personal statements, letters from ex-detainees in exile and poetry, and sang songs. The organisers also invited former detainees to the event. Expressing his initial feelings upon receiving the invitation, Tan Tee Seng, an ex-detainee of Operation Spectrum, remarked, "[I] don't know how to react or respond".[27] Eventually, several ex-detainees participated, namely Vincent Cheng, Teo Soh Lung and Wong Souk Yee.[28]

Restart, rejuvenate, reclaim

Crucially, it was partly this first gesture from the youth that pushed ex-detainees to speak up. Tan Tee Seng ruminated, "People telling your story and you dare not tell your story, how can that be right?"[29] Thus, eight people, comprising ex-detainees from Operation Spectrum and some of their friends, founded Function 8 as a social enterprise in 2010. Their first attempt at registration was rejected because the applicants were alleged to be "a threat to national security".[30] It was only after appealing to then-Minister of Finance Tharman Shanmugaratnam that Function 8's application under the Singapore Companies Act was approved.[31]

Another trigger behind the formation of Function 8 is the launch of Teo Soh Lung's book, *Beyond the Blue Gate: Recollections of a Political Prisoner*. Initially, Function 8's first task as an enterprise was to be Teo's publisher to protect her against any retaliatory measures. However, when Function 8's registration was delayed, the book was first published by a Malaysian enterprise – the Strategic Information and Research Development Centre (Teo 2010a). Despite having completed the book in 1990, Teo only published her writings 20 years later because she was afraid of yet another re-arrest. She eventually published the book to inform the public on Operation Spectrum.[32] Teo's book, launch at The Legends Hotel, attracted 150 attendees, some ex-detainees included (The Online Citizen 2010).

Elephant in the room

Coincidentally, the year following Function 8's establishment marked Singapore's inaugural participation in the Universal Periodic Review (UPR). Among the local civil society groups that submitted reports in 2011, three had highlighted the continued use of arbitrary detention via the ISA, with Function 8 making the abolishment of the ISA their sole focus (Teo 2010b), whereas MARUAH (2010) and Think Centre (2010) listed ISA as one of many human rights violations. All three organisations detailed the abuses of ISA by describing the government's arrests of political prisoners. This is juxtaposed to the submission from the Singapore Institute of International Affairs (SIIA). As an independent, non-governmental think-tank, SIIA also admitted to detention without trial in Singapore but stopped short of describing the actual abuses under the ISA, mentioning only the possibility of its abuse (SIIA 2010). The Singapore government also submitted a National Report, citing the ISA as "necessary to pre-emptively neutralise threats to national security such as racial and religious extremists, espionage and subversion", and thus "not punitive but preventive" (Ministry of Foreign Affairs 2011).

It is doubtful that the UPR was effective in inducing change pertaining to Singapore's laws of arbitrary detention. With the exception of Slovenia which urged Singapore to "ensure that (the ISA) [...] does not violate the right to a fair trial", other UN member countries in the Working Group Report did not recommend that Singapore review the ISA (UNGA 2011). The Singapore government itself is similarly bland in response, simply stating that the recommendations will "form the basis for the next review in 2016" (Ministry of Foreign Affairs 2011). This was not overlooked by Human Rights Watch (2011), which lambasted the government for showing "little inclination to reform". MARUAH President Braema Mathi also observed that civil society has been invited to dialogues with the government to discuss human rights issues, but although the government has been receptive towards addressing rights such as disability rights, the discussion on arbitrary detention is always put on the back burner.[33]

Three months later, some 12 former ISA detainees – detained during Operation Coldstore, the Euro-Communist arrests and Operation Spectrum – issued a statement in support of Function 8's UPR submission. The signatories re-emphasized the call for the ISA's abolition (Lim *et al.* 2011).

Activism diversified

Function 8, comprising Spectrum detainees, organised its first major event two years post-inception – commemorating the twenty-fifth anniversary of Operation Spectrum. "That We May Dream Again" was launched in collaboration with MARUAH and saw 600 participants turn up in 2012 (Liew and Pang 2015). Apart from the regular speeches and songs, the event was unique in re-enacting the detention facility at Whitley Road; makeshift interrogation rooms and prison cells were set up with the aid of cardboard boxes. By displaying personal items such as the detainees' writings, sketches and calendars, visitors were able to contextualise Operation Spectrum better and empathise with the cause for anti-arbitrary detention.

In 2012, Achtung! Productions, an entirely student-led initiative, staged a play entitled *Chiam's Finest Hour*. One of the actors, Jewel Philemon, explains that the play was an enactment of ex-Member of Parliament Chiam See Tong's motion to call for the release of the alleged Marxist conspirators during a 1987 parliamentary sitting. The impetus for seven students to reflect upon history stemmed from reading Chiam's parliamentary speech on The Online Citizen (2011).[34]

Function 8 – having first commemorated Operation Spectrum's twenty-fifth anniversary – continued its series of public events a year later by commemorating Operation Coldstore's fiftieth anniversary. The event saw some 600 participants[35] – including ex-detainees – gather at Hong Lim Park. Poh, detained for a total of 17 years, gave a speech noting the difference in political atmosphere:

> Today, the unimaginable has happened. That we can stand, tall and straight, at Hong Lim Park, in this bright sunshine exactly 50 years after the sinister mass arrest of February the second and say loud and clear: we the survivors of 2.2, we are vindicated of our youthful ideals of 1963.
> (Poh 2013)

In 2014, film director Tan Pin Pin was scheduled to screen her film *To Singapore, with Love* at the 2014 NUS Arts Festival, but not before the Media Development Authority (MDA) imposed a ban under the "Not Allowed for All Ratings" category (Tan 2014). The Media Development Authority (2014) claimed that "the contents of the film undermine national security", stating that the film's subjects had subscribed to the Communist Party of Malaya which "sought to overthrow the legitimate elected governments of Singapore" (Tan 2014). The response was poignant; 41 members of civil society signed a joint statement urging the MDA to reconsider its decision. What is noteworthy is the spill-over effect to the public. Two days later, hundreds of Singaporeans chartered four buses, crossing the causeway to watch Tan's production in Malaysia (Yahoo! News 2014). Despite this, the Films Appeal Committee remained unperturbed by these gestures of civil disobedience, reasserting the MDA's decision in November 2014 (Tan 2014).

In 2015, another film, *1987: Untracing the Conspiracy*, was premiered. Director and producer Jason Soo commissioned the film as an initiative to "portray the best and the worst of Singapore",[36] in which the best refers to the various forms of social work that the ex-detainees were engaged in (whether directly through organisations such as Geylang Catholic Centre, or indirectly through social criticism in plays and books), and the worst as the arrests of these same activists during Operation Spectrum. During their detentions, detainees were forced to appear on national TV in exchange for their release, giving them little control over their speech content. Soo remarked, "In this film I try to reverse it. I let them have some kind of control".[37] At the time of writing, the MDA had given the film an R21 rating for screening during Singapore's Freedom Film Festival in November 2015 (TODAY 2015). The film attracted a full audience at The Projector, with some even standing or sitting on the staircases (Ho 2015).

Bread and butter, no room for others

Civil society members behind anti-ISA events comprise many ex-detainees themselves, civil society members of other causes or older members of the public. Members of civil society have remarked that patrons of anti-ISA events are often regulars, describing their events as "preaching to the choir" at times. However, on exceptional occasions when youths took the initiative, the support from anti-ISA civil society is positive. More importantly, the impact of youth outreach has even spurred silent ex-detainees to engage in reflective discourse.

However, the impact of outreach upon the general public is ambiguous. Compared to the period 1963 to the late 1990s, the intensity of the climate of fear has diminished. First, the ISA has not been leveraged upon for mass political arrests recently, but only for cases of alleged involvement in terrorist activities. Second, human rights lawyer Peter Low argues that the Internet and social media have broken the government's previous control over the media.[38] Social media have provided greater transparency towards the non-government narrative. Today, people are no longer apprehensive about discussing the ISA for fear that their livelihoods would be threatened, but residual fear towards the authorities remains. A "shadow of fear still hangs among (ex-)detainees in Singapore".[39] Even those that have stepped up were once strongly apprehensive, such as Teo Soh Lung's 20-year hiatus in publishing her book. However, fear is not exclusive within ex-detainees. In staging the student-led play *Chiam's Finest Hour*, Philemon speaks of an incident in which a student pulled out just a few days before its premiere: "I think ultimately he was kind of scared of the whole prospect of talking about the ISA because it is still kind of a raw subject".[40]

However, generally speaking, Peter Low[41] observes that youths are unencumbered by the emotional baggage of past ISA detentions. This distance from fear comes at a trade-off – the increase in apathy. An Institute of Policy Studies (2015) survey shows that only 18.5 per cent and 16.6 per cent of respondents are aware of Operation Spectrum and Operation Coldstore respectively, while 88.7 per cent of them know about Lee Kuan Yew crying on national TV over the separation from Malaysia. Film director Jason Soo, who has approached many ex-detainees, said that the reluctance of the older generation to share with their descendants mutes political awareness. Thus, learning only of the official version of history in educational institutions, the current generation is apathetic towards the alternative narrative that many ex-detainees harbour.

To be or not to be (an activist)

One's identity as an anti-ISA activist is fluid. To some, it is straightforward. Martyn See, a socio-political blogger and filmmaker, considers himself to be an activist; he highlights that "I'm working, I'm speaking, I'm doing things to affect some kind of change in policies, or to affect some kind of change in how politics and social policies are conducted in Singapore".[42] However, not all who have contributed towards anti-ISA activism identify themselves as activists, citing the extent of involvement and prioritisation of primary professions. Soo said: "Compared to real activists, I am just making a film. The film doesn't directly help people that need urgent help [...]. There's only so much a film can do to push for any kind of systematic change".[43] Similarly, Philemon does not consider herself as an activist, as "there are so many other people who have a lot more experience and a lot more skills".[44] For different reasons altogether, Teo – an ex-detainee and a vocal advocate against the ISA – sees no clear distinction between politics and activism, and "[doesn't] think [she] was ever an activist" (The Online Citizen 2009b), calling herself an "accidental activist"[45] if she is perceived as one. One's intent behind activism has proven to be a dominant factor in determining one's identity as an activist, shadowing the actual act of activism itself.

Conclusion

The ISA has evolved throughout history, and its current incarnation – valid since 1989 – sees no sign of amendment or abolition. The CLTPA (1955) and MoDA (1973) have also remained intact since their legislation. With all three forms of arbitrary detention holding steadfast in Singapore's laws, civil society has not succeeded in pressing for legislative reform.

However, Singapore's civil society not only focuses its attention on abolishing arbitrary detention; activists highlight the lack of public education towards arbitrary detention and are addressing this issue. Civil society groups have organised local forums, discussions and commemorative events surrounding the ISA. Bringing the matter to global attention, some have also initiated submissions to the UN-UPR. However, compared to the ISA and CLTPA, activists have not cited arrests under the MoDA as examples of arbitrary detention in Singapore.

There is an observable trend of activists engaging with the public to raise awareness towards arbitrary detention in Singapore. External to civil society, events held successfully in the public show that the government has made concessions to civil society. Internally, ex-detainees themselves have become more receptive towards sharing their experiences. But, while anti-ISA activism has been effective in promoting reflective discourse among ex-detainees, its impact in eliciting public concern towards arbitrary detention is ambiguous.

Currently, anti-ISA activist groups are not as prominent or influential relative to activist groups such as those championing migrant workers' or women's rights. Activists have repeatedly raised the issue of apathy, attributing the phenomenon to the public's priority towards 'bread-and-butter' issues such as retirement savings and housing, detracting attention from arbitrary detention. Besides, given today's global threats, such as the alleged al-Qaeda 9/11 hijacking and recent ISIS attacks, the shift in the use of the ISA away from political dissidents to purported radicalised Islamists sways public preference towards conservative laws.

Regardless, the prevalence of public apathy does not translate to the loss of relevance of campaigns against arbitrary detention. In principle, the ISA is a "suspension of all laws",[46] or some would even call it "lawlessness within law" (Soo 2015). Peter Low argues that the ISA is a fundamental departure from the rule of law and principles of good governance. "It suspends the protection of personal liberty guaranteed in the Constitution [the highest law of the land]".[47] In practice, the civil liberties of ISA detainees cannot be guaranteed. As ex-detainees such as Poh and Teo Soh Lung reflect, officers at their detention facility had told them that "it's only privileges – no rights".[48]

To effectively further the cause of erasing arbitrary detention from Singapore's legal framework, civil society needs to liaise with the government – namely actors with access to resources in political institutions. In 2011, both civil society and the government submitted human rights reports to the UN-UPR. Although both efforts are parallel in their engagement with the international community yet divergent in their contents, the government has never engaged civil society in their submissions. But the government *can* engage with civil society, for example, when the AWARE rape study committee collaborated with the government via multiple discussions to improve the police handling of rape cases[49] (AWARE 2015b). Activists of arbitrary detention has never benefited from a similar vein of dialog.

The supply of anti-ISA activism is abundant from activists; but from the public the demand is lacklustre. With ex-detainees engaged in conversation, and events for the public diversified, activism against arbitrary detention in Singapore is nascent. Public apathy may eventually be chipped away, but as of now, remains the stumbling block. Succeeding in stimulating public discourse on arbitrary detention as an encroachment of civil liberties is what will amass public demand for government accountability to push forward the campaign against arbitrary detention.

Notes

1. UN General Assembly, Universal Declaration of Human Rights, 10 December 1948, 217 A (III).
2. Commission on Human Rights Resolution 1997/50: UN Office of the High Commissioner for Human Rights (OHCHR).
3. Fact Sheet No. 26, The Working Group on Arbitrary Detention (Vol. 26). Geneva: United Nations Office of the High Commissioner for Human Rights (OHCHR). Available at www.ohchr.org/Documents/Publications/FactSheet26en.pdf (accessed 28 December 2016).
4. Ibid.
5. Criminal Law (Temporary Provisions) Act (Cap 67, 1987, rev. edn) s 30(a).
6. Misuse of Drugs Act (Cap 185, 2001, rev. edn) s 34(1).
7. Misuse of Drugs Act (Cap 185, 2001, rev. edn) s 18(2).
8. Personal interview, Braema Mathi, 3 November 2015, Singapore.
9. P.T. Thum (2013). "Operation Coldstore". The Online Citizen, YouTube.
10. Email interview, Gopalan Raman, 1 December 2015, Singapore.
11. Personal interview, Poh Soo Kai, 9 September 2015, Singapore.
12. Ibid.
13. Personal interview, Poh Soo Kai, 9 September 2015, Singapore.
14. Email Interview, Gopalan Raman, 1 December 2015, Singapore.
15. Poh Soo Kai was first arrested under Operation Coldstore in 1963 and released in 1973.
16. Email interview, Gopalan Raman, 1 December 2015, Singapore.
17. Personal interview, Tan Tee Seng, 16 September 2015, Singapore.
18. F.H. Tay (1989, 2015). "A detainee remembers". Available at www.singaporewindow.org/tfhmemo.htm.
19. Personal interview, Teo Soh Lung, 1 October 2015, Singapore.
20. Constance Singam, Guest Lecture for POSC317 Special Projects with International Organizations, organised by Jiyoung Song at Singapore Management University, 19 September 2015, Singapore.

21 Tang Fong Har had left for the United Kingdom and was not re-arrested.
22 Personal interview, Alvin Tan, 12 October 2015, Singapore.
23 Ibid.
24 Personal interview, Martyn See Tong Ming, 26 September 2015, Singapore.
25 Films Act (Cap 107, 1998, rev. edn) s 35(1).
26 M. See (2013). "Martyn See to Yaacob: Lift ban on films featuring ex-ISA detainees". *Singapore Rebel: To build a democratic society based on justice and equality [...]* Available at http://singaporerebel.blogspot.sg/2013/11/martyn-see-to-yaacob-lift-ban-on-films.html (accessed 18 November 2015).
27 Personal interview, Tan Tee Seng, 30 September 2015, Singapore.
28 J. George (2009). "Photos of Remember 21st May event at Hong Lim Park". *Jacob 69er*. Available at https://jacob69.wordpress.com/2009/05/23/photos-of-remember-21st-may-event-at-hong-lim-park/ (accessed 20 September 2015).
29 Personal interview, Tan Tee Seng, 30 September 2015, Singapore.
30 Ibid.
31 Ibid.
32 Personal interview, Teo Soh Lung, 1 October 2015, Singapore.
33 Personal interview, Braema Mathi, 3 November 2015, Singapore.
34 Personal interview, Jewel Philemon, 2 October 2015, Singapore.
35 Function 8 (2013). "Operation Coldstore". Available at https://fn8org.wordpress.com/silenced-history/operation-coldstore/ (accessed 13 October 2015).
36 Personal interview, Jason Soo Teck Chong, 26 September 2015, Singapore.
37 Ibid.
38 Email interview, Peter Cuthbert Low, 5 October 2015, Singapore.
39 Personal interview, Martyn See Tong Ming, 26 September 2015, Singapore.
40 Personal interview, Jewel Philemon, 2 October 2015, Singapore.
41 Email interview, Peter Cuthbert Low, 5 October 2015, Singapore.
42 Personal interview, Martyn See Tong Ming, 26 September 2015, Singapore.
43 Personal interview, Jason Soo Teck Chong, 26 September 2015, Singapore.
44 Personal interview, Jewel Philemon, 2 October 2015, Singapore.
45 Personal interview, Teo Soh Lung, 1 October 2015, Singapore.
46 Personal interview, Tan Tee Seng, 16 September 2015, Singapore.
47 Email interview, Peter Cuthbert Low, 5 October 2015, Singapore.
48 Personal interview, Poh Soo Kai, 9 September 2015, Singapore.
49 See note 27.

References

Alagappa, M. (2004). *Civil Society and Political Change in Asia: Expanding and Contracting Democratic Space*. Redwood City, CA: Stanford University Press.
Ali, M., R. Chandran, E.B. Lee, K.S. Lim, R. Pestana and J. Sam (1963). "The swop began at 3am". *The Straits Times*.
AWARE. (2015). "History & achievements". Available at www.aware.org.sg/about/history-achievements/ (accessed 14 October 2015).
Benenson, P. (1963). Letter from Peter Benenson (Amnesty International) to David Marshall. London: Amnesty International, p. 1.
Blackburn, K. (2007). "Ex-political detainee forum at Singapore in 2006". *OHAA* **29**.
Cheong, D. (2006). "Selling security: The War on Terrorism and the Internal Security Act of Singapore". *The Copenhagen Journal of Asian Studies* **23**(1).
Chew, M. (1996). *Leaders of Singapore*. Singapore: Resource Press.
Chin, C.C. and K. Hack (2004). *Dialogues with Chin Peng: New Light on the Malayan Communist Party*. Singapore: NUS Press.

de Silva, G. (1977). "My campaign of hate – Arun". *New Nation*.
Duhaime, L. (n.d.). "Duhaime's Law Dictionary: Lettre de Cachet Definition".
Emergency Committee for Human Rights in Singapore (1987). The International Christian Connection, Emergency Committee for Human Rights in Singapore.
Florida State University (1983). *Fijar: Circular Letters and Other Statements*. Leiden.
Function 8 (2011). "ISA detainees final". Available at https://fn8org.files.wordpress.com/2011/08/isadetainees-final.pdf (accessed 14 October 2015).
Function 8 (2013). "Operation Coldstore". Available at https://fn8org.wordpress.com/silenced-history/operation-coldstore/ (accessed 13 October 2015).
Her Majesty's Stationery Office (1958). *Exchange of Letters: Between the Government of the United Kingdom and the Government of the Federation of Malaya about the Representative of the Government of the Federation of Malaya on the Internal Security Council to be Established under Part VII of the Singapore (Constitution) Order-in-Council*. London: Her Majesty's Stationery Office.
Ho, C.H. (2015). FFF & SGAAB DAY 2 (Photo 20/32).
Hong, L. (2015). "Revisiting Malaya: Malayan dream or Singapore Nightmare". *Inter-Asia Cultural Studies* 16(1): 24–34.
Huang, J. (2006). "Positioning the student political activism of Singapore: Articulation, contestation and omission". *Inter-Asia Cultural Studies* 7(3): 403–430.
Human Rights Watch (2011). "Singapore: adopt UN rights recommendations". Available at www.hrw.org/news/2011/09/21/singapore-adopt-un-rights-recommendations (accessed 14 October 2015).
Institute of Policy Studies (2015). *IPS Survey on Perceptions of Singapore's History*, Institute of Policy Studies, Lee Kuan Yew School of Public Policy.
Internal Security Council (1963). Statement of the Internal Security Council: Presented to the Legislative Assembly by the Prime Minister, Lim Bian Han, Acting Government Printer: 6.
International Commission of Jurists, International Federation of Human Rights and Asian Human Rights Federation (1987). *Report of the International Mission of Jurists Singapore*.
Kutty, N.G. and P. Jansen (1977). "Ex-review man Ho held by ISD". *The Straits Times*.
Lee, K.Y. (2014). *The Battle for Merger*. Singapore: Straits Times Press.
Liew, K.K. and N. Pang (2015). "Fuming and fogging memories: Civil society and state in communication of heritage in Singapore in the cases of the Singapore Memories Project and the 'Marxist Conspiracy' of 1987". *Continuum: Journal of Media & Cultural Studies* 29(4): 549–560.
Lim, H.S., S. Zahari, S.K. Poh, G. Raman, B.C. Ong, K.Y. Koh, S.L. Teo, W.H.N. Yap, Y.L. Low, T.S. Tan, V.K.C. Cheng and S.Y. Wong (2011). Universal Periodic Review – Singapore, Function 8.
Loh, K.S., E. Liao, C.T. Lim and G-Q. Seng (2012). *The University Socialist Club and the Contest for Malaya: Tangled Strands of Modernity*. Amsterdam: Amsterdam University Press.
Loh, M.P. (2015). "Political detainees in Singapore, 1950-2015". Function 8.
Lyons, L.T. (2008). "Internalized boundaries: AWARE's place in Singapore emerging civil society". *University of Wollongong Research Online*.
Marshall, D. (1963). Letter from David Marshall to the Minister of Internal Security: 2.
Marshall, D. (1964). Letter from David Marshall to the Secretary General of Barisan Sosialis.

Marshall, D. (1971). Letter from David Marshall to Ernst Becherer (Amnesty International) re: Mr Kerk Loong Sing.

Martin, B. (2007). "Activism, social and political". In *Encyclopedia of Activism and Social Justice*, edited by G.L. Anderson and K.G. Herr. Thousand Oaks, CA: Sage.

MARUAH (2010). Universal Periodic Review Singapore – Submission of MARUAH, MARUAH.

Media Development Authority (2014). "MDA has classified the film *To Singapore, With Love* as Not Allowed for All Ratings (NAR)". Media Development Authority, Singapore.

Ministry of Culture (1962). Transcript of the Broadcast on 13 August at 10.30 p.m. over Radio Singapore – Being a speech made by the Finance Minister, Dr Goh Keng Swee n 26 July before the United Nations Special Committee on Colonialism, and a summary of the case of the Singapore Government by the Prime Minister, Mr Lee Kuan Yew, disposing of points made by the representatives of the 19 Singapore assemblymen who appeared before the Committee earlier in the morning of the same day.

Ministry of Foreign Affairs (2011). *National Report for Singapore's Universal Periodic Review*. Ministry of Foreign Affairs.

Ministry of Foreign Affairs (2015). "Singapore Universal Periodic Review". Available at www.mfa.gov.sg/content/mfa/media_centre/special_events/upr.html (accessed 14 October 2015).

Ministry of Home Affairs (1977). Singapore Government Press Statement. Ministry of Home Affairs, Ministry of Home Affairs: 5.

Ministry of Home Affairs (1987). Ministry of Home Affairs Press Release. Ministry of Home Affairs.

Ministry of Home Affairs (1988). Statement Issued by the Ministry of Home Affairs. Ministry of Home Affairs.

Ministry of Home Affairs (2002). A Singapore Safe for All. Ministry of Home Affairs. Singapore, Times Books International: 7, 11.

Ministry of Home Affairs (2003). White Paper: *The Jemaah Islamiyah Arrests and the Threat of Terrorism*. Ministry of Home Affairs (Singapore), cmd. No. 2.

Ministry of Home Affairs (2015). Arrest and Detention of Self-Radicalised Singaporeans under the Internal Security Act, Ministry of Home Affairs.

Ministry of Information Communication and Arts (2007). Press Statement, Ministry of Information, Communication and Arts: 1.

New Nation (1977a). "Kwon Ping held". *New Nation*.

New Nation (1977b). "Lawyer Khoo now in London". *New Nation*.

New Nation (1977c). "Lawyer Raman detained by police". *New Nation*.

NLB (2014). "Internal Security Act". Available at http://eresources.nlb.gov.sg/infopedia/articles/SIP_2014-10-13_105937.html.

NLB (n.d.). Internal Security Act. *Singapore Infopedia*, National Library Board, Singapore.

Ooi, S.M. (2010). *The Transnational Protection Regime and Democratic Breakthrough: A Comparative Study of Taiwan, South Korea and Singapore*. Political Science Department, University of Toronto.

Parliament of Singapore (1956). Singapore Legislative Assembly Debates Official Report Second Session of the First Legislative Assembly **2**.

Pettinicchio, D. (2012). "Institutional activism: Reconsidering the insider/outsider dichotomy". *Sociology Compass* 6(6): 499–510.

Poh, S.K. (1975). "Dr. Poh Soo Kai speaks at FUEMSSO". London, *Journal of Contemporary Asia*.

Poh, S.K. (2013). Dr Poh Soo Kai's speech (in English). YouTube.
Poh, S.K. (2014). "Commemorating May 13 1954". Available at https://fn8org.word press.com/in-memory/commemorating-may-13-1954/ (accessed 10 November 2015).
Poh, S.K., ed. (2015a). *Comet in Our Sky: Lim Chin Siong in History*. Selangor: Vinlin Press.
Poh, S.K. (2015b). "Dr Poh Soo Kai: Lee Kuan Yew is a political pimp". Available at www.allsingaporestuff.com/article/dr-poh-soo-kai-lee-kuan-yew-political-pimp (accessed 28 November 2016).
Poh, S.K. (2015c). "Detention without trial: Going beyond Coldstore?" Available at www.theonlinecitizen.com/2015/02/detention-without-trial-going-beyond-coldstore/ (accessed 15 September 2015).
Poh, S.K., K.F. Tan and L. Hong, eds (2013). *The 1963 Operation Coldstore in Singapore: Commemorating 50 Years*. Kuala Lumpur: Strategic Info Research Development.
Raman, G. (1977a). Statement by G. Raman, Ministry of Culture.
Raman, G. (1977b). Extracts from further statement by G. Raman.
Rerceretnam, M. (2006). "The 1987 ISA arrests and international civil society: Responses to political repression in Singapore". *The Copenhagen Journal of Asian Studies* 23(1).
S/PORES (2009). "A public oral history of the Singapore Left in 2006".
Salient (1975). "Lee Kuan Yew's justice". *Salient* 38. New Zealand, Victoria University College Students' Association.
Sam, J. (1966). "Pathetic 30 turn up for 'the mass struggle' as Mr. Chia talks of taking the fight outside Parliament". *The Straits Times*.
SBC (1987). *Tracing the Conspiracy*. Singapore: NC.
See, M. (2013). "Martyn See to Yaacob: Lift ban on films featuring ex-ISA detainees". *Singapore Rebel: To build a democratic society based on justice and equality* [...]. Available at http://singaporerebel.blogspot.sg/2013/11/martyn-see-to-yaacob-lift-ban-on-films.html (accessed 18 November 2015).
Seow, F. (1998). *The Media Enthralled: Singapore Revisited*. Boulder, CO: Lynne Rienner Publishers.
SIIA (2010). SIIA – Individual UPR Submission – Singapore – May 2011 (11th Session). Singapore Institute of International Affairs.
Singapore Law Report (1988). Chng Suan Tze vs. Minister for Home Affairs and others and other appeals – [1988] 2 SLR(R) 525. Singapore Academy of Law.
Singapore Special Branch (1956). Translation of a speech made by Lim Chin Siong in Hokkien at a meeting organised by the PAP at the Beauty World Park, Bukit Timah Road, on the evening of 25 October. Singapore Special Branch.
Soo, J. (2015). Director Statement. Available at http://1987untracing.wix.com/1987 untracing#!director-statement/qqfpr (accessed 14 October 2015).
Tan, B.H. (2014). "The Films Appeal Committee upholds MDA's decision to classify 'To Singapore, With Love' as Not Allowed for All Ratings (NAR)". Films Appeal Committee.
Tay, F.H. (1989, 2015). "A detainee remembers". Available at www.singapore-window.org/tfhmemo.htm.
Teo, S.L. (2010a). *Beyond the Blue Gate: Recollections of a Political Prisoner*. Singapore: Function 8.
Teo, S.L. (2010b). *Universal Periodic Review Singapore – Submission by Function 8*. Singapore: Function 8.
The Catholic News (1987). "2,500 pray at Mass for detainees". *The Catholic News*: 1.
The Online Citizen (2009a). "'Zahari 17 Years' continues to be banned in Singapore – BFC".

The Online Citizen (2009b). *Teo Soh Lung – In Her Own Words (Part Two)*.
The Online Citizen (2010). "An open wound".
The Online Citizen (2011). "29 July 1987: *Chiam's Finest Hour* (Part One)".
The Singapore Free Press (1954). "Boys stay in school all night". *The Singapore Free Press*.
The Straits Times (1954a). "Law from Monday". *The Straits Times*.
The Straits Times (1954b). "Schoolboys call off protest". *The Straits Times*.
The Straits Times (1954c). "Warning to students". *The Straits Times*.
The Straits Times (1956a). "Student bodies keep Red Day". *The Straits Times*.
The Straits Times (1956b). " 'Operation Liberation' begins: Mr Lim pledges to fight tyranny". *The Straits Times*.
The Straits Times (1956c). "Chief Minister: 'First task to restore order – do nothing to impede it' ". *The Straits Times*.
The Straits Times (1961). "Anson: Unionists support PAP". *The Straits Times*.
The Straits Times (1963). "Siew Choh cables a protest to Thant". *The Straits Times*.
The Straits Times (1977a). "9 more held in anti-Red swoop". *The Straits Times*.
The Straits Times (1977b). "My part in Red Plot: Arun". *The Straits Times*.
The Straits Times (1987a). "Tan Wah Piow hopes to set up Marxist regime". *The Straits Times*.
The Straits Times (1987b). "16 held in security swoop". *The Straits Times*.
The Straits Times (1987c). "Marxist plot uncovered". *The Straits Times*.
The Straits Times (1987d). "Raja: Marxist threat not over". *The Straits Times*.
The Straits Times (1988a). "Marxist plot a bid by CPM to exploit English-educated". *The Straits Times*.
The Straits Times (1988b). "Francis Seow detained under the ISA". *The Straits Times*.
The Sunday Times (1956). "Mass arrest of middle school leaders". *The Straits Times*.
Think Centre (2002). "15th anniversary of May 21 ISA arrests".
Think Centre (2010). Universal Periodic Review on Singapore – Prepared by the Think Centre.
Thio, L.A. (2009). "Singapore human rights practice and legal policy". *Singapore Academy of Law Journal* 21(1): 326–362.
Thum, P.T. (2013). "Operation Coldstore". The Online Citizen, YouTube.
Thum, P.T. (2014). "Lim Chin Siong was wrongfully detained". Retrieved 15 October 2015, 2015. Available at www.theonlinecitizen.com/2014/05/lim-chin-siong-was-wrongfully-detained/ (accessed 15 October 2015).
TODAY (2015). "R21rating for film on Marxist conspiracy". *TODAY*, MediaCorp.
UNGA (2011). Report of the Working Group on the Universal Periodic Review – Singapore. UNG Assembly, United Nations General Assembly: 24.
Wong, K.S. (1996). Speech by Mr Wong Kan Seng, Minister for Home Affairs, at the Singapore Ex-Political Detainees Association's Thirtieth Anniversary cum Singapore's Thirty-First National Day Celebrations. National Archives of Singapore Library.
Wong, K.S. (2003). Speech by Minister for Home Affairs at the ISD Intelligence Service Promotion Ceremony. Media Division, Ministry of Information, Communications and the Arts.
Yahoo! News (2014). "Defiant Singaporeans view banned film in Malaysia".

5 Socio-economic rights activism in Singapore

Catharine Smith, Kimberly Ang and Bryan Gan

Introduction

Socio-economic rights involve a wide spectrum of basic human rights, including the right to education, housing, work, social security and health (UN 1966). A country with Singapore's level of development and state capacity has relatively high expectations of meeting these basic rights, which enable citizens to lead a dignified life with adequate living standards, free from discrimination.

Singapore went through its first Universal Periodic Review (UPR) in 2011. Many have accepted Singapore's exceptional position as a multi-religious and multicultural society that makes it difficult to adhere to the exact obligations in some international human rights covenants, such as the International Covenant on Economic, Social and Cultural Rights (ICESCR) (UPR 2011). Some areas where Singapore does not adhere to the agreements of international human rights include the Central Provident Fund (CPF) as a social security net and the absence of policies to tackle discrimination and unequal treatment respecting the right to work.

With policies focused on improving the nation's economic performance, and demonstrating success through progression in the standard of living for the majority of the population, the status quo is satisfactory to many (Chang 2011); therefore, the level of activism in the socio-economic sphere has been relatively low. Various groups touch on economic rights as part of their greater goals, such as women's rights organisations campaigning for a better economic position, but there is almost no organisation whose brand of activism focuses specifically on socio-economic rights. Given the relative absence of activism, academics and economists participate in debates over specific policies, and how these affect the economic welfare of Singaporeans. In addition, due to the political sensitivity of human rights issues in Singapore, most advocates for socio-economic rights work within the system of OB Markers[1] and argue primarily on the basis of economics and social justice rather than within a human rights framework.

This chapter focuses primarily on the arguments concerning social security, housing, trade unions and wages in Singapore. While there are perhaps other areas in which arguments might be made concerning the infringement of economic and social rights, these areas have seen the most debate. In addition, we will discuss activism in previous decades and reasons for the low levels of activism concerning these issues.

In making any effective call for policy change, one necessarily requires verifiable evidence in order to generate political and social impetus for one's cause. This is especially true in the realm of economics and perhaps more so in Singapore's technocratic, top-down approach to policy-making. According to the Associate Dean at the Lee Kuan Yew School of Public Policy, Donald Low, "analysts of government have frequently noted how Singapore's policies are grounded in rigorous economics thinking [and] policies are designed to be economically efficient even if they are not always popular" (Low 2011). This relegates most arguments without such a level of economic rigour, analysis and data to a lesser status. Public support is further discouraged by the typical counter-narrative claiming that Singapore's poor are a minority that are already well taken care of.

This is a key stumbling block facing activism in the socio-economic field of human rights; calls for action to help segments of the population are reduced to either general statements about the need to alleviate poverty or extremely specific, emotionally charged examples of poverty-stricken individuals with detailed descriptions of their everyday hardships. The latter argument is observably more prevalent than the former, presumably because activists deem it more effective to make an emotional appeal rather than un-demonstrable claims about poverty levels in the country. The reason for this is simple; the data required to formulate an argument for policy reviews regarding socio-economic rights are virtually impossible to obtain in Singapore. An activist may wish to make the case for more medical coverage, yet cannot find information on numbers of people turned away at hospitals when they are unable to afford healthcare. Therefore, the activist is unable to demonstrate the importance of his or her cause. Even data that would give a vague indication of poverty levels, such as the number of people residing in rental flats, are absent; when looking on the Housing Development Board (HDB) website, only the vague eligibility criteria for rental flats are available.

There have been calls by non-profit organisations for more demographic data on Singapore's poverty-stricken households, as well as other relevant indicators, for two reasons. First, their philanthropic efforts may be more effective if informed by accurate data. Second, they might acquire more impartial information on both the success of their work and the success of government schemes.[2] This issue of data unavailability in these critical areas of socio-economic rights activism is a recurring theme throughout this chapter, simply because it affects both activism and academic inquiry; activists trying to determine how many people are unable to afford healthcare stumble in the dark just as their peers who seek to understand the state of Singapore's low-income households do.

CPF and the right to social security

The issue of Singapore's social security system is an example of where the public has expressed increasing impatience with the lack of transparency, leading to some activism. The CPF system began in 1955 as a way of assuring retirement support for Singaporean citizens and permanent residents.[3] It evolved from being solely a mandatory savings scheme for retirement, to a multi-tiered scheme, covering major life events such as home purchases and education. In 1984, the Medisave Account was created, further expanding the purposes of CPF to include healthcare. While this multi-account system is intended to cover more areas of Singaporeans' lives, expanding the purpose of mandatory savings has depleted the retirement savings that CPF was originally intended to provide, thus leading to several debates over retirement adequacy.

Transparency

Much activism concerning CPF has had to do with the system's lack of transparency and the erosion of trust in the government due to the rules regarding CPF being changed periodically, without public consent. The lack of transparency and the government's failure to maintain agreements regarding its management fails to meet the standards set in General Comment No. 19 on Article 9: "the right of individuals to seek, receive and impart information on all social security entitlements in a clear and transparent manner" (UN 2008a).

While sweeping changes to the CPF scheme have always prompted public debate, some voices stand out. Toh Chin Chye, long-time PAP minister, professed misgivings about CPF during his term. Following his retirement, he continued to be a vocal critic of the scheme, particularly when the government announced major changes such as setting aside monies for Medisave[4] and raising the minimum age at which people could access their funds.

In 1984, Toh criticized plans to raise the minimum age:

> I think fundamental principles are being breached. The CPF is really a fixed deposit or a loan to Government, which can be redeemed at a fixed date when the contributor is 55 years old. If I were to put this sum of money in a commercial bank and, on the due date I go to the bank to withdraw the money, the manager says, "I am sorry, Toh, you will have to come next year", there will be a run on the bank!" It is as simple as this, that the CPF has lost its credibility, the management of it.

Toh's primary concern was that the CPF system had the potential to damage public trust in the government, given that the government was quite unilaterally changing the rules under which it was managing citizens' savings (The Online Citizen 2015). He argued that actions without public consultation would cause people to lose faith in the government's management of the funds.

His concerns became reality in 2014, when blogger Roy Ngerng began to question the government's management of CPF on his blog, TheHeartTruths. Ngerng's blog covered various issues, from social spending to CPF management and transparency.[5] Prime Minister Lee Hsien Loong sued Ngerng in June 2014 for accusing him of "criminal misappropriation of the monies paid by

Singaporeans to the CPF" in a blog post, where Ngerng questioned the government's management of CPF funds. Ngerng's objection to the CPF system was the lack of transparency in its management.

An activist in his own right, Ngerng's experience with the CPF debates demonstrates Toh's initial concerns: that the lack of transparency and shifting contracts concerning the funds would undermine public trust in the system. The traction that Ngerng's activism gained suggests that there was a significant basis for Toh's concerns. Ngerng spoke at "Return Our CPF" protests on 7 June, 12 July and 23 August regarding the transparency and accountability of the CPF (*Wall Street Journal* 2015). Thousands attended the protests, which in turn pressured the government to look at a possible review of the scheme. To calm the situation, the government formed an advisory panel to suggest improvements to CPF (Ministry of Manpower 2015). Forums were also organised by the Institute of Policy Studies regarding CPF.

Access to and maintenance of benefits

Beyond the issues of transparency in the CPF system there are also concerns about how well CPF functions as a social security system. The right to social security[6] encompasses the right to access and maintain benefits when there is "a) a lack of work-related income caused by sickness, disability, maternity, employment injury, unemployment, old age, or death of family member; b) unaffordable access to healthcare; and c) insufficient family support, particularly for children and adult dependents" (UN 2008a). General Comment No. 19 in Article 9 includes "the right to access and maintain benefits", which the CPF system often fails to meet.

The CPF system fails to meet these standards largely because it is not a defined contribution or benefits system but a mandatory savings scheme. That it is a savings scheme consisting of contributors' own earnings is a central point in debates – the right to access and maintain benefits when in need, as opposed to the few specific situations in which one is entitled to access pre-specified amounts. This also makes the individual the duty-bearer for his or her fundamental human rights via his or her financial situation. This undermines the very idea of fundamental human rights, which are not intended to be dependent on financial ability.

The Singapore government has enacted criteria such as a minimum age and minimum sum that must be present in the CPF account before funds can be withdrawn.[7] Furthermore, as a response to demographic changes, the government has periodically changed the rules for people to access their savings; policy changes that often do not rest easily with Singaporeans. The Association of Women for Action and Research (AWARE) has argued that raising the minimum age and the minimum sum is too great a hardship for low-income elderly Singaporeans who likely need to access their CPF funds.

Healthcare and social security

The extension of the CPF scheme beyond retirement support and into healthcare has also introduced human rights concerns. Toh, discussed above, spoke out against the use of CPF for Medisave:

> The provision of health care facilities must be accepted as a social responsibility. It is not that an individual who has the misfortune to be inflicted with some particular disease is solely responsible for searching the facilities to cure his illness. This is a social responsibility that is accepted by governments all over the world. This is part and parcel of the organization of individuals into societies. It is a measure of the degree of civilization.[8]

This objection to CPF invokes socio-economic rights language; he argues that healthcare is a basic right of citizens. Access to healthcare should not depend on an individual's financial capacity in the form of CPF and Medisave; as higher income leads to higher CPF funds there will be easier healthcare access for wealthier Singaporeans.

This system fails to adhere to Article 12(1) and (2d) in ICESCR, "the right of everyone to the enjoyment of the highest attainable standard of physical and mental health", and the steps taken by the state parties to the present covenant to achieve the full realisation of this right shall include those necessary for the creation of the conditions which would assure the necessary medical attention in the event of sickness. Singapore's healthcare system goes beyond Medisave, and there are provisions for low-income families. However, even with these additional programmes there are different standards of healthcare for different income strata of society.

Medishield was introduced in 1990 and started out as a low-cost medical insurance plan that helps patients cope with large bills and covers up to 80 per cent of B2 and C ward class hospital bills. About 75 per cent of Singaporeans are currently covered under this insurance plan or other Medisave-approved plans (Ministry of Health 2014). However, its limitations are on the age of the policy holder as well as pay-outs in order to ensure the affordability of the premiums.

Medifund was set up in 1993 to provide assistance to those in serious need of financial help even after receiving government subsidies. This covers large hospital bills in public hospitals and selected costly outpatient treatments such as kidney dialysis and chemotherapy for cancer (Ministry of Health 2013). However, one has to go through rigorous financial means testing to get the funding, which may deter individuals, given that means testing includes family members who would then be responsible for their relatives' high medical bills.

Finally, subsidies are an important aspect for low- to middle-income Singaporeans, as programmes such as the Community Health Assist Scheme (CHAS)[9] and Pioneer Generation Package (PGP)[10] provide aid even for normal check-ups at participating private General Practitioners and dental clinics. The PGP specifically targets the elderly (Lim and Tan 2011). Furthermore, low-income

Singaporeans are also entitled to a subsidised rate for various long-term care services, for example, at day rehabilitation centres, for home care and in nursing homes. However, rigorous means testing makes it difficult to access.

> While the Government has successfully mitigated the risk of wanton state spending, the consequence arguably is that financial risk from medical catastrophe has been passed to individual citizens and their families, with resultant anxiety. Support from Medifund is possible, but only upon application and on a case-by-case basis with no certainty of coverage, complete or otherwise. Subsidies for C-class wards can be as high as 80 per cent, but even paying the remaining 20 per cent may be impossible for hefty bills; 20 per cent of S$50,000 is still too heavy a burden for low-income Singaporeans.
>
> (TODAY 2013a)

Even though the government have remained adamant regarding means testing to obtain aid, they have widened the depth and scope of Medishield insurance coverage to increase pay-outs, remove the age criterion and increase extensions towards outpatient treatment of chemotherapy and kidney dialysis.

Retirement adequacy

It has been argued that CPF savings alone are insufficient to sustain Singaporeans through retirement (*The Business Times* 2015). Indeed, studies often demonstrate that this demographic relies on support from children and other sources to a greater degree than on CPF. Hui Weng Tat argued that CPF is unlikely to sustain most income groups through retirement, particularly when factoring in wage stagnation, unemployment and large purchases from CPF accounts (Hui 2013). Hui argues that lower income groups may have a better chance at an appropriate income replacement rate, but not if they have made large purchases from their accounts. A study commissioned by the Ministry of Manpower found that CPF can provide adequate support for retirement, so long as people have made responsible choices during their lives regarding major purchases and housing. It concluded:

> [The] majority of young Singaporeans will receive adequate payouts in retirement. It also underscores that retirement adequacy is premised on individual responsibility. Individuals have to work consistently and make prudent decisions so as to set aside adequate savings for their retirement.
>
> (Chia and Tsui 2013)

The premise that the guarantee of a living in relative comfort and dignity during retirement must depend on a series of responsible decisions throughout people's lives places the onus of retirement support on the individual's personal capacity and financial soundness rather than on the state as the duty bearer.

The CPF system links retirement support to employment, categorising itself outside the parameters of social security envisioned by the ICESCR (UN 2008b). That CPF is a savings scheme which is tied to employment leaves certain members of society financially vulnerable in their retirement years. Many women have no access to CPF funds in retirement, as they had been homemakers instead of working. This issue has been brought up by various advocacy groups, and by some Members of Parliament. Grace Fu, a Minister in the Prime Minister's Office, raised concerns that the CPF would not provide adequate retirement support for homemakers (*The Straits Times* 2015c). Her concerns apply to many Singaporean women; according to the Labour Force Report 2014:

> Women made up the majority (65% or 0.69 million) of residents outside the labour force. They most commonly cited family responsibilities (housework, childcare or care-giving to families/relatives) (41%) as their main reason for not participating in the labour force.
>
> (Ministry of Manpower 2014)

AWARE actively advocates for more coverage for Singapore's elderly, focusing on women who have little or no CPF savings (TODAY 2013b). AWARE budget proposals frequently call for more social spending, with a focus on the impact of changes to the CPF system upon low-income elderly women.

The government has recently taken steps to respond to calls for greater support for older Singaporeans. The PGP and Silver Support Scheme,[11] introduced in 2014, provides additional subsidies, health coverage and helps those with lower CPF cope with retirement. AWARE has acknowledged these steps taken, and has offered its support of these new policies while also calling for further action.

CPF and the right to housing

Because of the way the CPF is structured, the right to housing is inextricably tied to concerns about retirement support. Part of one's CPF account – the Ordinary Account (OA) – is typically used to fund the purchase of an HDB flat in Singapore. This choice of flat is often the "responsible decision" that is referred to in debates about retirement adequacy of CPF savings – if a family purchase a small and inexpensive flat, they will have more savings for their retirement years. In Singapore, the right to housing is linked to the right to retirement support, and both rest on an individual's finances.

By many measures, the HDB scheme has been a phenomenal success. Singapore boasts that it has over 80 per cent of its population in public housing (Housing Development Board 2015a), and that public housing is not stigmatised the way it is in most other countries. As with other policies, however, HDB policies exclude certain members of the population. Furthermore, HDB policies deliberately exclude these people: HDBs are subsidised according to specific conditions that promote the formation of certain family types, and encourage certain types of behaviour (Tan and Naidu 2014).

HDB subsidies are designed to promote the 'ideal' situation of a Singaporean man and woman forming a family unit (*The Straits Times* 2015a). When a couple plan to marry, they apply for an HDB subsidy – typically through the Family Nucleus section such as the Fiancé/Fianceé Scheme, Parenthood Priority Scheme subsidy and many others, which partially cover the cost of an HDB unit (Tu 1999). Additional subsidies are available for couples who apply for flats near their parents, in the hope that the proximity implies an intention to provide care (Housing Development Board 2015a). A different perspective would be that this care provision for the elderly again removes some responsibility from the state when it comes to providing for this growing segment of the population.

Other than purchasing subsidised housing, the HDB also provides opportunities for rental housing. Unlike a typical 'rental market', it is strictly means tested to ensure that only very low-income Singaporeans are eligible. Currently, there are around 51,000 rental units in Singapore, with an approximate six-month waiting period for a rental application approval (*The Straits Times* 2015c).

Discrimination and public housing

Certain groups are excluded from the benefits of public housing in Singapore, particularly if they do not follow the "normal" course. Citizens who do not plan to marry are excluded; they are entitled to purchase subsidised flats after the age of 35, but must seek other options for accommodation until then (Smith 2015). Many continue to live with their parents or rely on the meagre rental market. LGBT rights groups such as Sayoni have been advocating for equal rights, including housing (Sayoni 2011).

More worrying is housing exclusion following a divorce, which discriminates based on an individual's marital status. If a couple divorces within five years of purchasing a subsidised flat, this can result in one spouse ending up homeless. Sharon Quah explained at a roundtable session conducted by AWARE that:

> Firstly, HDB flats must be returned after divorce if the occupation period was shorter than five years. Additionally, divorced couples had to pay a penalty charge to the HDB. Second, long waiting periods are involved in applying for a new flat. However, due to financial difficulties and a long waiting period for a flat, occupying one's own flat was often seen as an inaccessible or faraway prospect.

It is difficult to get a new flat after selling the previous flat, and many subsidies tend to be available only once (Housing Development Board 2015b). Such policies are in place to prevent 'gaming the system' by marrying only to qualify for the subsidy for the flat. While this policy may go some distance to prevent this, it is also likely that it discourages people from seeking divorce. AWARE has argued that these HDB policies are likely to keep women in dangerous relationships so that they would avoid losing their flats.

Single parents also suffer as a result of HDB policies. Unmarried parents are ineligible for HDB subsidies. Housing is notoriously difficult for this group; they are disproportionately more likely to be in the lower income band, and therefore only eligible for rental housing. However, even rules for this include the criterion that occupants must form a 'family unit', which single parents do not. These family types must often rely on the advocacy skills of social workers to appeal to the HDB on their behalf (Jalote 2014). Again, this transforms a basic, fundamental right into a commodity dependent on the individual's financial capacity regardless of his or her circumstances, or bestowed upon by a charitable third party.

Rental housing and public housing

The rental housing experience is fraught with uncertainty. Rental leases typically last two years at a time, so families in rental housing are under the impression that they cannot remain in their accommodation for long. In reality, the HDB extends leases for people who can demonstrate some effort to improve their financial position to eventually afford home ownership, but this is never a certainty. Uncertain housing situations also make it difficult for families to achieve the sorts of networks, employment opportunities, school support, etc. that can help them get out of the poverty cycle (Glendinning *et al.* 2015).

There is also the problem of moving from 'temporary' rental housing into purchased flats. If a family ends up in rental housing after having sold their previous flat (essentially a downgrade in an attempt to access needed funds), they would not qualify for any HDB subsidies to purchase another. This means that families already living in poverty wishing to purchase a flat must possess even more finances than those who are not. But they cannot remain in rental flats for long either, as there are strict income limits for eligibility. Therefore, if a family's income rises to a certain level, they may find themselves ineligible for rental housing but unable to afford to purchase an HDB flat, particularly when one takes into account the required down-payments and income-level eligibility. This essentially means that while poor families are encouraged to improve their financial position, there is actually a structural disincentive for them to do so.

The HDB often points out that some exceptions are made for families who "do their best".[12] Even so, there is still no guarantee that low-income families will have housing. The fact that it relies so heavily on social advocacy underscores the lack of a guarantee, and again highlights the disconcerting fact that a basic right is arbitrarily handed out to the 'deserving'.

For this reason, economists such as Yeoh Lam Keong and Donald Low have proposed that Singapore develop a rental market (Low 2014). While the HDB system was designed to promote home ownership for all Singaporeans, it is also important to guarantee some possibility of housing for those unable to afford home ownership. As there is currently a shortage of rental housing even for those on a very low income, there is surely a need for a system by which families can rent housing with some guarantee of not being evicted because of shifts in their income, a two-year tenancy, etc.

The right to housing also concerns migrant workers in Singapore, who typically rely on their employers to provide housing. While this chapter deals largely with citizens' rights, it is important to note that human rights are both universal and inalienable; anyone working and living in Singapore is entitled to basic human rights.

Singaporean workers' rights and trade unions

In 1952, Lee Kuan Yew fought one of his first cases for the Postal and Telecommunications Uniformed Staff Union. He gave them advice, drafted their press statements and negotiated settlements with employers, fighting for better conditions and benefits (Lim 2015). After the PAP came into power in 1959, however, the government enacted amendments to the Trade Unions Ordinance with the aim of balancing the demands of workers with the needs of the industrialising economy. The Industrial Relations Ordinance standardised collective bargaining, and set up the Industrial Arbitration Court (IAC) for compulsory arbitration of trade disputes (Leggett 2005). The Trade Union Registrar is also empowered to deregister or reject the formation of trade unions deemed to be acting against workers' interest without any appeal (Fernandez and Loh 2009).

Many Singaporeans remember the Hock Lee bus strike in May 1955. Unions went on strike for both economic and political reasons – in 1955, half of the 275 strikes were sympathy strikes, while in 1965, 90.3 per cent of the 31 strikes were due to economic reasons (Fernandez and Loh 2009). As Singapore embarked on industrialisation, the stability of its labour climate was crucial in attracting foreign investment. Thus, Singapore began to remove power and influence from unions and relegated them under the government's wing. According to Tan (2013), "This change in approach was born out of necessity. It began when a self-governing Singapore in 1959 embarked on the path to industrialisation".

According to Siddiqi (1968), the unions complacently supported them, even though the changes "made arbitrary decisions unassailable by shutting downs to an appeal in court". Many trade unions deregistered, while those that shared similar goals merged or joined the Singapore Trade Union Congress (STUC) (Fernandez and Loh 2009).[13] There was also little chance of setting up a new union with other workers at one's workplace, as the government reserved the right to reject any registration it deemed unfit.[14] Furthermore, a union member does not have the right to accept or reject collective bargaining agreements negotiated by their representatives.[15]

When the leftists within the PAP broke away to form Barisan Sosialis in July 1961, the trade union movement previously headed by STUC was split into two factions: the Pro-Barisan Socialist Singapore Association of Trade Unions (SATU) and the Pro-PAP National Trade Union Congress (NTUC) (Balakrishna 1976). Fernandez and Loh (2009) discussed the history of trade unions, explaining,

A systematic crackdown eradicated alternative sources of power by trying left-wing union leaders for misusing union funds and deregistering union leaders who were found guilty. These de-registrations caused many workers to be left stranded without any protection from trade unions.

Considering the NTUC's success[16] and the workers' interest in tangible economic benefits rather than politics, many of the stranded workers went over to the NTUC.

While most countries only require that more than 50 per cent of those present at a meeting vote to strike, Singapore requires that more than 50 per cent of those registered in the union vote to strike. Those with criminal records or non-Singaporeans were barred from taking up union posts. Besides imposing voting requirements for strikes, Singapore made strikes illegal for essential services such as water, electricity and gas. For semi-essential services, such as transport, etc., workers must give 14 days' notice before striking.[17] This could be the main reason that strikes are so unusual in Singapore.

In 2002 and 2003, there was a series of disputes between Singapore Airlines and its pilots, and the government weighed in with open threats of repercussions for the would-be strikers (TODAY 2003). As Lee Kuan Yew, then-Senior Minister in Singapore's Cabinet, said in a speech in December 2003,

> We are telling them, both managements and unions, "you play this game, there are going to be broken heads […]". If we sit back and do nothing and allow this to escalate and test the wills, then it is going to lose hundreds of millions of dollars in one, two, three months of nastiness. We are not going to have that.

This open threat of punitive action by the government in a labour dispute, alongside the prioritisation of lost revenue over workers' rights, signals the strong presence of the government in labour issues.

In 1986, Secretary General of NTUC Ong Teng Cheong, sanctioned a strike in the shipping industry. Even though it was organised without Cabinet approval, the Hydril Strike was a peaceful one that eventually reached an amicable and effective settlement without significant negative consequences. While Singapore cannot claim to be completely strike-free, the Hydril strike he sanctioned shows how successful and peaceful strikes can be conducted without the many negative outcomes associated with such strikes in the Singapore narrative.

Currently, the Singapore system is tripartite: unions develop solutions alongside employers and government agents (Soh 2012). The parties generally involved are the NTUC, the Ministry of Manpower (MOM), the Singapore National Employers' Federation (SNEF) and the National Wage Council (NWC) (Tan 2013). The International Organisation of Labour (ILO) has praised the tripartite for its stability and for attracting multinational companies with its business-friendly environment.

However, many have pointed out the deficiencies of tripartism. The tripartite model focuses on the nation's economic growth, unlike the labour movement in the 1940s to 1960s, which emphasised social justice and worker solidarity to bring about self-respect and dignity to the working class (Fernandez and Loh 2009). Furthermore, the NTUC has "close, almost inseparable ties" to the leaders of the PAP, despite starting out as an independent federation. This could lead to some question of a conflict of interests of those who are meant to be advocating for labour, causing the NTUC to take positions that are both unusual and somewhat troubling. For example, the NTUC chief has spoken out against a minimum wage, based on arguments involving productivity and economic growth.[18]

In short, the NTUC head expresses inordinate amounts of concern about employers rather than workers, casting some doubt over the impartiality of the latter's representation. At one point, the Executive Secretary of the National Transport Workers' Union was also a board member of the SMRT Corporation, and stood for election as a PAP representative in the General Election of 2011. This points out that the roles of those involved in these decisions often call into question where their interests may lie.[19] It is certainly reasonable to question the impartiality of someone involved with both business and government when it falls upon him or her to advocate for workers' rights.

Minimum wage

In addition to meagre labour rights, Singapore also lacks a minimum wage, thereby violating Article 7a of the ICESCR which includes the right of all people to enjoy just and favourable conditions of work, and which ensures remuneration to provide all workers with a decent living for themselves and their families in accordance with the provision of the present covenant.

In the absence of a minimum wage, Singapore has implemented other approaches towards increasing low wages. In 2006 and 2007, the government introduced the fourth pillar of Singapore's social protection system, the Workfare Income Supplement (WIS) scheme, to issue wage bonuses. Locals over the age of 35 earning an average monthly income of S$1,700 or less over a period of three months will be entitled to annual income supplements depending on their age, income and employment duration during the reference year.[20] The objective of this scheme was to increase workforce participation and incentivise productivity growth in order to receive additional pay-outs (Ministry of Manpower 2015b).

In 2012, Singapore also implemented the Progressive Wage Scheme (PWS) in place of a minimum wage. This is similar to the minimum wage system, but enables the government to target certain industries and regulate increases. Higher wages would be earned through skills upgrading and productivity improvement. The NTUC had successfully pushed for the adoption of a progressive wage in sectors such as cleaning, landscaping and security (e2i 2014). With this, low-income workers would be able to obtain increments over time.

However, the progressive wage model is not mandatory. This in turn affects its effectiveness, as the only incentive for companies to follow through is the maintenance of good relations in the tripartite system of Singapore.

However, the PWS has sparked responses from the public that it is insufficient for an adequate standard of living.[21] Yeoh has also claimed that the WIS and PWS are insufficient and that the government can afford to increase the pay-outs to strengthen their effect.[22] Bloggers like Roy Ngerng, Han Hui Hui, Leong Sze Hian and journalist Kirsten Han have also been writing on the issue of the minimum wage on new media such as The Online Citizen and their own blogs in the hope of raising the awareness of fellow Singaporeans. On 3 May 2014, Han, Ngerng, Leong, Jolene Tan, Victor Wijeysingha and Tan Kin Lian led a protest regarding labour issues at Hong Lim Park.[23] However, mainstream media covered this rally only briefly. Videos of the rally were instead shared on social media.

Conclusion

Socio-economic activism in Singapore is generally less active than human rights activism in other areas, such as that of women's rights or migrant workers' rights. First, given how Singapore's public policy discussion has always been informed by strong economic theory, many activists without academic or corporate backgrounds are readily dismissed by both government and society. Thus, there is little constructive public policy debate. Second, involvement in socio-economic issues is largely restricted to philanthropic, charitable efforts rather than to advocate activism. This mostly interactional activism, as opposed to institutional activism, perpetuates a self-reinforcing cycle in the socio-economic rights sphere in Singapore. The state is less averse to the former because it does not threaten its policy-making capacity, so more groups tend towards interactional activism. By doing so, they also inadvertently shift the duty-bearing role away from the state. Finally, many Singaporeans may well be ignorant of these issues. They have little knowledge of human rights and the process to claim them (The Online Citizen 2009). If people do not know what they are entitled to, they do not see the problem of their welfare being short-changed by the state.

As many socio-economic rights violations are a result of inadequacy in public policy, many activists tread on the edge while advocating for certain change in society. CPF activist Ngerng pointed out that the advocacy in this sector is immature compared to what it is in other areas.[24] He measures maturity by the level of conversation and negotiation conducted between civil society and government. Even though there are several platforms such as the National Conversation[25] and REACH,[26] where citizens can voice such concerns, the discussions generally do not go beyond platitudes and broad calls for and promises to do right.

In Singapore's current situation of stability and comfort, protests do not seem as popular and effective as they may have been in the past. In the case of the "Return My CPF" protest, the trend of the decline in attendees may be seen in the three sessions at Hong Lim Park. Direct, confrontational approaches are a rarity and are often seen by Singaporean society at large as disruptive and unproductive activities, rather than as advocacy for a legitimate cause.

Online advocacy, however, through platforms such as The Online Citizen and Five Stars and A Moon, is on the rise. This is because it has helped activists meet the objectives of raising awareness and garnering mass support and participation. New media and high Internet penetration rates in the nation[27] are some of the reasons for this (Infocomm Development Authority of Singapore 2014). This is a hasty and over-optimistic conclusion to draw, however. New media also shift socio-political dialogue from "collective goal formation to aggregation of individual preferences with minimal deliberation" (Curran 2005), which again makes it difficult to correlate online behaviour with actual support for causes. Individuals are able to express themselves freely with little effort, and while it means that more people are speaking up and speaking out, not everything they are saying can be interpreted as advocacy or participation.

Think-tanks like the Institute of Policy Studies Singapore have been engaged by the government to evaluate policies such as CPF and the minimum wage. However, Yeoh[28] has pointed out a significant problem in the engagement of think-tanks – they are sponsored by the government, allowing regulation of the topics researched, discussed and published.

Arguably the most effective activism in Singapore comes from those who are able to discuss and make their arguments in economic terms in a more politically acceptable, reconciliatory way. These arguments are not necessarily framed in a human rights aspect. Examples include Professor Lim Chong Yah or Ex-GIC economist Yeoh Lam Keong, who share their ideas through talks and forums, generating a substantial amount of discussions and awareness. These two social commentators are effective in the Singapore context because they are recognised as experts in their field, and have some relationship with the Singapore government. This insider/outsider approach towards activism in the socio-economic sphere appears to resonate more with Singaporeans than traditional, straightforward approaches to activism that are discussed in other chapters. However, Yeoh also recognises, realistically and sadly, that these academics fight in isolation and may not be enough to make a difference in the short term.

Notes

1 OB Markers, also known as "out-of-bounds markers", is a term used in Singapore to denote what topics are permissible for public discussion.
2 Guanyinmiao's musings (2014). "Poverty data will help non-profits". Available at https://guanyinmiao.wordpress.com/2014/10/08/poverty-data-will-help-non-profits/ (accessed 27 October 2015).
3 A. Lim (2015). "Lee Kuan Yew's other legacy – the Original Union". *alvinology.com*. Available at http://alvinology.com/2015/03/29/lee-kuan-yews-other-legacy-the-original-unionist/.
4 Medisave, introduced in April 1984, is a national medical savings scheme which helps individuals set aside part of their income into their Medisave accounts to meet future

personal or immediate family's hospitalisation, day surgery and certain outpatient expenses. Under the scheme, every employee contributes 8 to 10.5 per cent (depending on age) of his or her monthly salary to a personal Medisave account.
5. R. Ngerng (2015). "How PAP tried to hide what they are doing with your CPF". *The Heart Truths*. Available at http://thehearttruths.com/2015/09/09/how-the-pap-tried-to-hide-what-they-are-doing-with-your-cpf/.
6. The states parties to the present Covenant recognise the right of everyone to social security, including social insurance.
7. J. Cuellar (2014). "An Ex-CPF employee exposes the 3 biggest complaints Singaporeans have about their CPF accounts". *MoneySmart.sg*. Available at http://blog.moneysmart.sg/kao-peh/3-biggest-complaints-singaporeans-have-about-cpf/.
8. Singapore. Parliament of Singapore. Parliamentary Debates (30 August 1983), Vol. 43, col. 1 (Toh Chin Chye).
9. The CHAS was introduced by the Ministry of Health in 2012. The scheme enables Singaporeans from lower to middle-income (gross income per person lower than S$1,800, if no income, annual value of residence on NRIC lower than S$21,000) households, as well as all pioneers, to receive subsidies for medical and dental care at participating General Practitioner (GP) and dental clinics.
10. The PGP recognises the pioneer generation (aged 16 and over in 1965 or who obtained citizenship on or before 31 December 2014) for their significant contributions in the early days of our nation-building by providing additional subsidies and benefits like Medisave top-ups and disability assistance.
11. Silver Support will aim to support the bottom 20 per cent of Singaporeans aged 65 and over, with a smaller degree of support extended to cover up to 30 per cent of seniors. This is similar to how Workfare supports the bottom 20 to 30 per cent of Singaporean wage earners (Singapore Budget Speech 2015, Assurance in Retirement. E33–49).
12. H.L. Lee, Prime Minister, National Day Rally Speech (2015). Prime Minister's Office.
13. The unions that operated between 1948 and 1953 were non-political and moderate, such as the Singapore Trade Union Congress (STUC) established by V.K. Nair and Lim Yew Hock in May 1951, which conceded under British pressure the right to organise strikes and prohibited its officials from joining political organisations.
14. Trade Unions Act, rev. edn (Cap 333 s.14 (2014)).
15. Trade Unions Act, rev. edn (Cap 333 s.27 (2014)).
16. The NTUC, from a 'pathetic' initial position, adapted the tactics of the militant unions to labour's changing mentality in the 1960s. NTUC-led strikes, focusing on economic issues, caused the loss of more man-hours between 1961 and 1963 than the SATU unions and won tangible benefits for its members. The NTUC was partly responsible for the rise in 1962 in the average weekly and hourly earnings of manual workers by 11 per cent and 10 per cent respectively, although this was also due to the SBHEU's actions. These strikes led many workers to believe that the NTUC was independent of the government and served their interests.
17. Criminal Law (Temporary Provisions) Act, rev. edn (Cap 67 s.6 (2010)).
18. H. Cai (2011). "NTUC Chief opposes mimimum wage". *Justice For Workers, Singapore*. Available at http://justice4workerssingapore.blogspot.sg/2011/01/ntuc-chief-opposes-minimum-wage.html.
19. A. Lee (2015). What is a labour chief doing in cabinet? *Five Stars And A Moon*.
20. Ranging from S$150 (for workers aged between 35 and 44 earning S$1,600 per month) to S$2,800 (for workers aged 60 and over earning S$1,000 per month) depending on their age, monthly income and employment duration during the reference year.
21. Phillip Ang (2013). "Minimum wage: Open letter to Mr Lim Swee Say". The Online Citizen. Available at www.theonlinecitizen.com/2013/03/minimum-wage-open-letter-lim-swee/.

22 Personal interview with Yeoh Lam Keong, 18 October 2015, Singapore.
23 Hui Hui Han (2014). Personal blog. Available at http://huihui247.blogspot.sg/2014/05/our-rights-to-fair-wage.html.
24 Personal interview with Roy Ngerng, 13 October 2015, Singapore.
25 The committee held the first of an estimated 30 dialogue sessions with Singaporeans on 13 October 2012, involving "about 60 people from all walks of life, including taxi drivers, professionals, full-time national servicemen, university undergraduates and retirees".
26 REACH (reaching everyone for active citizenry @ home) is the lead agency in facilitating whole-of-government efforts to engage and connect with our fellow citizens on national and social issues that are close to our hearts. They engage Singaporeans through multiple platforms such as social media and toll-free hotlines.
27 Eighty-eight per cent of households have Internet access.
28 Personal interview with Yeoh Lam Keong, 18 October 2015, Singapore.

References

Balakrishna, V.R. (1976). *A Brief History of the Singapore Trade Union Movement*. Singapore: National Trades Union Congress.
Cai, H. (2011). "NTUC Chief opposes minimum wage". *Justice for Workers, Singapore*. Available at http://justice4workerssingapore.blogspot.sg/2011/01/ntuc-chief-opposes-minimum-wage.html.
Chang, R. (2011). "Over 90% of Singaporeans happy with quality of life". *McClatchy – Tribune Business News*, Washington.
Chia, N.C. and A. Tsui (2013). "Adequacy of Singapore's Central Provident Fund payouts: Income replacement rates of entrant workers". SCAPE Working Paper Series, Paper No. 2013/02, Department of Economics, National University of Singapore.
Cuellar, J. (2014). "An Ex-CPF employee exposes the 3 biggest complaints Singaporeans have about aheir CPF Accounts". *MoneySmart.sg*. Available at http://blog.moneysmart.sg/kao-peh/3-biggest-complaints-singaporeans-have-about-cpf/.
Curran, J.P. (2005). *What Democracy Requires of the Media*. Oxford: Oxford University Press.
e2i (2014). "NTUC pushes for adoption of progressive wage model in the cleaning, landscape and security sectors".
Fernandez, M. and K.S. Loh (2009). *The Left-Wing Trade Unions in Singapore, 1945–1970*. Hawaii: University of Hawaii Press.
Glendinning, E., C.J. Smith and M.M. Kadir (2015). "Single parent families in Singapore: Understanding the challenges of finances, housing and time poverty". *SMU Change Lab*, Lien Centre for Social Innovation, Singapore Management University.
Housing Development Board (2015a). "Buying together/near parents or married child". *HDB Grants*. Available at www.hdb.gov.sg/cs/infoweb/business/estate-agents-sales persons/buying-a-resale-flat/buying-together-near-parents-or-married-child.
Housing Development Board (2015b). "Conditions after buying". Available at www.hdb.gov.sg/cs/infoweb/residential/buying-a-flat/new/conditions-after-buying.
Hui, W.T. (2013). "Economic growth and inequality in Singapore: The case for a minimum wage". *International Labour Review* **152**(1): 18.
Infocomm Development Authority of Singapore (2014). "Facts & figures". *Tech Scene & News*. Available at www.ida.gov.sg/Tech-Scene-News/Facts-and-Figures (accessed 18 March 2015).

Jalote, S. (2014). "Housing policy must reflect commitment to equality". Association of Women for Action and Research (AWARE).

Lee, A. (2015). "What is a labour chief doing in cabinet?" *Five Stars And A Moon*.

Leggett, C.J. (2005). *Strategic Choice and the Transformations of Singapore's Industrial Relations*. Thesis for Ph.D. in Philosophy at Griffith University.

Lim, A. (2015). "Lee Kuan Yew's other legacy – The Original Union". *alvinology.com*. Available at http://alvinology.com/2015/03/29/lee-kuan-yews-other-legacy-the-original-unionist/.

Lim, J. and C. Tan (2011). "Strategic orientations in Singapore healthcare". *Ethos* (9).

Low, D. (2011). *Behavioural Economics and Policy Design: Examples from Singapore*. Singapore: World Scientific Publishing Co Pte Ltd.

Low, D. and Yeoh, L.K. (2014). "Beware the inequality trap". In D. Low and S. Vadaketh (eds) *Hard Choices: Challenging the Singapore Consensus*. Singapore: National University of Singapore Press.

Ministry of Health (2013, 30 October 2013). "Singapore healthcare system". Available at www.moh.gov.sg/content/moh_web/home/our_healthcare_system.html (accessed 18 October 2015).

Ministry of Health (2014, 30 October 2013). "Financing approach". *Costs and Financing*. Available at www.moh.gov.sg/content/moh_web/home/costs_and_financing/schemes_subsidies/financing_approach.html (accessed 18 October 2015).

Ministry of Manpower (2014). *Labour Force Report 2014*. Manpower Research and Statistics Department.

Ministry of Manpower (2015a). CPF Advisory Panel.

Ministry of Manpower (2015b, 5 September 2015). "Schemes for employers and employees". Available at www.mom.gov.sg/employment-practices/schemes-for-employers-and-employees/workfare.

Ngerng, R. (2015). "How PAP tried to hide what they are doing with your CPF". *The Heart Truths*. Available at http://thehearttruths.com/2015/09/09/how-the-pap-tried-to-hide-what-they-are-doing-with-your-cpf/.

Sayoni (2011). *Report on Discrimination against Women in Singapore based on Sexual Orientation and Gender Identity*. UN Convention on the Elimination of All Forms of Discrimination against Women.

Siddiqi, S. (1968). *The Registration and Deregistration of Trade Unions in Singapore*. Unpublished Master of Law Thesis. Faculty of Law, University of Singapore.

Smith, C.J. (2015). *A Handbook on Inequality, Poverty and Unmet Social Needs in Singapore*. Lien Centre for Social Innovation.

Soh, T.M. (2012). "The future of tripartism in Singapore: Concertation or dissonance?" *Ethos* (11).

Tan, C.L. (2013). *The Story of NWC: 40 years of Tripartite Commitment and Partnership*. Singapore: Straits Times Press.

Tan, S.B. and V.L. Naidu (2014). "Public housing in Singapore: Examining fundamental shifts". Lee Kuan Yew School of Public Policy.

The Business Times (2015). "CPF rethink needs to structure retirement adequacy". *The Business Times*.

The Online Citizen (2009). "Human rights 101". *The Online Citizen*. Available at www.theonlinecitizen.com/2009/11/human-rights-101/.

The Online Citizen (2015). "'CPF has lost its credibility, the management of it' by late Dr. Toh Chin Chye in 1984". *The Online Citizen*. Available at www.theonlinecitizen.

com/2015/02/cpf-has-lost-its-credibility-the-management-of-it-by-late-dr-toh-chin-chye-in-1984/.

The Straits Times (2015a). "Changing Singapore family and what it spells for the future". *The Straits Times*, Singapore.

The Straits Times (2015b). "Singapore Budget 2015: More public rental flat applicants used to own their homes". *The Straits Times*, Singapore.

The Straits Times (2015c). "Strengthen support for stay-home mothers with little CPF savings: PAP Women's Wing". *The Straits Times*, Singapore.

TODAY (2003). "SM Lee warns pilots". *TODAY*, Singapore.

TODAY (2013a). "Low-income women should have more positive ageing, less anxiety". *TODAY*. Singapore.

TODAY (2013b). "Spend more, to keep healthcare affordable". *TODAY*, Singapore.

Tu, Y. (1999). "Public homeownership, housing finance and socioeconomic development in Singapore". *Review of Urban & Regional Development Studies* 11(2): 100–113.

UN (1966). *International Covenant on Economic, Social and Cultural Rights*. Geneva: United Nations.

UN (2008a). *Frequently Asked Questions on Economic, Social and Cultural Rights*. Office of the United Nations High Commissioner for Human Rights. Geneva: United Nations.

UN (2008b). General Comment No. 19: The right to social security (art. 9). Committee on Economic, Social and Cultural Rights.

UPR (2011). *Report of the Working Group on the Universal Periodic Review*. Human Rights Council, United Nations, Eighteenth Session: 24.

Wall Street Journal (2015). "Protesters assail Singapore pension system". *Wall Street Journal*.

6 Shifting boundaries

State–society relations and activism on migrant worker rights in Singapore

Evelyn Ang and Sheena Neo

Introduction

Singapore is no stranger to migrants: over the past 50 years, the country has been a destination for both labour migrants and asylum-seekers alike. Migrant rights activism here has concentrated on the first group, however, and focuses on the unequal relationships between employers and migrant workers. As a small state constrained by the size of its local workforce, Singapore has had a long history of dependence on foreign labour (Ministry of Manpower 2014). Foreign workers were instrumental in growing the nation's pool of labour as early as the 1970s, and between then and now their numbers have risen to approximately 1,358,200, forming more than one-third of the total workforce (Ministry of Manpower 2015).

Despite this, Singapore's system of foreign manpower continues to deny these migrants basic labour rights such as job mobility and adequate legal protection against exploitation. Common problems reported include exorbitant recruitment fees, wage theft and unreasonably long working hours, among others (Humanitarian Organization for Migrant Economics 2014). Domestic workers are excluded from major employment protections, and migrant workers in general are denied the right to form their own unions and engage in collective bargaining (Transient Workers Count Too 2012).

Although a number of the laws and regulations governing migrant workers in Singapore were first contested by Catholic social workers in the 1980s, local activism in this area was brought to an abrupt end by the political arrests of Operation Spectrum in 1987, and began anew only after 2001. The first decade of the new millennium saw the emergence of several civil society organisations focusing solely on migrant worker issues, and repeated calls throughout for legislative changes to secure these workers' labour rights. In particular, activists have argued that the current frameworks create and perpetuate various workplace problems for migrants while rendering avenues of recourse somewhat inaccessible.

Despite years of advocacy, changes have been slow. A new requirement in 2012 now mandates a weekly day off for domestic workers, but these and other minor improvements have not fundamentally altered a system that fails to guarantee workers' basic rights to begin with.[1] As we trace the origins and progression of migrant rights activism in Singapore, however, what emerges from this history is a distinct sense of how local activism is circumscribed by shifting state–society relations. Notwithstanding the growth of alternative news media and increasing pressure from non-profit groups, the government has not changed its stance on migrant labour policies – but it has changed how it engages with local activists on these issues.

This chapter outlines the history of local activism of migrant workers' rights in Singapore since its independence in 1965. We categorise it into three periods: (1) forging new paths in 1965 to 1979; (2) the Geylang Catholic Centre era in 1980 to 1987, and (3) more organised and secular activism in 2000 to 2015. Between (2) and (3) was the dark age of Singapore human rights activism for migrant workers. Drawing upon interview data with human rights activists in this field, the final section offers an assessment of the legacies of their advocacy work and concludes with some thoughts on the future challenges and opportunities local activists are likely to face.

Forging new paths, negotiating invisible lines: 1965 to 1979

Social activism for migrant workers in Singapore first began during the 1970s, with efforts to both advocate for these workers and organise them to advocate for themselves. One of the earliest known instances of such attempts occurred in February 1973, when Malaysian labourers working in a plywood factory in Jurong (an industrial area in the western part of Singapore) found themselves embroiled in a dispute. The workers were supposed to receive paid leave for the Chinese New Year holiday, during which most of them returned to their families in Malaysia. They did not receive their pay for this period.

The workers approached the factory's managers to settle the issue, but discovered that this was futile – their employers were adamant that the instruction had been given. Seeking help from the trade union proved similarly ineffective, as the union was not particularly interested in assisting non-citizens. A strike seemed to be their last option. Following discussions guided by an 'undercover' social worker, it was finally agreed that the migrants would simply down tools if they received less than their due on payday, and – crucially – spread a rumour about this beforehand so that their employers would be effectively warned.[2]

The plan worked: every worker received his due on payday without salary deductions. Through collective action, the migrant workers succeeded in thwarting their employer's plan. The man who helped steer this process, however, was soon forced to leave his employment at the factory due to his role in organising the workers: Vincent Cheng, at the time a community organiser with the Jurong Industrial Mission (JIM), had sought employment at the factory to determine whether the many employment-related complaints he heard from migrant workers in the industrial estate were in fact true. JIM had been set up in 1968 under the auspices of the National Council of Churches of Malaya and Singapore, and the East Asia Christian Conference – a regional body with which the National Council was affiliated – had provided its staff training in American grassroots activist Saul Alinsky's 'Community Organisation' (CO) tactics a year later. In Singapore, such socially conscious, community service-oriented activities by both Protestant and Catholic groups began in the mid-1950s and continued through the 1970s and early 1980s (Goh 2010). It was first met with suspicion, and ultimately with decisive state censure.[3]

In retrospect, the reasons seem simple. Jurong was the centrepiece of the PAP government's economic strategy for newly independent Singapore, and its success was by no means a foregone conclusion in the 1970s. Set in this context, JIM placed further constraints upon state actors overseeing the development process there, since Alinsky's CO methods involved mobilising people as communities to solve their own problems by leveraging collective strength vis-à-vis other actors.[4] Using these methods, the Mission called on Jurong's governing authorities to meet infrastructural needs such as school facilities and public transportation – and, through small-scale efforts, sought to educate workers on their rights. A large proportion of the residents there were Malaysian workers who had little recourse to help through either the law or the unions, so the staff and volunteers at the JIM organised sessions to explain what workers could do to resolve issues like arbitrary salary deductions or work injuries.

Tensions soon arose. Cheng recalls unpleasant encounters with officers at the Ministry of Labour (MOL), and feedback from the workers that MOL officers were displeased about workers approaching the Ministry in pairs or groups, as advised by the JIM staff to ensure witnesses to whatever an officer said.[5] Civil servants overseeing the development of Jurong resented both the confrontational tactics of the Mission, as well as the perception that these tactics had lent it a popularity that in turn threatened their leadership. Two years after it started, the Mission was warned against allowing its premises to be used for non-religious purposes, and later closed in 1972 due to "complaints of [JIM's] interference in industrial disputes" (National Archives Singapore 1987). A line had been drawn: the government's unease with CO tactics signalled a constraint upon activists' strategies. In the years following JIM's closure, other attempts to navigate these invisible lines gradually shed more light on their precise contours – though sometimes with heavy costs.

The Geylang Catholic Centre era: 1980 to 1987

Activists paid a price, most notably when unforeseen mistakes eventually culminated in the 'Marxist Conspiracy' crackdown by the state. This occurred during a second period of activism that stands out as significant in the development of human rights advocacy in Singapore, which centred on the Geylang Catholic Centre (GCC) for migrant workers and the extensive social services it provided. It was a period during which the lines demarcating politically permissible activities from unacceptable ones were still being drawn – and the Geylang Catholic Centre's crossing of ambiguous boundaries ultimately helped clearly draw a line in the public consciousness.

Like the prevailing Protestant theology of the period, liberal Catholicism called for social action from churches in modernising Asian societies. Desiring to help the 'forgotten ones', a young French priest from the Paris Missions Society, Fr. Guillaume Arotçarena, obtained approval from his superiors to set up a centre for the needy at Lorong 19 Geylang, where he himself would live (Arotçarena 2015).

The Geylang Catholic Centre opened its doors on 1 June 1980. Although Arotçarena did not intend to focus exclusively on any particular group of people, the Centre served largely migrant workers due to its location. Geylang in the 1980s was one of the poorer districts in Singapore, and thus also one in which Singapore's rapidly growing migrant population was concentrated, due to the draw of low property rental costs for both migrant workers and the employers who housed them. In fact, the Centre's first 'clients' were its neighbours – 20 Chinese female workers from Malaysia who lived on the floor above them in an informal dormitory that Arotçarena quickly realised was common in Geylang.

Broadly speaking, the Centre served migrants in two ways: (1) through its case work and advocacy, and (2) through its recreational activities which were run by young professionals and other volunteers from tertiary institutions. A key difference between the GCC and JIM was the type of advocacy work each did. A great deal of the issues which Arotçarena and his team dealt with concerned foreign domestic workers (FDWs) – a group that increased in numbers during the 1980s, after a government scheme for their recruitment was launched in 1978 (*The Straits Times* 1978). This was a new population of migrant workers with problems similar to yet distinct from workers in other sectors, but the key point to note is that Arotçarena directly helped resolve workers' issues to begin with: the JIM's CO methods of mobilising workers to advocate for themselves had proven unfeasible in Singapore's political climate at the time.

Instead, the GCC worked with the relevant authorities to resolve these issues, and also brought migrants' issues into the public eye through court trials for specific cases that were handled by lawyers volunteering at the Centre. Its work gave the government a view from the 'ground' as various state agencies struggled to navigate issues raised by Singapore's new influx of migrant labour, but interactions between these agencies and the GCC also allowed the Centre's social workers to obtain both concessions and clarifications through consultations with the MOL (Arotçarena 2015).

Like the JIM, however, the GCC did not last long. Arotçarena recalls strange events in the mid-1980s: an indirect warning from a civil servant friend about wiretapping, official visits from government personnel who appeared not to be from the departments they claimed they were, and even a visit from two strangers who suggested that he start a trade union for migrant workers (Arotçarena 2015). What followed is by now well-established: Operation Spectrum in May 1987 saw the political arrests of 22 individuals linked both directly and indirectly to the Geylang Catholic Centre, and the subsequent explanation of these extra-judicial acts by the Internal Security Department (ISD) as the defeat of a 'Marxist Conspiracy'. This was traced back to the JIM, which the government alleged "was used by leftists and Marxists like Tan Wah Piow [and] Vincent Cheng [...] as a cover to stir up industrial unrest in the Jurong factories in the early 1970s" (National Archives Singapore 1987).

Barr argues that Christian organisations' engagement with socio-political issues threatened the state's monopoly on setting the agenda for national development in public discourse (Barr 2008). This seems probable: groups like the Catholic Students Society and Young Christian Workers, for instance, had been involved in public campaigns related to the state's socio-economic policies, and *Aquinas*, the Catholic Church's newsletter, had evolved into a publication that disseminated analyses of current affairs, including articles that criticised government policies (Goh 2010). Like the JIM, the GCC itself was doing work that impinged directly upon a matter of great importance to Singapore: labour. Altogether, the liberal theological ideas about democratisation that produced such vibrant civil society activity thus challenged the ruling elites' imagination of the nation. Unlike the official discourse that pictured Singapore as a vulnerable state in a hostile environment and accordingly demanded political quiescence in the name of national security, the ideas espoused by Christianity demanded a society in which policy-making was not the prerogative of the state, but a duty to be shared with an active citizenry.

Over the next decade, very little occurred in the area of migrant rights' advocacy. Operation Spectrum was the third wave of political arrests in Singapore's early years, and its message was clearly understood by the people. Its legacy would prove to be remarkably (and unfortunately) enduring.

Organised and secular activism by TWC2 and HOME: 2000 to 2015

On 1 December 2001, a 19-year-old Indonesian domestic worker, Muawanatul Chasanah, collapsed in a pool of her own vomit and died the following day in hospital from peritonitis (*The Straits Times* 2002a). She had been hit by her employer Ng Hua Chye on the face, chest and back shortly before fainting, but her autopsy showed more than 200 injuries on her body, inflicted by punches, kicks and burns from both cigarettes and hot water, among others (*The Straits Times* 2002b).

In the days and months which followed, the press ran articles and letters that generated an unprecedented level of discussion about Singapore's foreign domestic workers. Journalists and readers alike raised various questions, but many of these focused on two unsettling facts: how had the doctors who performed Chasanah's mandatory biannual medical checks missed or failed to report her injuries, and why did Ng's neighbours choose not to intervene or report him to the police? Did the same "culture of fear" that had made Singaporeans so "conditioned to distancing ourselves from politics" explain these failures to act morally (TODAY 2002)?

Chasanah's death thus raised questions that extended beyond social issues related exclusively to migrant workers. However, tragedy spurred action. The

Working Committee II – which was to become Transient Workers Count Too (TWC2), one of the key migrant labour civil society organisations – was formed in direct response to this incident. It started as a discussion among friends who were members of the women's rights group Association of Women for Action and Research (AWARE). Specifically, a comment by one of Ng's neighbours, a Mr Neo, galvanised them into action. The man had told *The Straits Times* that he would not have intervened, even if Ng's abuse of Chasanah had been obvious, since it was not his business; justice, he implied, was up to the gods (*The Straits Times* 2002b). These activists were adamant that it should not be so, and launched a campaign to promote the rights of migrant domestic workers.

The formation of TWC2 represented a turning point in the local history of migrant-related social activism. Although the Archdiocesan Commission for the Pastoral Care of Migrants & Itinerant People (ACMI, then CMI) as well as UN Women Singapore (then UNIFEM) had both existed since 1998, neither made public advocacy of migrant workers' rights a consistent priority. As a Catholic organisation, the ACMI concerned itself more with pastoral care.[6] Whatever advocacy efforts it made – such as those with Ministry of Manpower (MOM) officers in the course of case work – tended to be done behind closed doors, because of concerns about provoking the Singapore government. Even then, Bridget Tan, the then-Chairperson of CMI, revealed that this was done without permission from the church, and that the church leaders would have been "alarmed" if they had known she had done anything beyond pastoral care for migrants.[7]

By 2003, UN Women had in fact already organised various activities concerning migrants and human trafficking, but these tended to focus on trafficked migrants in Southeast Asia rather than on those in Singapore. When it became officially registered as a society on 18 August 2004, TWC2 was thus the first NGO to focus exclusively on issues concerning migrant labour, and it was joined a month later by the Humanitarian Organisation of Migration Economics (HOME).

TWC2's status as a registered society was initially made contingent upon its adherence to two conditions: that its constitution clearly state that it would not become a trade union or partake in "trade union-like activities", and that it would not "[network] with foreign organisations that could prove detrimental to Singapore's national interests" (Gee and Ho 2006). The second condition was overcome through dialogue, and TWC2 had no problem complying with the first condition.

HOME faced similar constraints when it was finally registered as a society in September 2004: it was not allowed to be a "proxy, branch or affiliate" for any foreign organisations (Humanitarian Organization for Migration Economics). HOME's founder Bridget Tan was the ex-chairperson of the ACMI (then called CMI). As the church was not able to support a shelter and case advocacy due to perceived political sensitivities, Tan believed that the next logical step was to set up an organisation independent of the church. She decided to call it a 'humanitarian organisation', to show the government that it was not a political organisation and would focus on welfare activities. Since there was a gap in direct service provisions for migrants at the time, Tan believed that it was important to start an organisation focused on this area. She knew through her experiences chairing ACMI that advocacy work on the issue of migrants was sensitive, and wanted to successfully register the organisation first before getting more actively involved in public advocacy.[8]

The Working Committee II's campaign in 2003

During its inaugural nine-month-long campaign in 2003, TWC2 focused its advocacy efforts on public education, organising press conferences, forums and writing letters to the press to discuss the situation of migrant domestic workers. From July to August, for instance, an essay competition for primary schoolchildren was held that garnered over 2,000 entries on topics concerning their experiences with domestic workers at home. This experience was one of several that underscored the potential challenges faced by activists at the time. TWC2 encountered a curious hesitance from schools it had approached to collaborate with: preliminary calls made by the organisers found that school "principals often asked if MOE had given permission to conduct such a competition", and MOE's subsequent endorsement of the initiative was thought to have partly accounted for the overwhelmingly positive response (Gee and Ho 2006). During the same period, proposals for Housing and Development Board (HDB) block parties that were sent to all residential committees nationwide as part of TWC2's 'Sundays Off' campaign yielded only a few replies and one positive response. Similarly, plans for artworks from the HouseWORK Project to form a travelling exhibition at Community Development Councils (CDCs) were scrapped after only two CDCs responded to reject the proposal – even though the exhibits merely explored the value of household chores, and seemed as innocuous as could be.

This is not to say that every single initiative remotely related to migrant workers was met with disapproval, or ignored outright. Indeed, TWC2's 'A Day Off' exhibition that showcased six photographers' pictures of domestic workers at work and during leisure received the support of the Land Transport Authority, and was presented to the public at the Toa Payoh bus interchange as well as in various public libraries. Nevertheless, it would be remiss not to acknowledge that both cautiousness due to self-censorship from citizens and wariness from the state posed difficulties with which TWC2, HOME and other groups working in the area of migrants' rights have had to contend.

New actors, growing cooperation and renewed state contestation: 2005 to 2010

Raising awareness about the plight of migrants through their stories of hardship and exploitation was identified as an important goal in the early years of

HOME's activism, as it was felt that change could only come about when there was sufficient public awareness. To this end, its social workers and volunteers who provided employment advice, legal aid and shelter to workers lobbied reporters, particularly from two of Singapore's major English dailies, *The Straits Times* and *The New Paper*. From 2007, with the establishment of the sociopolitical news website *The Online Citizen*, HOME and TWC2 also actively engaged social media portals to write commentaries, share stories and generally raise awareness of migrant rights issues. In all of these efforts, direct service provision helped complement advocacy. HOME consciously used its direct services and contact with abused migrants to add weight and credibility to its public advocacy efforts, as well as in its dealings with government officials. Similarly, TWC2 launched a crisis helpline in 2006 and started to become more involved in direct services in addition to its research work, with the establishment of a free meal programme – the Cuff Road Project – in 2008.

Momentum on issues concerning migrants' rights was slowly building, and new groups soon joined the activist scene. Migrant Voices started in 2005 as a CD project featuring songs, spoken word performances as well as interviews with activists, and established itself formally as an organisation the following year. Its focus was to engage migrant workers and use the arts to raise awareness of issues affecting migrants – in some respects, objectives that echoed HOME's idea of advocating for migrants through storytelling. Among other activities, volunteers at Migrant Voices taught migrant workers photography, organised art exhibitions, and performed plays with themes about abuse and exploitation (*The Straits Times* 2007).

When the Day Off campaign for domestic workers was relaunched in 2007, the NGO organisers were called to a meeting with the MOM and warned against starting a parliamentary petition on the issue. They were told to remove campaign posters which had already been placed in the country's underground railway stations, and objections were also raised to the use of the word 'slavery' in its campaign message to describe domestic workers who did not have any days off at all.[9] Activists involved later learned from friends working in schools that Ministry of Education (MOE) circulars had been sent to instruct them not to engage with the NGOs – according to the government, the NGOs' attempts to turn students into activists would have a negative impact upon Singapore's bilateral relations with its neighbours.[10] Despite the fact that the government seemed to favour a mandatory day off during private talks with NGOs, it was concerned about a backlash from Singaporean employers and that any aggressive campaign on this issue would polarise the Singapore public and thus lead to 'social instability'.

In 2010, HOME, TWC2 and Migrant Voices decided to organise a vehicle lorry procession to raise awareness of the number of construction workers who had died in traffic accidents that year. It also proposed to pass out flyers on the United Nations International Convention on the Protection of the Rights of All Migrant Workers and Members of Their Families, to raise awareness of international migrant rights standards. Permits for both activities were denied, and the NGOs wrote an open letter in protest. The event was still not allowed to proceed, however, with the Ministry of Home Affairs citing "law and order problems" as well as "disruptions to the community as reasons" (Ministry of Home Affairs 2010). It would appear that so long as activists did not stray into the realm of asserting their civil liberties, such as organising outdoor protests, the government was prepared to allow them some space to raise public awareness of issues and critique government policies.

A new political climate: 2011 to 2015

Several years into their advocacy work, it was more than evident to local activists that they faced several challenges and constraints from both the government and society at large. Nevertheless, the year 2010 seemed to herald a new political climate for civil society. In 2011, the elections demonstrated that the government had yet to win over a more sceptical younger generation of voters, or to compete effectively with new media platforms that were becoming increasingly popular as alternatives to the mainstream media. Faced with citizens' concerns about issues like job security and the rising costs of living, the government has been under mounting pressure to restore public trust and engage more actively with the citizenry.

During this period, the government upped its ante in public engagement. An NGO relationship manager was appointed by the MOM around this time, and government officials more frequently took the lead in initiating meetings with NGOs. Groups like HOME and TWC2 were also encouraged to bring cases of aggrieved migrants to the attention of the government, instead of publicising these cases to the media (Wham 2015).

Contesting the state publicly

In February 2012, over 200 mostly Bangladeshi workers who had not been paid their salaries for several months went on strike at a construction site in Tampines (*The New Paper* 2012). In August that same year, 100 workers from a Panasonic plant started up and publicised a petition to protest poor working conditions and exorbitant recruitment fees (*The Straits Times* 2012a). November 2012 saw almost 200 bus drivers from the government-linked corporation SMRT go on strike to protest poor working conditions and wage discrimination by nationality (*The Straits Times* 2012b). The following month, another group of construction workers refused to work over unpaid salaries (*The Straits Times* 2012c). Two Chinese construction workers from a separate company embroiled in a wage dispute also protested in December by climbing up a crane and refusing to come down (*The Straits Times* 2012d).

These incidents cast doubt on the conscientiousness and efficacy of the MOM's policies and mechanisms for redress, and occasionally produced tensions between the Ministry and civil society. The executive director of HOME, Jolovan Wham, has experienced this personally. MOM had attempted to intimidate HOME by asserting that Wham would be held responsible if the workers took any collective action (Wham 2015), to which the Ministry responded quickly online to deny this. Its claim that Wham had made "baseless allegations" was accompanied, moreover, by lengthy statements that implicitly chided NGOs for unprofessional and "counter-productive" engagement while simultaneously emphasising its own support for such groups. HOME was subsequently reprimanded for this, and its Executive Director was forbidden from criticising government policies publicly (Wham 2015).

Elsewhere, the government acted similarly to defend its public image. When the SMRT bus drivers' strike occurred, the MOM's repeated insistence that the workers should have resolved their concerns through the proper channels foreclosed any substantive discussion of the state of industrial relations in Singapore, or about the efficacy of such avenues of recourse (*The Straits Times* 2012e). All in all, the state's emphasis on the illegal nature of the strike, its criminalisation of the workers, and swift repatriation of 29 individuals without trial (as well as imprisonment of four workers), summarily affirmed its refusal to evaluate the current tripartite industrial relations and fundamentally review protections for workers.

Interestingly, the state's narrative about the bus drivers' strike was not strongly challenged by the key migrant labour NGOs at the time. This led to the formation of a new, temporary advocacy group – Workfair Singapore – that mainly comprised activists Stephanie Chok, Jolovan Wham, Shelley Thio, Vincent Wijeysingha, among others. The group believed that the bus drivers' perspectives were missing from the press coverage, and accordingly set out to provide these, in addition to critical commentary on the state's actions as investigations progressed. A week after the swift deportation of 29 drivers who were alleged to have been active participants in the strike, Workfair published the first of its many online blog posts, a *Civil Society Statement of Solidarity* that called on the state to grant the bus drivers a fair trial and more broadly to "redress the imbalance of power between corporations and workers".[11] Subsequent articles also exposed the limitations of state mechanisms of redress and questioned the effectiveness of the government's investigations into allegations of police brutality. This led to a strongly worded statement from the government accusing the activists of exploiting vulnerable foreign workers for their own political ends (Ministry of Manpower 2013). Equally significant, however, was the fact that HOME and TWC2 were conspicuously absent among the signatories to Workfair's published statements.

If HOME and TWC2 hesitated to become involved in advocating for the bus drivers, though, it was because they rightly foresaw the political sensitivities of such involvement (Wham 2015). At least three activists from Workfair had reported being followed by unnamed individuals who they suspected to be Internal Security Department (ISD) officials (Wham 2015). Two of these activists had directly helped the former bus drivers during the police investigation process, and the drivers also reported being followed by unidentified men, presumably from the ISD. It appeared that the government's accusation that the activists had a political agenda stemmed from genuine suspicion about these individuals' motives, as opposed to being a mere tactic to silence these critics.

On 8 December 2013, approximately 300 South Asian migrant workers rioted in response to a bus accident which killed an Indian worker (*The Straits Times* 2013). Two weeks later, 57 of these men were similarly deported without trial, and 28 were charged in court for rioting. TWC2 and HOME again remained largely inactive in publicly advocating for the workers who were allegedly involved in the riot.[12] Instead, Workfair stepped in to fill the gap. In the aftermath of the riot, Workfair publicly called for the 57 workers to be tried in court rather than arbitrarily deported, and even filed a complaint concerning this to the UN Special Rapporteur for the Human Rights of Migrants.[13] It also expressed concerns about the independence of the Committee of Inquiry (COI) set up to investigate the riot's causes, as well as the appropriateness of the Public Order (Additional Temporary Measures) Bill that granted the MHA expansive powers to police Little India even before the COI's findings were released.[14] In comparison to its work on the SMRT strike, these efforts seemed to elicit a less robust response from the authorities, although the government rebutted the activists' assertion that the deportation was unjust.

These incidents all tested the limits of migrant rights activism. Where they have provoked strong reactions from the government, it appears that some NGOs are less willing to take an openly confrontational stance, leaving it to individual activists acting in their individual capacity to tackle these issues.

Legacies of contemporary activism

Leading legislative changes

Looking back on various developments since Singapore's independence, we find the local history of migrant rights' activism to be one of both continuity and change. Even as amendments to labour laws have incorporated positive measures which activists have long called for, the state has continued to parry online criticism from NGOs in ways that challenge the credibility of activists at times.

No fundamental change in labour policy has occurred to date, although the government has made small reforms in policies and practices related to the governance of migrant labour. For example, after almost a dozen domestic workers fell to their deaths within the first half of 2012 while doing window cleaning and hanging laundry, and following a campaign organised by HOME (*The Star* 2012) to ban these practices, local authorities implemented stricter regulations and doubled the existing penalty for employers who violated this law (Ministry of Manpower 2012). A year earlier, in response to concerns about FDWs being exploited by employment agencies, the government also revised several provisions under the Employment Agencies Act in 2011 so that agency personnel were legally required to be certified, registered, and thus regulated by more stringent rules concerning fee refunds, such as in cases where workers were prematurely dismissed from employment (Ministry of Manpower 2011).

Other significant changes have resulted from comprehensive reviews of the EFMA and EA in 2012 and 2013 respectively. Up until 2012, for instance, it was not an explicit requirement for employers to provide food and lodging for workers awaiting case resolution at MOM before repatriation. Nor were they required to ensure that the In-Principle Approval (IPA) letter workers receive before departing their country was in their native language (Ministry of Manpower 2011). It is also now against regulations to attempt to repatriate workers when they have outstanding employment claims which they wish to file with the Ministry of Manpower.[15] More recently, the government has enacted changes to make pay slips and detailed employment records compulsory (*The Straits Times* 2015).

These are all important changes; however, none of them really addresses the three fundamental issues that enable foreign workers' basic human and labour rights to be violated, as outlined at the beginning of this chapter. By extension, none of these truly challenges or undermines the current status quo in industrial relations either.

What all of this amounts to, in effect, is the "technocratic management and resolution of political conflict" (Bal 2013a). Workers are encouraged to resolve their workplace issues through the MOM, and are discouraged from collectively contesting their rights as enshrined in state legislation. Their grievances are channelled into official sites of resolution and then "resolved administratively", despite the fact that only changes in legal structures offer the possibility of renegotiating the power asymmetries between employers and employees that are a root cause of most workplace disputes (Bal 2013a). Seen in this light, the minor changes made to various laws over the past five years are a long step away from systemic change, and instead represent a mere expansion of "the scope of [the MOM's] complaints mechanisms" available – the tweaking of a creaky system so that it might run a little more smoothly. This, coupled with the swift suppression of any large-scale collective action by workers, seems intended to maintain the status quo, not revise it.

Several things lend credence to this view; the first is the growing capability of the government-linked MWC (which launched a mobile office in February 2015), while the second is the activists' estimates of the low prosecution rates of employers who infringe labour laws. Neither the 2011 case of *Lee Chiang Theng v. Public Prosecutor* nor the joint MOM-MWC survey of foreign worker satisfaction in 2014 inspire much confidence in the state's willingness to safeguard workers' rights within the current framework, let alone restructure the system to do so (*The Straits Times* 2014). And despite the state's continuing engagement of civil society on various policy issues (such as its drafting of a second anti-trafficking national plan), it remains reluctant to enable more productive consultations with NGOs by sharing its own data.[16]

Increased prosecution of errant employers would ostensibly mean greater deterrence against contraventions of the law and hence better economic productivity, while a mutual exchange of information between state and civil society actors would clearly benefit the government in its policy-making role. From the perspectives of long-time activists, however, part of the answer lies in the state's concerns about national security. Bal's (2013b) analysis of how Singapore's foreign manpower legislation developed identifies the state's objective of preventing irregular migration as the key motivation behind various laws. Local activists have also pointed out separately that many laws seem crafted to ensure that labour migrants here are "law-abiding temporary immigrant[s] rather than [workers] whose needs are recognised as entitlements" (Humanitarian Organisation for Migration Economics *et al.* 2011). Ultimately, though, little can be said conclusively without further research to understand how security concerns are framed in relation to human rights within official discourse.

The more, the better: public awareness through the media

Since public education has been a key priority for both HOME and TWC2, we wanted to find out if the burgeoning activism of migrant workers since the formal inception of both organisations in 2004 was reflected in an increased visibility within mainstream media. To this end, we conducted an analysis of the news articles produced by the main news outlets in Singapore from 2001 to November 2015 – specifically, those published in English-language newspapers. Using keywords related to migrant rights activism, a range of relevant articles was found that included quotes by activists and discussions about activities organised by the NGOs, among others. As seen in Figure 6.1, a general upward trend may be observed. There was an average of 4.5 articles published between 2000 and 2004. Following the formation of TWC2 and HOME, however, analysis showed that there has been an average of 27 articles published yearly from 2005 to 2015. In other words, a positive correlation exists between the growth

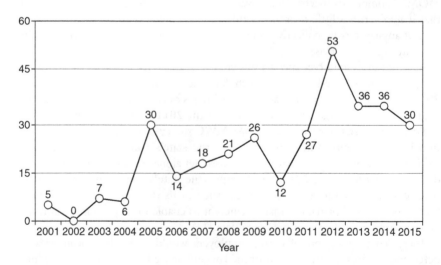

Figure 6.1 Number of migrant labour activism-related articles produced per year.
Source: created by authors using data from Factiva.

of activism relating to migrant workers and its visibility in the mainstream media. Interestingly, the year 2012 was an anomaly, with 53 articles produced – twice the annual average. This outlier could be reflective of the increase in migrant worker-related incidents in 2012 which, as discussed earlier, included two different strikes and one public petition to protest working conditions.

Campaign strategies and networks

We interviewed 15 local activists[17] and sought their views on a range of issues concerning their activism, including advocacy strategies. These conversations revealed that some favour closed-door negotiations with the government for better results, while others prefer questioning policies and state actions in an open public space.

Such differences exist not only between individuals, but also between organisations: HOME and TWC2 adopted slightly different approaches vis-à-vis the government when both organisations were beginning their respective activities, and more recent events such as the 2012 strike and the 2013 riot have thrown such distinctions into sharper relief. Activists like Jolovan Wham and Alex Au, for instance, appear more sharply critical of the government in their public comments than others, and Workfair's formation confirmed that significant differences in individual convictions exist not only across advocacy groups but also within them. Two questions might be asked: (1) why individual activists hold the convictions that they do, and (2) what impact such differences have had on the overall movement.

Based on the interviews, we observed that the activists' ideas about which sorts of advocacy strategies they should use were influenced by two factors. The first concerned activists' goals, including (more broadly) self-perceptions of their activist work and what it entails. Second, decisions about what strategies would best achieve specific goals were mediated by activists' perceptions of the government – a key target of their work. Together, these two factors formed a straightforward rational calculus that determined their choices.

Although no causality can be established, we noted that activists who saw the government in a more negative light tended to adopt or favour a more openly critical stance than others in their public advocacy. One such activist indicted the government for not being genuinely consultative, for instance, which contrasted with another's remarks that "the form of [consultation and dialogue] is actually more important than having no form at all", since "[w]ith an avenue to engage, it creates a basis for future updates and checks back which serve to build confidence and trust over time".[18] Some emphasised adopting a nonconfrontational, relationship-building approach to create trust between the government and civil society, while others believed that because certain government policies were inherently flawed, relations between state and civil society have in reality been unable to escape a persistent sense of wariness from government actors who are acutely conscious of the need to maintain a positive public image.

For the most part, however, we found that local activists shared very similar perceptions of the government. The second variable thus appears equally important in explaining variation in advocacy strategies used; we attribute such differences to the fact that the local activists we interviewed likely had similar goals in mind but different priorities. A useful (though crude) distinction can be made between goals related to a narrowly defined social cause – in this case, labour rights – and goals related to broader societal issues beyond this field (e.g. transparency in governance). We have thus far referred to those involved in advocating for migrant workers as 'activists', but this label potentially obscures subtle differences among individuals in terms of what change it is exactly that they are striving to create – whether, for instance, they see their work as primarily labour rights-focused or as indivisible from other human rights.

That said, a few qualifications should be noted. For starters, activists operating within organisations necessarily focus on different areas of work for the whole group to function smoothly. A person might spend most of his time on direct services, for instance, but it would be misleading to immediately conclude therefore that he is less supportive of advocacy work and perhaps even of strategies that include harsh public criticism of the government. In addition, people may and often do hold more nuanced views: one interviewee appeared to favour diplomacy so as to cultivate good relationships with state officials, but at the same time differentiated this approach from ACMI's private, closed-door representations to the government. Another activist mused that her previously unapologetic attitude about openly shaming the government was in retrospect "naïve" and "counter-productive", but believes that closed-door discussions "make your countrymen more stupid". Moreover, the organisation under her leadership has currently placed certain forms of public advocacy on hold in order to focus on building a community of workers who can advocate for themselves in the future.[19]

As the above examples indicate, advocacy strategies are better described in terms of continuums rather than as clear dichotomies such as public versus private advocacy, diplomatic versus tactless, etc. It would be unfair to conclude that those who determinedly avoid vocal criticism of the government must naturally disparage these actions by other activists, but thinking in such absolutes also overlooks the possibility that one approach might legitimise another. State actors might see the task of maintaining a public image that is consultative as desirable, for instance, partly because certain NGOs are seen as better alternatives to other, more publicly critical ones.

Conclusion

Although it may seem dispiriting to conclude that few significant legislative changes have been achieved through social activism, our examination of the history of state–civil society interactions – including the government's continued resistance to substantive change – offers reasons as to why this is so. Local activists have made great strides in other ways: many agree that much change has occurred in the realm of public education, while the main NGOs' development of their capacity as well as expertise in advocating for and serving migrant workers is itself an achievement to celebrate.

The history of local activism concerning migrants' rights is one marked by constraints upon forms of advocacy and fear about potential consequences of public advocacy, both within civil society and from the government. Moving forward, one key challenge stands out: the question of how to redraw the lines that ostensibly distinguish the political from the social. Diversity in advocacy strategies is inevitable, even desirable; but how can local activists stand in greater solidarity publicly to achieve their shared goals? At this juncture – having achieved so much and yet so little, but also having new opportunities for advocacy with the Internet and a more informed public – this seems more important for progress than ever before.

Notes

1. J. Wham (2013). "Still struggling for a weekly day off". *Workfair Singapore*. Available at https://workfairsingapore.wordpress.com/2013/06/15/still-struggling-for-a-weekly-day-off/.
2. Personal interview with Vincent Cheng, 16 May 2015, Singapore.
3. Ibid.
4. Ibid.
5. Ibid.
6. Personal interview with Bridget Tan, 8 September 2015, Singapore.
7. Ibid.
8. Ibid.
9. Personal interview with Jolovan Wham, 8 May 2015, Singapore.
10. Ibid.
11. Workfair Singapore (2012). "Civil society statement of solidarity on SMRT bus drivers". Available at https://workfairsingapore.wordpress.com/2012/12/08/civil-society-statement-of-solidarity-on-smrt-bus-drivers-labour-dispute/.
12. Personal interview with Vincent Wijeysingha, 6 May 2015, Singapore.
13. Workfair Singapore (2014a). "Workfair Singapore's response to the Little India COI Report". Available at https://workfairsingapore.wordpress.com/2014/07/08/workfair-singapores-response-to-the-little-india-coi-report/.
14. Workfair Singapore (2014b). "Public Order Bill disproportionate and ill-timed". Available at https://workfairsingapore.wordpress.com/2014/01/23/public-order-bill-disproportionate-and-ill-timed/.
15. Employment of Foreign Manpower Act (Chapter 91A).
16. StopTraffickingSG (2015). "Some thoughts on the Public Consultation on Trafficking in Persons". Available at http://stoptrafficking.sg/2015/06/23/some-thoughts-on-the-public-consultation-on-trafficking-in-persons/.
17. They include Vincent Cheng, Vanessa Ho, Melissa Kwee, Saleemah Ismail, Claudine Lim, Bridget Tan, Jolovan Wham and Vincent Wijeysingha.
18. Personal interview with Melissa Kwee, Saleemah Ismail and Claudine Lim, 17 June 2015, Singapore.
19. Personal interview with Vanessa Ho, 11 May 2015, Singapore.

References

Arotçarena, G. (2015). *Priest in Geylang: The Untold Story of the Geylang Catholic Centre*. Singapore: Ethos Books.

Bal, C. (2013a). "Production politics and migrant labour advocacy in Singapore". *Journal of Contemporary Asia* **45**(2): 219–242.

Bal, C. (2013b). *The Politics of Obedience: Bangladeshi Construction Workers and the Migrant Labour Regime in Singapore*. Murdoch University.

Barr, M.D. (2008). *Singapore's Catholic Social Activists: Alleged Marxist Conspirators*. Singapore: NUS Press.

Gee, J. and E. Ho (2006). *Dignity Overdue*. Singapore: Select Publishers.

Goh, D.P.S. (2010). "State and social Christianity in post-colonial Singapore". *Sojourn: Journal of Social Issues in Southeast Asia* (25): 54–89.

Humanitarian Organisation for Migration Economics, Transient Workers Count Too and United Nations Development Fund for Women (2011). "Made to Work".

Humanitarian Organisation for Migrant Economics (2014). Helpdesk Report (Q1 & Q2).

Ministry of Home Affairs (2010). Letter of reply. Humanitarian Organisation for Migration Economics and Transient Workers Count Too.

Ministry of Manpower (2011). *Changes to the Employment Agency Regulatory Framework*.

Ministry of Manpower (2012). "Enhanced & safe working conditions must be In place before FDWs allowed to clean window exteriors". Available at www.mom.gov.sg.

Ministry of Manpower (2013). Joint response to media queries on statements by NGOs/individuals and Former SMRT driver He Junling.

Ministry of Manpower (2014). *Labour Force in Singapore 2014*.

Ministry of Manpower (2015). *Foreign Workforce Numbers*.

National Archives Singapore (1987). Christian Conference of Asia (CCA).

StopTraffickingSG (2015). "Some thoughts on the public consultation on trafficking in persons". Available at http://stoptrafficking.sg/2015/06/23/some-thoughts-on-the-public-consultation-on-trafficking-in-persons/.

The New Paper (2012). "200 foreign workers hold protest in Tampines". *The New Paper*.

The Star (2012). "Group wants maids to be prohibited from cleaning outside of windows". *The Star Online*.

The Straits Times (1978). "Domestic servants: Govt confirms $10,000 scheme". *The Straits Times*, Singapore.

The Straits Times (2002a). "18 1/2 years, caning for man who abused maid". *The Straits Times*, Singapore.

The Straits Times (2002b). "Starved, battered, dead". *The Straits Times*, Singapore.

The Straits Times (2007). "A peek into their lives". *The Straits Times*, Singapore.

The Straits Times (2012a). "Panasonic workers demand better pay; they go online to protest against poor wages and working conditions". *The Straits Times*, Singapore.

The Straits Times (2012b). "Key grouse said to be over unequal salaries". *The Straits Times*, Singapore.

The Straits Times (2012c). "Foreign workers say firm has not been paying them". *The Straits Times*, Singapore.

The Straits Times (2012d). "Two Chinese workers arrested for unlawfully remaining at the place". *The Straits Times*, Singapore.

The Straits Times (2012e). "102 SMRT bus drivers protest against pay". *The Straits Times*, Singapore.

The Straits Times (2013). "Little India Riot: 27 nabbed, more expected to be arrested in hours and days that follow". *The Straits Times*, Singapore.

The Straits Times (2014). "Little India Riot: Survey by MOM, MWC shows foreign worker satisfaction levels remain high". *The Straits Times*, Singapore.

The Straits Times (2015). "Parliament: Employment Act amended to make payslips and employment terms more transparent". *The Straits Times*, Singapore.

TODAY (2002). "Is it apathy […] or fear". *TODAY*, Mediacorp.

Transient Workers Count Too (2012). "Worse off for working? Kickbacks, intermediary fees and migrant construction workers in Singapore".

Wham, J. (2013). "Still struggling for a weekly day off". *Workfair Singapore*. Available at https://workfairsingapore.wordpress.com/2013/06/15/still-struggling-for-a-weekly-day-off/.

Wham, J. (2015). Interview with Jolovan Wham. E. Ang.

Workfair Singapore (2012). "Civil society statement of solidarity on SMRT bus drivers". Available at https://workfairsingapore.wordpress.com/2012/12/08/civil-society-statement-of-solidarity-on-smrt-bus-drivers-labour-dispute/.

Workfair Singapore (2014a). "Workfair Singapore's response to the Little India COI Report". Available at https://workfairsingapore.wordpress.com/2014/07/08/workfair-singapores-response-to-the-little-india-coi-report/.

Workfair Singapore (2014b). "Public Order Bill disproportionate and ill-timed". Available at https://workfairsingapore.wordpress.com/2014/01/23/public-order-bill-disproportionate-and-ill-timed/.

7 Against a teleological reading of the advancement of women's rights in Singapore

Edwina Shaddick, Goh Li Sian and Isabella Oh

Introduction

As Singapore celebrates its 50 years as a sovereign nation in 2015, it takes stock of all it has achieved during this time. With regard to women's rights, organisations like the World Economic Fund (WEF) and the United Nations (UN) have lauded Singapore's progress in areas such as educational attainment, health and, to some extent, economic participation (United Nations Committee on the Elimination of Discrimination against Women 2011; World Economic Forum 2014).

Indeed, significant historical developments like the implementation of the Women's Charter, and other legal and policy developments such as the police handling of rape cases, do suggest that 'progress' has been made. Yet in this chapter, Goh Li Sian, Edwina Shaddick and Isabella Oh critically evaluate the teleological and even celebratory narrative implicit in many accounts of women's history in Singapore. It is argued that the benefits of advancement in women's rights over the past decades have often been distributed unevenly. Starting from the inception of the Singapore Council of Women (SCW) in the 1950s, the authors offer a unique interpretation of women's rights history in Singapore and reveal a more complicated picture than was previously envisioned.

Contemporary Singapore is a more gender-equitable society than Singapore in the past. At least, this statement has been repeated often, both by lay persons and women's rights activists, who either want to suggest that women in Singapore have much to be grateful for and should therefore be content, or perceive in this teleological narrative a promise of greater advancement towards the future end-point of a gender-equal utopia. Journalist Kirsten Han addressed the former attitude in her article "Considering feminism in Singapore": "there are even people who will say that the women have won. That, through the Women's Charter and the exclusion of women from National Service, women have successfully seized power and advantage from men".[1]

Despite being substantially better informed about the state of women's rights and gender justice in Singapore, however, there are certain similarities between that assumption and narratives perpetuated by histories of gender-equality activism in Singapore. For example, Singam argues (2007) that the present day represents an advancement for women's rights from the past, suggesting that the future holds out greater opportunity and justice for women. However, such a narrative is arguably questionable. Despite the many benefits of advancement in women's rights over the past decades that have undoubtedly materialised, these have often been distributed unevenly.

A teleological explanation of a thing or social phenomenon provides an account of that thing or phenomenon's given purpose. The teleological narrative, first developed by Ancient Greek philosopher Aristotle, was hugely influential over several thousand years of Western philosophy, notably prompting Hegel to develop his theory of world history. Hegelian thought, however, was oriented towards a supposed end-point in history, in which these various groups would eventually be subsumed into a form of life with no different identities and which left violent conflict behind.

Teleological accounts of societal and scientific phenomena have since fallen out of favour, and the reasons will not be recounted in full here. However, it may suffice to say that teleological accounts have been criticised for being reductive, exclusionary and even harmful. Yet when it comes to the claims of social justice and human rights, teleological narratives are tempting because they provide a utopian goal towards which to aspire – a world where justice prevails in social, economic and political relations between members of different groups, whether such groups are differentiated by characteristics of gender, race, class, sexuality, national origin, and other markers of status and belonging.

Beyond the optimistic 'forward-march' narrative of women's rights history, it could be suggested that the advancement of women's rights cannot be read as 'two steps forward, one step back' but rather 'some steps forward, an unknown number of steps back, and an equally undisclosed number of steps sideways'. This is without even considering the tensions and areas of contestation among multiple actors in Singapore's political arena: state actors, some of whom have varying attitudes towards the prospect of concession to feminist concerns and recommendations about social policy; civil society actors, who have used varying means and channels to achieve their goals, and international actors, who may be more or less keen to use their influence to bring about greater respect for women's rights in Singapore.

In the following sections, we recount the remarkable events of women's rights activism in Singapore, starting from the early years of independence. The term 'events', rather than 'advancements', is used, as it is questionable whether such changes were advancements in the first place. Even if they may be considered net gains for women in Singapore, a more complex narrative will be more easily embraced if we explore these changes in a deliberately non-celebratory manner before pausing to evaluate the impact of these 'events', and arguably uneven distribution of the benefits achieved.

Tracing women's rights activism

One would not be wrong in saying that there are many achievements to celebrate. At the most basic level, women in Singapore have seen tremendous improvement in terms of mortality and basic health due to socio-economic progress and developments in health technology (Phua 2010).

The passing of the Women's Charter (1961)

Perhaps the Women's Charter may be considered one of the more striking achievements brought about in Singapore's post-colonial era. The Women's Charter addressed gender imbalances by providing women with more protections in marriage and divorce, including outlawing polygamy. The Charter itself was a piece of legislation that the pioneering women's movement had been advocating for many years. Comprising prominent and passionate individuals like Shirin Fozdar, Mrs George Lee, Checha Davies and Elizabeth Choy, the SCW was a vocal advocate of women's rights from its inception in 1952. Indeed, the SCW was founded to serve a role that was different from the welfare groups of that era, which Fozdar noted "could not ameliorate the legal disabilities under which women have been suffering and which were the root causes of many of the social evils" (1951). In both their personal capacity and as representatives of the SWC, these women's rights activists voiced their opinions through letters (Fozdar 1955) and also lobbied legislators, associations (Lee 1954) and political parties.

The SCW found the most support for their cause in the People's Action Party (PAP), which in 1959 campaigned with the promise of "One Man One Wife" in their election manifesto. For this and several other reasons, the PAP won the elections by a landslide. Hence the passing of the Women's Charter may also be seen as a fulfilment of the PAP's election promises following their victory at the polls (Chew 1994).

While the abolition of polygamy was the cornerstone of the Women's Charter, it would be untrue to say that polygamy has been completely outlawed in Singapore. Polygamy remains legal and permissible for Muslims under the Syariah court in Singapore. However, the passage of the Charter did force the Muslim community to look into further means of improving the status of Muslim women through an amendment of the Muslim Ordinance in 1960. This amendment addressed the problem of maintenance for divorced Muslim women and restricted the practice of polygamy (Chew 1994). It may be said that the manner in which the issue of polygamy, and women's rights in general, was and continues to be addressed is typical of Singapore's model of multiculturalism and the state's long-standing approach to managing the Malay-Muslim community. Scholars like Noor Aisha binte Abdul Rahman have argued that the maintenance of Syariah in Singapore is not incompatible with ratifying human rights conventions like the Convention for the Elimination of All Forms of Discrimination Against Women (CEDAW), and that in "acknowledging the rights of the minority to determine and practice its own personal laws, the state has unwittingly compounded the problem by relying on dominant stakeholders predisposed to conservatism with adverse repercussions on women" (Rahman 2014).

Limited activism in the 1970s

Following the consolidation of power by the PAP in the 1960s, state mechanisms like the Internal Security Act (ISA), the Societies Act and the Sedition Act were exercised to control civil society organisations. Despite this curtailing of civil society, women's rights in Singapore did experience some advancement in the late 1960s to mid-1980s. This progress was most evident in the workplace and was largely brought about by the Employment Act enacted in 1969, which allowed for greater protection for women at work, including protection against the unfair dismissal of pregnant women as well as 16 weeks of paid maternity leave. Complementarily, the Foreign Domestic Worker (FDW) Law was passed in 1978, allowing families to hire foreign domestic workers (FDWs) to live in their homes and help with domestic work. This allowed more women to re-enter the workforce after having children, and coincides with an increase of women in the workplace, both in terms of the percentage of women who work as well as a percentage of the total labour force (Ministry of Labour 1995).

Yet viewing these two Acts as part of the same forward progression of women's rights is questionable. Although more Singaporean women have been able to enter the workforce as a result of domestic workers taking over care duties in the home, it has not been an improvement on the state of women in Singapore insofar as FDWs who work in Singapore have few legal rights which are poorly enforced. According to a recent research study by the Humanitarian Organization for Migration Economics (HOME), significant gaps exist in the content and enforcement of legislation relating to FDWs. On a similar note, Chapter 6 of this volume argues that the exclusion of FDWs from the Employment of Foreign Manpower Act (EFMA) and the Work Injury Compensation Act (WICA) in Singapore denies FDWs basic employment-related rights.

Overall, it has been suggested that the progression of (middle- to higher income, professional) women's rights in Singapore has been made possible by the devaluation of other groups of women, including those with less education, lower income and those not from Singapore, but also by valuing institutions above the welfare and rights of individual women. Scholars such as Shirlena Huang and Brenda Yeoh (1996) have described how wealthier women are able to "transfer their previous subordination onto their hired help" because they are "simply exploiting economically disadvantaged women in the same way that men used women to free themselves of reproductive responsibilities and advance in the productive sphere". More recently, Teo (2014) noted how this progress comes at the expense not only of FDWs but also of lower income Singaporean women. It is not just that women from low-income groups do not benefit from the extra help that comes from having a domestic worker; they are doubly punished because government policy creates a status quo where having such a worker is expected and the norm (Teo 2014). Thus, it is arguably harder now for low-income women to balance both caregiving duties and productive labour in the policy era of domestic workers in Singapore.

The formation of SCWO (1980)

It should be noted that the Singapore Council of Women's Organisations (SCWO) was conceptualised towards the end of the 1970s as an umbrella body to unite the smaller women's organisations in Singapore, which ranged from business groups (e.g. Business & Professional Women's Association) to community groups (e.g. Singapore Muslim Women's Association) and advocacy groups (e.g. Society Against Family Violence). Since its formation, the SCWO has provided services in line with its focus on economic empowerment and family violence. The SCWO also represents Singapore on regional and international platforms such as the Association of Southeast Asian Nations (ASEAN) Confederation of Women's Organisations. In May 2014, the SCWO was granted special consultative status to the United Nations Economic and Social Council (ECOSOC), allowing attendance by the SCWO at events and conferences, the use of UN facilities and submission of written statements to UN agencies. While the SCWO considers itself to be a part of civil society in Singapore, the organisation has not engaged in much activism for women's rights. This may be attributed to its mandate as the national coordinating body of women's organisations in Singapore and the practical constraints that come with being an umbrella body for many different women's organisations.

The re-emergence of activism for women's rights in the mid-1980s

As the population policies of the 1960s and 1970s began to bear fruit, the 1980 Census indicated that better-educated women were having fewer children than less-educated women, and that many graduate women were remaining single (Wong and Yeoh 2003). This trend alarmed the state and their response to it revealed attitudes and mindsets that were deeply eugenic. This translated into the devaluation of certain groups of women by the state, while collective goals were prioritised above the welfare and rights of individual women, made clear during the 1983 National Day Rally Speech and the Great Marriage Debate that followed. In a way, these events also played a role in reawakening the women's rights movement and civil society in general.

In his 1983 National Day Rally speech, then-Prime Minister Lee Kuan Yew worried that, if this trend continued, the following generation might be "depleted of the talented". Mr Lee's comments sparked a public controversy, which the press dubbed the Great Marriage Debate. Indignant Singaporeans argued that they were being treated like "second-class citizens", and even the more highly educated citizens felt insulted by his comments (Lyons 2007). Still, the government pushed on and introduced a slew of eugenicist policies the following year as steps towards encouraging graduate women to marry and have more children. For example, the Graduate Mothers' Priority Scheme was introduced, where children of graduate mothers, beginning from the third child, would receive priority in Primary One registration in a school of their choice.

In addition to questions of which socio-economic groups were more fit to reproduce, the Great Marriage Debate also involved a discussion of women's roles. During his speech, Mr Lee Kuan Yew bemoaned the fact that giving women and girls equal opportunities in education and employment had "affected their traditional role as mothers":

> Equal employment opportunities, yes, but we shouldn't get our women into jobs where they cannot, at the same time, be mothers [...]. You just can't be doing a full-time heavy job like that of a doctor, engineer and run a home and bring up children [...] their contribution to the next generation [...] is more important than their contribution to this generation.

Graduate women, rather than graduate men, were singled out for not reproducing. Vivienne Wee recalls receiving a phone call in 1984 from the Singapore Broadcasting Corporation. She was asked if she would like to go on television to explain why, as a graduate woman, she did not have children. Wee hung up.[2]

The inception of AWARE (1985)

Against the backdrop of the Great Marriage Debate, the voices of concerned citizens and would-be activists began to consolidate, organise and collectively speak out on the rights of women in Singapore (AWARE 2015a). The National University of Singapore Society held a forum in November 1984, "Women's Choices, Women's Lives", bringing together women from different professional backgrounds such as orthopaedic surgeon Kanwaljit Soin, director of the National Library Hedwig Anuar and deputy Sunday editor of the *Singapore Monitor* Margaret Thomas. During the forum, participants voiced their concerns regarding the government's family and population policies, in particular how women were being singled out as being responsible for the falling fertility rate.

"Many of us felt the injustice of being ordered around, being told to do this or that, but never being consulted [...]. I think that we were all at boiling point when that forum was held", Lena Lim said in an interview in 2005 (Lyons 2007). Following the forum, it was felt that there was a need for an organisation that would specifically focus on improving women's social and legal statuses in Singapore. The Association of Women for Action and Research (AWARE) was launched in 1985 and immediately began its activism via research and advocacy work on a number of issues, from violence against women to sexist media representations of women.

Landmark amendments to the Women's Charter (1996)

The Women's Charter as passed in 1961 outlawed polygamy but was silent on domestic violence. This changed in 1996, when the Charter was amended to include new provisions to protect women against 'family violence', expanding protection for victims and including emotional and psychological harm on top of physical harm. Victims could also obtain Personal Protection Orders (PPO) from a newly established Family Court. The Court could issue mandatory counselling for both victims and perpetrators, and penalties were also increased.

The success of these new provisions may be attributed to nearly a decade's worth of activism by AWARE and support by the SCWO, culminating in the tabling of the Family Violence Bill in 1995 by Nominated Member of Parliament Kanwaljit Soin, a founding member and former president of AWARE. In 1986, the first Task Force for the Prevention of Violence was launched, chaired by the SCWO and AWARE. In the following year, the Task Force partnered the National Crime Prevention Council in organising a public forum and a year-long public education programme (Singam 2002).

In the years that followed, AWARE continued to actively advocate on the issue of violence against women. The handbook *Men, Women and Violence* was published in partnership with the Singapore Association of Women Lawyers (SAWL); Rape Awareness Week was launched in collaboration with *The New Paper*; and more forums and study groups were organised by AWARE (Singam 2002). In 1995, Soin moved a private member's Bill on Family Violence. The Bill was defeated. However, the government later incorporated many of Soin's suggestions into its 1996 revision of the Women's Charter, dealing specifically with more protection for victims of domestic violence.

Reflecting on the defeat of the Bill, Soin notes (2011),

> [S]ome good things did come about from this aborted bill. Firstly, it generated a great deal of media attention and this brought the subject of family violence very much into public consciousness. [...] Secondly, some important legislative and practice changes were implemented as a result of the Family Violence Bill. At the second reading of the bill on 1 November 1995, Mr Wong Kan Seng [then-Minister for Home Affairs] said "Since April last year, an interagency Work Group on Spousal Violence was formed by my Ministry to recommend measures to improve and co-ordinate the management of spousal violence cases and to find innovative ways of dealing with them. Here I would give credit to Dr Soin for the impetus in setting up this Work Group.

Changes to migration and citizenship laws (1999)

Prior to 1999, there was a stark difference in the immigration policy: there were no preconditions for foreign wives to be sponsored for permanent residency by their Singaporean husbands, while foreign husbands could only obtain permanent residency on their own merit (i.e. by finding full-time employment that would qualify them for a work visa). The implication was clear: foreign wives could depend on their husbands to provide, but foreign husbands had to show their ability to earn an income. The same difference applied when it came to the citizenship of children: children born to Singaporean fathers received citizenship by descent, whereas those born to Singaporean mothers had to apply for citizenship.

After years of lobbying by AWARE and other groups, a change in policy allowing Singaporean women to sponsor their foreign husbands for permanent residency was enacted in 1999 and gender-neutral citizenship by descent was introduced in 2004. While this equalisation of citizenship laws between the genders should be acknowledged as an advancement of women's rights in Singapore, it must be noted that difficulties remain for transnational couples, and have played out in a specifically gendered manner. Since the mid-2000s, there has been a surge in the number of Singaporean men taking foreign brides. Hailing from other parts of Asia, news reports suggest that such women had and continue to have difficulties in ensuring a right to remain in Singapore, with immigration passes that remain valid for only up to a year or less.

The precariousness of the right to remain is known to create a power imbalance in the marital relationship, creating certain conditions in which domestic violence flourishes. In 2005, Channel NewsAsia reported that AWARE had been receiving more calls for help from foreign brides who had been victims of abuse and emotional harassment (Channel NewsAsia 2005). AWARE followed up with a position paper in 2006 on foreign brides, looking into the practices of international matchmaking agencies, coming up with recommendations to implement more regulation and protection for women (AWARE 2006). In 2012, the government created two new visa categories: the Long-Term Visit Pass (LTVP) and the Long-Term Visit Pass Plus (LTVP+), which is meant to offer foreign spouses a path towards permanent residency, thus preventing the need to rely on short-term Social Visit Passes. In 2015, more measures were implemented to help foreign spouses stand a better chance of finding work and being financially independent from their Singaporean spouses.

However, difficulties still remain for some transnational families, particularly those from lower income backgrounds. Although long-term passes allow foreign spouses time to remain in Singapore, even though they may be unable to receive permanent residency, these passes are still in regular need of renewal, and often do not provide a level of stability and peace of mind that families need.

Women's rights activism in the twenty-first century

Persistent eugenicist mindset by the state

Although the Graduate Mothers' Priority Scheme of 1984 was scrapped relatively quickly, the eugenicist and elitist worldview it embodied has arguably persisted, most notably in a support scheme for young low-income families introduced in 2004. According to the Ministry of Social and Family Development (2015), the Home Ownership Plus Education (HOPE) scheme "aims to give […] families a head start to improve their socio-economic status by upgrading their skills and investing resources in their children's education".

The benefits of the HOPE scheme are indisputable – there is a S$60,000 housing grant and a S$1,000 once-off grant to offset utilities charges, as well as annual education bursaries for each child. Employment and training incentives are also provided, as well as ongoing employment and family support. However, in order to be eligible for these benefits, each family must have no more than two children.

The attempt to control the reproductive destinies of women, though no longer aimed at highly educated women to have more children, is still apparent in such a policy which discourages women who are on a lower income, and less likely to be highly educated, from having more children. Ironically, this policy exists alongside the general exhortation by the government to encourage Singaporeans to have more children. In essence, the upshot is that while children from middle- and upper-class households are encouraged, children from lower income households are treated as unwelcome burdens on societies, and support for lower income families is made conditional upon there being a limited number of such persons. Such unequal treatment of reproductive decisions also has an ethnicised dimension: as of September 2012, it was reported that 45 per cent of women in the HOPE scheme were Malay, while 33 per cent were Chinese and 15 per cent Indian (Singapore Parliamentary Report 2012).

Solving Singapore's demographic woes cannot realistically only focus on encouraging well-off families to have children. Moreover, extending incentives to lower income households to start families will be more effective than providing financial incentives to already well-off people. Yet such thinking seems not to have made any headway in Singapore's population policies which continue to be drawn along class lines, denying reproductive justice to lower income women who want larger families, while Singapore experiences unprecedented levels of socio-economic inequality.

The institution of marriage

Beyond whether or not women possess certain characteristics desired by the state, women's rights and their value is outweighed by the value of institutions, namely marriage. This may be seen from two examples: the legality of marital rape and the treatment of single mothers.

Marital rape

Marital rape, or non-consensual sex between husband and wife, is not considered an offence, and to this day, immunity is provided to men who rape their spouses due to the all-important preservation of the family unit. In response to No to Rape, a campaign to abolish marital immunity, which gathered 3,000 signatures for its petition to criminalise marital rape in 2009, the Ministry of Community Development (2010) stated:

> A balance needs to be struck between various interests, such as that of protecting vulnerable women and preserving the institution of marriage.

> The Government believes that such a balanced and calibrated approach is a better one than abolishing marital immunity altogether and will continue to retain sections 375(4) and 376A(5) in the Penal Code.

Following these comments, the government reiterated its family-focused approach again in its report to the UN Committee for CEDAW in 2011. Elaborating upon the amendments to the laws governing marriage and divorce under Article 16 (Marriage and Family Life), the government accounted for the calibrated approach to marital rape by stating: "Abolishing marital immunity entirely may change the whole complexion of marriage in our society".

Single mothers

The rights of single mothers are also curtailed for a similar reason. In 2015, it was announced that the government was reviewing the discrepancies in benefits for unwed mothers in different areas (Kok 2015). Yet less often noted is the fact that the discrepancy in housing eligibility was introduced only in 1994. Prior to that, single parents had always been able to buy flats directly from the HDB by forming a family unit with their child.

In 1994, this policy stopped. Single parents could thenceforth only buy their flats on the open resale market, where flats are more expensive. Housing policy was used to express disapproval of unmarried mothers, and provide an obvious disincentive against having a child out of wedlock. The announcement was made by then-Prime Minister Goh Chok Tong in his National Day speech (Ministry of Information and the Arts 1994): "This is wrong. By removing the stigma, we may encourage more women to have children without getting married".

Kong and Yeoh (2003) also pointed out that there is the same refusal to support single mothers who are separated or divorced from their husbands. Although they will be considered to form a family unit together with their children in buying flats directly from the HDB, the fact that such parents are "treated in much the same way as all other applicants, with no special considerations for their special circumstances in the buying or renting of flats", in itself disadvantages such women and their families.

Co-option by the state

The ambiguity of ascertaining the progress of women's rights in Singapore stems not only from the fractured nature of who benefits, but also that it sometimes comes at the expense of other rights (Lim 2015). In fact, advocacy pursuing the protection of women has at times been co-opted by the state to reduce other civil liberties. Two notable examples include the Prevention of Human Trafficking Act and the Protection from Harassment Act in 2014.

The Protection from Harassment Act (POHA)

AWARE had previously advocated for this piece of legislation, hoping that it would help move to reduce sexual harassment in the workplace. Instead, the state has most recently used the Act to charge a 16-year-old boy for an online video he made. Amos Yee, who was sentenced to a four-week jail term for posting an obscene image online, as well as content intended to hurt the religious feelings of Christians, was not eventually charged under the Act. AWARE subsequently released a statement expressing its concern over this inchoate abuse of the Harassment Act, arguing among other things that (2015):

> There were no other people referred to by Yee who might be said to be victims of harassment. We urge the Attorney General's Chambers to ensure that POHA is not extended beyond its intended remit – the protection of individuals who would otherwise be vulnerable to harm.

Although the harassment charge was dropped, the prospect of the state using a gender-progressive law which AWARE, a women's rights civil society organisation, had advocated for, to cases involving the government, or an extremely wide category of supposed victims, is dispiriting.

Prevention of Human Trafficking Act

Prior to the Prevention of Human Trafficking Act 2014 being passed in Parliament, a coalition of NGOs known as StopTraffickingSG interested in trafficking raised several criticisms of the draft bill as it had been tabled by MP Christopher de Souza (2014). This coalition comprised AWARE, Healthserve, HOME, Transient Workers Count Too (TWC2), MARUAH and UN Women. StopTraffickingSG took directional cues from HOME, Healthserve and TWC2, as these NGOs had firsthand experiences from working with victims of human trafficking, while the other groups provided resources and administrative support.

In their campaign, StopTraffickingSG argued that the protection and assistance offered to victims by the then-Bill were not adequate. In order to provide a strong basis for countering trafficking in Singapore, the overall Act needed to be more sensitive towards victims' rights (Wee and Goh 2014). The Act granted a huge extension of discretionary powers to police and non-police enforcement officers, allowing them to arrest and forcibly gain entry to premises without warrant. The coalition argued that such powers, if exercised to their fullest extent, would result in the secondary traumatisation of vulnerable victims of trafficking.[3] The coalition offered critiques of the proposed Bill, only to see it pass without amendment through Parliament. Since then, it has concentrated on urging the Inter-Agency Task Force to implement the Trafficking Act in ways that measure up against international standards, such as the USA's annual Trafficking in Persons (TIP) Report.

The role of international human rights conventions

Having thus debunked the teleological narrative we suggest is unwarrantedly pervasive in women's rights in Singapore, its assurance of a more gender-equal future thus falls away. What may lie ahead then for the state of women's rights in Singapore? In addition to understanding the nature of progress of women's rights, an understanding of why it may have happened can help us understand if it is likely to continue.

The focus on socio-economic or 'pragmatic' concerns, as opposed to the rights for their own sake, suggests that the exclusive nature of progress, dependent on the value that women can provide to the state, and defined by the state, will have continued dominance. That said, if gender-equitable policies are a key result of negotiations between civil society and the state, and not the result of some inexorable march of progress, and what 'progress' has been achieved is limited, subject to regression, and in itself contested and ambivalent, a further implication is the role played by international human rights conventions in negotiations between state and civil society.

State–society interactions, anthropologist and founding AWARE member Vivienne Wee argues, are crucial to democratisation (2015): "In the context of such interactions, civil society emerges as a force that can shape public opinion and monitor public authority". In particular, international human rights conventions constitute a critical device for this public monitoring of state authority. Despite the predominance of Singapore exceptionalism (Thompson 2006), the Singapore state has proven susceptible to certain forms of international rights pressure. These certain rights tend to be socio-economic rather than political in nature. Of the nine UN Core International Human Rights treaties, Singapore has signed and ratified three: Convention on the Elimination of All Forms of Discrimination Against Women (CEDAW), the Convention on the Rights of Persons with Disabilities (CRPD) and the Convention on the Rights of the Child (CRC). The rights protected by these three conventions lie squarely in the realm of the socio-economic (insofar as the division between socio-economic and political rights is tenable).

In response to a parliamentary question about whether the government would consider acceding to and ratifying major human rights treaties and conventions, the Law Minister K. Shanmugam responded:

> Singapore takes its treaty obligations seriously and prefers to become a party to Conventions when we are sure that we are able to comply fully with all of the obligations [...]. If we accede to a treaty and yet make reservations that detract from the object and purpose of the treaty as a whole, it becomes an exercise in mere optics. That is not our approach.
>
> (Ministry of Law 2014)

Singapore's approach to safeguarding the rights of women

The Singapore government ratified CEDAW on 3 October 1995. Following the ratification, an Inter-Ministry Committee (IMC) on CEDAW was set up to monitor its implementation. In 2002, the Women's Desk was established as the national focal point for women matters as well as the secretariat for CEDAW.

Singapore subscribes to the philosophy that the family undergirds society and that close-knit and supportive families make for a cohesive nation. Therefore, many policies in Singapore safeguard the rights of women by promoting the healthy development of families. Other key considerations in safeguarding the rights of women in Singapore include the maintenance of a multiracial and multi-religious society (Ministry of Community Development 2009).

Despite ratifying CEDAW, the government has entered reservations to key articles in the Convention, namely Articles 2, 11 and 16, stating the following justifications for entering these reservations: that Singapore is a multiracial and multi-religious society and should respect the freedom of minorities to practise their religious or personal laws (Articles 2 and 11). In 2011, Singapore partially withdrew its reservation and agreed to enforce Article 2, "so long as it did not interfere with the rights of minorities to practise their religious or personal laws", more specifically referring to the Syariah court system.

However, AWARE has pushed for the removal of all current reservations, arguing with respect to Article 2 (the core provision of CEDAW) that it "calls into question Singapore's commitment to CEDAW" (2014). Indeed, it is difficult to reconcile this particular reservation with the government's statement that Singapore's approach to major human rights treaties and conventions is not "an exercise in mere optics" (Singapore Parliamentary Report 2014).

Moreover, AWARE has argued that entering a reservation on Articles 2 and 16 on the interests of allowing minorities to practise their religious or personal laws is equivalent to suggesting that racial and religious minorities have a right to discrimination against women, or indeed that discrimination against women is inherent to the practice of such religious or personal laws (AWARE 2014). With respect to Article 11, Singapore's reservation was argued to be:

> disproportionately wide as it includes women, who are not in hazardous occupations as well as women who are not pregnant [...] employers are permitted to discriminate against women in terms of their right to work, promotion at work, job security, remuneration and benefits.
> (AWARE 2014)

The implications of CEDAW for women's rights in Singapore

Nevertheless, CEDAW has had some effect on state policies concerning women and has, to a certain extent, acted as a catalyst for domestic implementation efforts in Singapore. Similar effects of CEDAW have been observed in other countries such as Zimbabwe, Croatia, Bangladesh and the Philippines, where the convention has provided women with a powerful advocacy tool at the national level (Bayefsky *et al.* 2000). Indeed, the concluding observations of the Committee on the Elimination of Discrimination against Women noted several legislative reforms and government initiatives as positive aspects of CEDAW in Singapore.

However, there appears to be a lack of public consciousness about CEDAW and its application to women's rights in Singapore. In a 2007 forum entitled *Making CEDAW Work in Singapore*, organised by the Institute of Policy Studies (IPS), Constance Singam, then-President of AWARE, highlighted that the ignorance of public bodies towards CEDAW and gender equality was pervasive. She also voiced her concern about the efficacy of the Women's Desk in serving the needs and enhancing the status, contributions and well-being of women in Singapore. Speakers also noted that more work needs to be done to raise awareness about CEDAW among national institutions such as the judiciary and schools in Singapore.

The role of shadow reports

AWARE has been a party in the CEDAW reporting process since 2004, in which it submits shadow reports as a participating NGO. Since then, the reporting process has expanded to involve more civil society organisations in Singapore. During Singapore's last Periodic State Report for CEDAW in 2011, shadow reports and additional information were submitted by a total of seven civil society organisations. They included AWARE, Equality Now, International Disability Alliance (IDA), Sayoni, SCWO, TWC2 and the Global Alliance Against Traffic in Women.

Shadow reports play a critical role in highlighting loopholes and inadequacies, by providing supplementary information omitted in the State Report (Li 2011). They also provide perspectives from and insights into the frequently overlooked groups of people within the broader category of 'women'. For example, the 2011 Shadow Report submitted by Sayoni proved useful during the discussion on queer women, a topic not covered in the official State Report. With the information provided, the CEDAW committee was in a better position to engage in constructive dialogue with the government delegation. In addition, issues that were discussed tended to stand a greater chance of being reflected in the Committee's Concluding Comments and recommendations to the state (Poore 2011).

Interestingly, SCWO is currently in the early stages of leading various NGOs in Singapore in the writing of a consolidated Shadow Report for the upcoming fifth CEDAW report. If successful, this cooperation among civil society organisations in Singapore could be an indicator of progress for women's rights activism in terms of the ability to organise resources and collectively harness experiences in order to advocate on the rights of particular subsections of women.

Beyond the shadow reports

AWARE had in the past called upon the government to define trafficking and its indicators as a means of effectively addressing the phenomenon. Although activist responses to the Prevention of Human Trafficking Act (discussed above) were decidedly ambivalent, one could easily draw the conclusion that international pressure – with CEDAW being one of its sources – did play a part in the tabling and passage of the Bill. Mindful of this, AWARE then published an op-ed (2014) suggesting that by those very international standards, the Prevention of Human Trafficking Act did not recognise key elements of trafficking such as profiteering, and also offered little recognition of the rights to safety and livelihood necessary to encourage victims to report their cases, identify traffickers and testify against them.

Conclusion

In summary, international human rights conventions and standards provide a rare forum where governments have to defend their policies that do not meet human rights standards before international scrutiny. In a state like Singapore where civil society and human rights activism enjoys little space, this represents a precious site for governmental accountability and exchange between the state and civil society, as mediated by the international organisation at hand and the standards it sets out. Progress captured along these lines, however, has been incremental, even by the standards of Singapore activism. At the same time, the very interests and rights discourses employed by international actors are themselves open to interrogation, complicating an already complex understanding of progress, and any dreams or hopes we may have for it.

Notes

1 K. Han (2015). "Considering feminism in Singapore". Available at www.beaconreader.com/kirsten-han/considering-feminism-in-singapore.
2 Personal interview with Vivienne Wee and Emily Charissa Lim, 21 February 2015, Singapore.
3 StoptraffickingSG (2014). "The full story of our recommendations for the Prevention of Human Trafficking Bill (before it passes into law!)". Available at http://stoptrafficking.sg/2014/10/21/the-full-story-of-our-recommendations-for-the-prevention-of-human-trafficking-bill-before-it-passes-law/.

References

AWARE (2006). "Beyond 'Happily ever after': Making a match between Singapore grooms and foreign brides". Singapore.
AWARE. (2014). "Singapore's reservations". Available at http://cedaw.aware.org.sg/singapores-reservations/.
AWARE (2015a). AWARE statement on the prosecution of Amos Yee. Singapore.

AWARE (2015b). Singapore Memory Project (SMP).
Bayefsky, A.F., D. Reid and K. Balmforth (2000). "The CEDAW Convention: Its contribution today". *Proceedings of the Annual Meeting (American Society of International Law)*, American Society of International Law **94**: 6.
Channel NewsAsia (2005). "AWARE believes some foreign brides mum on spousal abuse". MediaCorp News Pte Ltd.
Chew, P.G.L. (1994). "The Singapore Council of Women and the Women's Movement". *Journal of Southeast Asian Studies* **25**(1): 28.
Choy, E. (1951). "The founding of the Singapore Council of Women". *Minutes of Ladies Meeting on 20 November 1951 at 352-A Tanjong Katong Road*. Available at Postcolonialweb.org.
Fozdar, S. (1955). Open Letter to David Marshall. *An Open Letter to Mr. Marshall, the Chief Minister, Singapore*. Singapore. Available at Postcolonialweb.org.
Han, K. (2015). "Considering feminism in Singapore". Available at www.beaconreader.com/kirsten-han/considering-feminism-in-singapore.
Huang, S. and B.S.A. Yeoh (1996). "Ties that bind: State policy and migrant female domestic helpers in Singapore". *Geoforum* **27**(4): 14.
Humanitarian Organization for Migration Economics (2015). "Home sweet home? Work, life and well-being of foreign domestic workers in Singapore". Singapore: 37.
Institute of Policy Studies (IPS) (2007). *Forum on Making CEDAW Work in Singapore*. IPS Conference Room.
Kok, X.H. (2015). "Government reviewing benefits for unwed mothers". *The Straits Times*, Singapore.
Kong, L. and B.S.A. Yeoh (2003). *The Politics of Landscapes in Singapore: Constructions of "Nation"*. New York: Syracuse University Press.
Lee, G. (1954). SCW Correspondence with the Chinese Advisory Board, 1954–1959. *Letter to the Chinese Advisory Board*. Singapore. Available at Postcolonialweb.org.
Lee, K.Y. (1983). "Talent for the Future". Speech delivered at the National Day Rally on 14 August.
Li, L. (2011). "Singapore questioned by the UN CEDAW Committee on gender equality and human rights". Available at www.theonlinecitizen.com/2011/08/singapore-questioned-by-the-un-cedaw-committee-on-gender-equality-and-human-rights/.
Lim, J. (2015). "Empowering citizenry, securing our future – WP urges voters to entrench alternative voices". Available at www.theonlinecitizen.com/2015/08/empowering-citizenry-securing-our-future-wp-urges-voters-to-entrench-alternative-voices/.
Lyons, L. (2007). *The Birth Of AWARE. Small Steps, Giant Leaps: A History of AWARE and the Women's Movement in Singapore*. M. Arora. Singapore: AWARE.
Ministry of Community Development, Youth and Sports (2009). Singapore's Fourth Periodic Report to the UN Committee for the Convention on the Elimination of all Forms of Discrimination Against Women. Singapore: 163.
Ministry of Community Development, Youth and Sports (2010). MCYS Response to No To Rape. F. Policy. Singapore.
Ministry of Information and the Arts (1994). National Day Rally, Address by Prime Minister Goh Chok Tong, Speech in English. Singapore.
Ministry of Labour (1995). *Profile of the Labour Force of Singapore 1983–1994*. Singapore: R.a.S. Department.
Ministry of Law (2014). Written Answer by Minister for Law, K Shanmugam, to Parliamentary Question on Human Rights Treaties and Conventions. Available at www.mlaw.gov.sg/content/minlaw/en/news/parliamentary-speeches-and-responses/

written-answer-by-minister-on-human-rights-treaties-conventions.html (accessed 28 December 2016).

Ministry of Social and Family Development (16 March 2015). "Home Ownership Plus Education (HOPE) Scheme". Available at http://app.msf.gov.sg/Assistance/Home-Ownership-Plus-Education-HOPE-Scheme.

People's Action Party (1959). *The Tasks Ahead, PAP's Five Year Plan 1959–64. Part 1.* Singapore: PAP.

Phua, H.P. (2010). "Trend in Adult Mortality in Singapore". *Information Papers*, 2015. Available at www.moh.gov.sg/content/moh_web/home/Publications/information_papers/2010/trend_in_adult_mortalityinsingapore.html (accessed 13 December 2011).

Poore, G. (2011). "Amazing responses by CEDAW to address LGBT discrimination in Singapore". Available at www.outrightinternational.org/content/amazing-responses-cedaw-address-lgbt-discrimination-singapore.

Rahman, N.A.B.A. (2014). "Convention on the Elimination of Discrimination Against Women and the Prospect of Development of Muslim Personal Law in Singapore". *Journal of Muslim Minority Affairs* **34**(1): 20.

Sayoni (2011). *Report on Discrimination against Women in Singapore Based on Sexual Orientation and Gender Identity.* Singapore: Sayoni.

Singam, C. (2002). "Working for gender equality: An AWARE experience". In *Building Social Space in Singapore: The Working Committee's Initiative in Civil Society Activism,* edited by C. Singam, C.K. Tan, T. Ng and L. Perera. Singapore: Select Publishing.

Singam, C. (2007). "Women's activism and feminism". In *Small Steps, Giant Leaps: A History of AWARE and the Women's Movement in Singapore,* edited by M. Arora. Singapore: AWARE.

Singapore Parliamentary Report (2012). *Home Ownership Plus Education (HOPE) Beneficiaries,* 12 September, **89**.

Singapore Parliamentary Report (2014). *Ratifying With Reservations Major Human Rights Treaties and Conventions.* **92**.

Soin, K. (2011). Keynote Address "Women's Charter to Family Charter". In *Singapore Women's Charter: Roles, Responsibilities, and Rights in Marriage,* edited by T.W. Devasahayam. Singapore: Institute of Southeast Asian Studies (ISEAS) Publishing.

StoptraffickingSG (2014). "The full story of our recommendations for the Prevention of Human Trafficking Bill (before it passes into law!)". Available at http://stoptrafficking.sg/2014/10/21/the-full-story-of-our-recommendations-for-the-prevention-of-human-trafficking-bill-before-it-passes-law/.

Teo, Y.Y. (2014). "Not everyone has maids: Work–life balance policies and their class differential effects in Singapore". *XVIII International Sociological Association's World Congress of Sociology,* Yokohama, Japan.

Thompson, E.C. (2006). "Singaporean exceptionalism and its implications for ASEAN regionalism". *Contemporary Southeast Asia: A Journal of International and Strategic Affairs* **28**(2): 23.

United Nations Committee on the Elimination of Discrimination Against Women (2011). Concluding observations of the Committee on the Elimination of Discrimination against Women (Singapore).

Wee, V. (2015). *State–Society Interactions in Southeast Asia (Forum).* Southeast Asian Studies Symposium, Sunway University, Malaysia, Project Southeast Asia.

Wee, V. and L.S. Goh (2014). "Anti-trafficking law: Singapore can do better". *The Straits Times,* Singapore.

Wong, T. and B.S.A. Yeoh (2003). "Fertility and the family: An overview of pro-natalist population policies in Singapore". *Asian MetaCentre Research Paper Series.* Singapore, Asian MetaCentre for Population and Sustainable Development Analysis, Asia Research Institute, National University of Singapore, **12**.

World Economic Forum (2014). *Global Gender Gap Report 2014.* Insight Report.

8 LGBTQ activism in Singapore[1]

Jean Chong

Introduction

In 1993, the former Minister of Foreign Affairs Wong Kan Seng at the World Human Rights Conference in Vienna framed human rights as a Western notion without relevance to Asian societies, and pointed out that

> [M]ost Singaporeans, and people in many other parts of the world do not agree that homosexual relationships is just a choice of lifestyle. Most of us will also maintain that the right to marry is confined to those of the opposite gender.
>
> (Wong 1993; Berry 1994)

He dismissed any discussion on the rights of LGBTQ (lesbian, gay, bisexual, transgender and queer). By 1993 there were hardly any organised LGBTQ movements in Singapore and same-sex marriage was certainly not a worldwide trend.

To date, the Singapore government has continued to preserve the old colonial law that criminalises sex between consenting men. Article 377A of the Penal Code states:

> [A]ny male person who, in public or private, commits, or abets the commission of, or procures or attempts to procure the commission by any male person of, any act of gross indecency with another male person, shall be punished with imprisonment for a term which may extend to 2 years.[2]

By maintaining 377A in the country's penal system, the state engages in the deliberate process of "othering" homosexuals and seeks to use homosexuality as a boundary marker to differentiate itself from the West, and to warn of the consequences of adopting a similar rights-centric approach.

It declares that the East is economically successful and morally superior due to its communitarian values and the West is heading in the other direction with its individualism, economic decline and social failures (Berry 1994; Offord 1999). This was seen in a parliamentary debate to retain 377A in 2007 where Prime Minister Lee Hsien Loong warned about the breakdown of marriage as an institution between a husband and a wife in Western Europe (Lee 2007). Then-Nominated Member of Parliament and a law professor, Thio Li Ann, compared homosexual sex to "shoving a straw up your nose to drink", denounced homosexuality as an agenda set by Western nations in an attempt to influence others, and asserted that "there is no need of foreign or neo-colonial moral imperialism in matters of fundamental morality" (Thio 2007).

This portrayal of LGBTQ rights as foreign and Western ideas helped shape the contemporary human rights discourse of gay citizens in Singapore. Homosexual rights are deemed as having an agenda from the imperialistic West and a threat to the nation's sovereignty, which is harmful to its community and heterosexual family-centred value system, social order and economic enjoyment of the population (Tan 2011). As seen from the speeches, homosexuality is believed to originate from the individualistic West and is the result of Western liberal democracy which caused the degeneration of its social construct (Offord 1999).

LGBTQ Singaporeans not only have to contend with the array of regulations and policy tools used against them to limit their human rights, but also with the weight of public opinion. Religious and cultural beliefs such as Christianity, Islam and "hetero-patriarchal obligations and familial responsibilities" play a central role in influencing the landscape (Yusop 2005; Chan 2008; Obendorf 2013). A national survey conducted by Our Singapore Conversation (OSC), a government outreach programme with a sample size of 4,000 in 2013, found that 47 per cent of Singaporeans reject the "gay lifestyle", versus 26 per cent of acceptance and 27 per cent undecided. There was even less acceptance of same-sex marriage at 55 per cent rejection, 21 per cent acceptance and 24 per cent undecided (Institute for Policy Studies 2013). However, there was much criticism of the government's intentional use of the words "gay lifestyle" without definition to suggest deviancy which inevitably skewed the survey. Furthermore, "gay lifestyle" is deemed offensive to the gay community, suggesting that LGBTQ persons live a life of choice and can be cured (Yahoo! News 2013). Nevertheless, it is important not to underestimate the political apathy of Singaporeans towards LGBTQ rights and to be mindful of the state's capacity to steer and influence public opinions or values on controversial issues to its own purpose (Wee 2007; Chan 2008).

This chapter examines a very short history of human rights activism on LGBTQ rights in this peculiar historical cultural and political context of Singapore. It divides the period into each decade since 1980: (1) the awakening in the 1980s; (2) organising in the 1990s, and (3) strategising in the 2000s.

A new beginning: from the past to the future

1980s: the awakening

The 1980s was perhaps known as the decade that gave birth to the emergence of the LGBTQ community in Singapore. In the broader economic, social and political landscape, it was a time of change. The opposition parties saw a breakthrough over the stronghold of the ruling party, the People's Action Party (PAP) in 1981 by J.B. Jeyaratnam of the Workers' Party (WP) (*The Straits Times* 1981), and in 1984 Chiam See Tong won another seat for the Singapore Democratic Party (SDP) which contributed to a vote share drop of more than 12 per cent (*The Straits Times* 1984). By the end of the decade, Goh Chok Tong had taken over as Prime Minister from Lee Kuan Yew and promised a "kinder and gentler Singapore" in response to the better educated and changing electorate (Tan 2007).

The arts was the first frontier for gay political expression and experimentation in the 1980s. Gay scriptwriters became bolder and explored the boundaries for queer discourse, and a number of attempts to push the boundaries were considered so audacious that three scripts were subsequently banned for normalising and justifying homosexuality. However, true to his words on a kinder and gentler Singapore, then-Prime Minister Goh Chok Tong liberalised the culture policy and the plays were all subsequently staged. From then on, homosexual artists that engaged in this indirect and pragmatic activism saw the blossoming of the theme of homosexuality in a variety of artistic work, literature, films, books and political essays (Heng 2001).

The slow opening up of the socio-political climate also saw the flourishing of non-governmental organisations (NGOs) in Singapore. Of significance was the HIV/AIDS epidemic that was sweeping across the globe, and gay persons responded to this challenge by rallying around the issue and setting up an NGO, Action For AIDS (AFA) in 1985. Even though it has never identified itself as a gay organisation for pragmatic reasons like funding from the government and in avoidance of resistance from the public, AFA has provided a training ground for LGBTQ Singaporeans in taking their first baby steps into activism (Heng 2001; Chua 2014). On the other hand, due to their participation in AFA by these activists, this created the impression that HIV was a homosexual disease that would cost them in the public sphere in the later decade (Tan 2003).

This was the decade of hope that saw the slow awakening of the LGBTQ community to the possibilities that then-Prime Minister Goh Chok Tong's administration had presented to them. Unbeknown to then-Prime Minister Goh Chok Tong, his leadership style of a "kinder and gentler Singapore came with a gay subtext" that went on to jump-start a series of tactics and social movements from the LGBTQ community in Singapore (Heng 2001).

1990s: the organising

If the 1980s were characterised by the LGBTQ community as an awakening, the 1990s should be depicted as the decade of organising. A few individuals started discussing informally the need for a gay support group to address the discrimination towards homosexuality in Singapore and soon decided to name itself People Like Us (PLU). In the midst of the discussion-driven meetings of the group, an incident soon gave PLU the momentum to consider further actions (Lo and Huang 2003).

On 30 May 1993, the disco Rascals held its weekly gay night event and was raided by the police. Although raids on gay bars were commonplace in the 1990s, there was something different in this incident. The police intimidated the party-goers and further detained 20 gay persons without identity cards in police stations but did not formally charge them. Outraged by this legally groundless treatment, 20 gay men issued a letter of complaint to the police and sought an apology, even though most of the signatories were not hopeful of getting any kind of response from the authorities. To the pleasant surprise of many, an apology was given by the police on their unprofessional behaviour and assurance was provided of stopping the legally baseless practice of the detention of persons without identification cards (Heng 2001; Chua 2014).

This first positive contact with the authorities spurred PLU to consider shifting their tactics by attempting to educate and create awareness for the LGBTQ community of their rights. This was done through organising monthly public meetings and other activities such as newsletters (Heng 2001). Through these activities, a sense of community was forming and an awareness was building on the various ways laws are used to curtail their human rights through using legal means to limit their freedom of assembly, speech and association (Chua 2014).

Inspired by the response from the Rascals bar raid, LGBTQ activists decided to continue strengthening the community by holding events which became popular. However, it was becoming apparent that police surveillance of their activities was increasing. Media outlets like *The New Paper*, an English tabloid, were planning to sensationalise and uncover PLU's activities. This led to the decision by the activists to scale back on the events and rethink tactics (Heng 2001).

From this chaotic environment, activists from PLU then decide to be pragmatic and creative in their approach. They decided that even though confrontations were the tactics often used in Western democracy, in particular the historic Stonewall riots in America (Duberman 2013), it was not the right way to proceed with gaining rights. In order to operate safely and to be sustainable in 1995, activists in PLU decided that registering it as a business would give it some legal cover to exist. To their dismay three months later, their application was rejected with the justification that "the proposed company is likely to be used for unlawful purpose or for purposes prejudicial to public peace, welfare or good order in Singapore" and that it was "contrary to the national security or interest for the proposed company to be registered" (Heng 2001).

By now it was clear to PLU that the government knew exactly who they were, so there was no need to mask their true identity. A second attempt was launched in 1996 to register PLU as a society instead under the Societies Act, but this, too, was no easy task. After a number of police interviews, six months later the group was again rejected and no reason was given. PLU then decided to escalate their tactics with the goal of engaging the state publicly to advance the discourse of the LGBTQ community. They first wrote to ask the Registrar of Societies for an explanation, appealed to the Ministry of Home Affairs, and then finally went all the way to the Prime Minister's Office. This process ran its course in May 1997 when the state refused to engage them in any other ways than through official channels. Despite the precarious situation, a silver lining soon appeared on the horizon over the coming decade (Offord 1999; Heng 2001; People Like Us 2003a).

The cyber age

Faced with the failure of attempting to obtain legal status and told by the authorities to cease their activities and to disband, pragmatism again took over for the sake of survival. PLU retreated and found the creative solution they needed: the Internet (Phillips 2008, 2014; Chua 2014).

The Internet is an important tool in the activist's toolbox. Its ability to circumvent traditional roadblocks placed by the authorities and to provide the freedom and space for "intersubjective and intercultural communication which allows discourse around citizenship and notions of belonging and participation" inspires the LGBTQ community in Singapore (Offord 2003).

In addition, one of the most important elements of the Internet was being able to provide a space for LGBTQ activists to strategise and to seek transformation. Kleinwaechter described the cyber world as follows: "the decentralised Internet is to a certain degree the most organised chaos in the history of mankind. It is unmanageable and uncontrollable. It is a new dimension, a new culture, a new way of communication" (Kleinwaechter 1998). It is through this technology that LGBTQ citizens of Singapore have been able to communicate with each other and it became the marketplace for all kinds of concerns, ideas and activities. Most importantly of all was that it offered the opportunity to the LGBTQ community to develop their own political identity and raise awareness on the socio-political culture of Singapore (Offord 2003).

On 15 March 1997, PLU decided that the best strategy was to start an online mailing list, called Singapore Gay News List (SIGNEL). In this way, PLU saw that they could creatively circumvent the authorities while continuing with community-building. In return, this would avoid the glare of public scrutiny which would in turn invoke government sanctions (People Like Us 2003b; Chua 2014). Empowered by the cover of the Internet and the previous actions by PLU, subgroups soon emerged from within SIGNEL. Other mailing lists with a diversity of approaches and ranges soon appeared. Some of these are Redqueen that catered to queer women in the year 1998, Safehaven, a gay Christian support group in the year 1998, Adventurers Like Us (ADLUS) for gay persons who were interested in sporting activities in the year 1999, Heartland for LGBTQ Buddhists in the year 1999 and so on (Phillips 2008; Chong 2011).

By the end of the decade, LGBTQ activists had retreated for survival, and organised and engaged in creative activism by using the Internet to expand their political and human rights discourse "without the usual socio-political constraints, beyond state and civil society's governance and surveillance of sexuality" (Offord 2003). Notably, as demonstrated later in the chapter, the Internet continues to play a significant role in the movement of the LGBTQ community today.

Different tactics in the late 1990s to the 2000s

The 1980s to the 1990s was a time of awakening and organising for the LGBTQ community. The introduction of the Internet in Singapore provided the means to survive without state intervention. It provided information, communication and ways to organise, and helped in the LGBTQ community's struggle against an authoritarian state. In this context, the late 1990s and the 2000s was a time of advancing, exploration and creativity (Chong 2011). Gay activists employed a variety of strategies and escalated their tactics with state and non-state actors for social change, leading to a number of significant milestones (Chua 2014).

The first surprise and hope

One of the defining moments that propelled activism forward in the coming decades for activists was a remarkable incident on 11 December 1998 that set out the position of the state for the first time. Then-Senior Prime Minister Lee Kuan Yew was asked live on television on Cable News Network (CNN) by an anonymous caller who said,

> I am a gay man in Singapore. I do not feel that my country has acknowledged my presence. As we move into a more tolerant millennium, what do you think is the future for gay people in Singapore, if there is a future at all?

To which Lee carefully replied,

> Well, it's not a matter which I can decide or any government can decide. It's a question of what a society considers acceptable. And as you know, Singaporeans are by and large a very conservative, orthodox society [...] completely different from, say the United States and I don't think an aggressive gay rights movement would help. But what we are doing as a government is to leave people to live their own lives so long as they don't impinge on other people. I mean, we don't harass anybody.
>
> (Peterson 2001; Reuters 2015)

While positive for many in the LGBTQ community, this statement from then-Senior Prime Minister Lee Kuan Yew hinged upon the state's position on communitarian values, human rights and in opposition to the liberal ethics of the West. He insisted it was "up to society to decide". Singaporeans are "a very conservative and orthodox society" and, "unlike the West in the United States", LGBTQ people will be left alone so long as they do not "impinge on other people" (Reuters 2015). Following this public declaration, political elites repeated the same rhetoric, providing further evidence on how entrenched this communitarian ideology is with the state (Goh 1989; Times 1993; Wong 2004; Lee 2007).

Nonetheless, the interview with Lee Kuan Yew on CNN gave many LGBTQ citizens a renewed sense of hope and encouraged the LGBTQ community to take further steps out of the closet. Along with the soaring penetrative rate of the Internet, online gay commercial website portals like *Trevvy and Fridae* were started in 2001. Both saw themselves as community sites for lesbian and gay Singaporeans, and provided a diversity of services ranging from news to casual chat rooms (Obendorf 2013). Subsequently, Fridae started venturing into the public sphere and organised the first gay circuit party in 2001 to be held in a public venue (Fridae 2006, 2015). Following a few successful years this was banned in 2005 after then-Health Minister Dr Balaji Sadasivan associated HIV with gays, and accused the circuit parties of spreading HIV by attracting "gays from high prevalence societies to fraternise with local gay men, seeding the infection in the local community" (*The Straits Times* 2005).

The second surprise and uncertain times

The second significant speech during this decade was again presented to foreign media via *Time* magazine by then-Prime Minister Goh Chok Tong in 2003. In an unusually pragmatic way, he told *Time* magazine, "in the past, if we know you're gay, we would not employ you, but we just changed this quietly", and he went on to hint at further tolerance by suggesting "so let it evolve and in time to come, the population will understand that some people are born that way [...] we are born this way and they are born that way but they are like you and me" (*New York Times* 2003).

As a result, there was a huge reaction from both for and against camps, with one side urging the government to rethink about hiring gays (*The Straits Times* 2003a) and asserting that gays are deviants (*The Straits Times* 2003b), while others called for an open mind and a respect for differing views (*The Straits Times* 2003c). Public debate became so impassioned that former Prime Minister Goh Chok Tong had to stop mainstream media publishing further on the issue (Tan 2009).

Despite this, Goh Chok Tong's speech drove PLU to submit a further application to become a registered society but it was rejected for a second time. In 2004, PLU was given the same reason as in 1995 why it was refused registration (People Like Us 2004; Phillips 2008). Evidently, Singapore tolerated the presence of the LGBTQ community but it was not prepared to recognise it as a sector; nor was it prepared to consider LGBTQ citizens to have rights.

Despite the setback and mixed signals given, activists remained optimistic that there would be an opportunity for dialogue with the government. However, two years after then-Prime Minister Goh Chok Tong's speech, in a surprising turnaround the state decided to ban the Nation Party, a public

LGBTQ circuit party event, and justified its actions by stating that it was a gay event. PLU responded with outrage and in response organised a string of forums, social and arts events called "Indignation" in August. In a statement on their website, PLU asserted that "gays and lesbians are indignant over what these say about their equal rights and their place in this nation" (Chua 2014; People Like Us 2015). Subsequently, "Indignation" became an annual pride event in August and was an exercise in creative activism by pushing the limits of public discourse and existing laws. In the course of organising events, numerous events were banned, censored and closely monitored by different government agencies (Phillips 2013).

Losing but winning: cyber activism despite the government's legal discrimination

Like trees being blown left and right in turbulent times, activists were again surprised by the government when it decided in November 2006 to conduct an open consultation with the public on its proposal to update the Penal Code. One such proposal was to amend Section 377 of the law that criminalised "carnal intercourse against the order of nature" (Chan 2007). However, the bad news was that the state intended to deliberately retain Section 377A of the Penal Code that specifically targets any sexual conduct between men (Chan 2007; Leong 2012). The consequence of this was that oral and anal sex will be legalised for heterosexual and lesbian couples while singling out gay men for discriminatory treatment under the law.

This soon led to public outcry from the LGBTQ community against this discriminatory action that targeted a minority class of people in Singapore. This was also the first time LGBTQ activists openly challenged the state over their rights and attempted to garner public support in its advocacy. Very quickly, activists organised an online petition against the retention of 377A of the Penal Code and submitted it to Parliament with 2,341 signatures. Countering this, a group of Christians who were in opposition to the repeal of 377A of the Penal Code also galvanised the public with an online petition, Keep377A.com webpage, on 19 October 2007, and collected about 15,559 signatures (Lee 2008; Chua 2011).

On behalf of the LGBTQ petitioners, then-Nominated Member of Parliament (NMP) Siew Kum Hong, in a parliamentary debate over the amendments, stated that "the amendment of 377 without also repealing 377A is therefore unconstitutional under Article 12(1) of the Constitution", which provides that "all persons are equal before the law and entitled to the equal protection of the law" and that "it does not satisfy the legal requirements for derogating from Article 12(1)".[3]

He went on to criticise the government's rationale for retaining 377A by stating that "the majority of Singaporeans disapprove of homosexuality [...] but reflecting the morality of the majority is not a stated aim of the Penal Code, nor is it an accepted objective of the criminal law" (The Online Citizen 2007).

Prime Minister Lee Hsien Loong responded with the familiar communitarian argument, saying,

> [B]ut homosexuals should not set the tone for Singapore society ... this is the way the majority of Singaporeans want it to be. So, we should strive to maintain a balance, to uphold a stable society with traditional, heterosexual family values, but with space for homosexuals to live their lives and contribute to the society.
>
> (Lee 2007)

Eventually, the chambers of power echoed Prime Minister Lee's statement and overwhelmingly supported the retention of 377A. However, an olive branch was held out to the LGBTQ community by the Prime Minister in the way of non-enforcement of 377A. Nevertheless, this was the first time activists had reached out to non-LGBTQ allies and the public to organise the parliamentary petition against the retention of 377A. It generated a great deal of media attention and discussion in the public sphere and forced politicians to consider questions of discrimination, and to acknowledge that 377A exists and is retained to target the sexual behaviour of gay men. This had the unintended consequence of broadening the political boundaries and at the same time expanding the human rights discourse in Singapore (Chua 2014).

In an attempt to pacify both camps, the state placed itself in an ambiguous position while making a mockery out of the rule of law by retaining 377A and at the same time promising non-enforcement (Hor 2012). Chua cynically claimed that the episode is merely "political theatre" in a country where "parliamentary proceedings are monologues by the single-party government" (Chua 2008). As discussed in earlier chapters, the state assumes the position of the promotion and protection of communitarian values where the community is prioritised over the individual, and while maintaining that social order is one where the heterosexual family is the building block of society.

Out in the open

Frustrated with this outcome and looking for a way to break the argument of the non-acceptance of society over homosexuals, activists continued to look for other creative avenues to navigate in a limited and controlled socio-political landscape. It was not long before another opportunity arrived. In September 2008, the government revised its licensing for Hong Lim Park's "Speakers' Corner" to include public demonstrations (*The New Paper* 2008). Seizing on the opportunity, gay activists soon came together to organise an event called "Pink Dot" with a non-confrontational message of the "Freedom to Love". Attendees were told to wear pink to represent the LGBTQ community and to form a human pink dot in the middle of Hong Lim Park (Chua 2011). It remains the biggest gay public event with 2,000 attendees in 2009 to claims of 28,000 attendees in 2015 (*The Straits Times* 2015).

Choosing not to follow similar pride events as seen in Western liberal democracies where pride marches are a commonality, and constrained in a park smaller than the size of two football fields, the organisers of Pink Dot were conscious of the need to comply with a reactionary government and popular opinion that deemed public demonstrations as disruptive. In addition, Pink Dot promoted notions of love in a family as diverse and inclusive which deconstructed state ideology towards the ideal family as heterosexual. By pitching the message "The Freedom to Love", activists emphasised love as unconfined, agreed with official rhetoric on family values but expanded the discourse to include other forms of family arrangements (Ramdas 2013).

By doing this, activists from Pink Dot chose to be creative about circumventing existing limitations, avoided all manner of direct confrontation, rights-based messaging such as gay rights is human rights and political association and used it to their own advantage. In addition, unable to get itself reported or promoted on media stream media, Pink Dot turned to the Internet and successfully marketed the event through videos, Facebook pages and its own website (Chua 2014).

Despite this, opposing voices stirred once more in 2014, this time led by an Islamic teacher Ustaz Noor Deros, who initiated an online "Wear White" campaign to protest against homosexuality and to reclaim the notion of "family values" (*The Straits Times* 2014). Subsequently, Christians from the Faith Community Baptist Church and Love Singapore, which is a network of churches, joined the campaign in a show of alliance and solidarity against their common enemy (The Online Citizen 2014).

In pursuit of their own agendas, activists had often used state discourse and rhetoric to challenge for their rights, with some success (Paul Tan and Lee Jack Jin 2007). However, Oswin argued that in reality events like Pink Dot that adopt an "assimilationist and homo-nationalist stance" is unlikely to change the current communitarian rhetoric which enshrines heteronormative logics that are "complex and deeply rooted and cannot be countered through appeals for LGBTQ inclusion alone" (Oswin 2014). Perhaps realising this, gay activists would continue to creatively construct new forms of tactics to challenge and take advantage of the existing institutional structure, rhetoric and resources.

Hence an alternative approach to activism soon emerged, this time through a queer women's research and advocacy organisation Sayoni, which adopted a rights-based approach in its activities. In 2011, after submitting their country Shadow Report, Sayoni, with the aid of International Women's Rights Action Watch Asia Pacific (IWRAW Asia Pacific), who work with women NGOs, went to the United Nations to lobby the committee for the Convention on the Elimination of All Forms of Discrimination Against Women (CEDAW). For the first time in the history of Singapore, the state had to directly address questions of discrimination towards the LGBTQ community in an international human rights arena (Poore 2011). Extraordinarily, the state claimed that gender and sexual orientation are protected under Article 12 of the Constitution of Singapore, when in reality it makes no mention of the word gender or sexual orientation (CEDAW 2011; Constitution 2015).

In spite of breaking away from the norm and choosing to escalate their tactics by using the global human rights platform, the actions by Sayoni activists remained within the boundaries of acceptable political norms and did not amount to disrupting "social order" or any socio-political ideologies that are held dearly by the government. They worked with existing legal procedures provided by CEDAW that the state ratified and used it to push the discourse on human rights. This is another exercise in the creativity of engagement while maintaining their legitimacy to the claims of rights. Furthermore, the activism by Sayoni that pushed the state to make a claim of inclusion under Article 12 of the Constitution planted the seed for further advocacy in the courts over 377A (Chua 2014).

As demonstrated in this chapter, there were various milestones during this decade in which the state was a crucial contributor in shaping how LGBTQ activists escalated their collective actions (D'Emilio 1998). Activists went from tiptoeing out of the closet in the earlier decade to open and public engagement that took the form of "creative activism", away from conventional methods of mobilisation (Davenport 2005).

However, in other repressive contexts, collective organising has emerged in other forms as alternatives to the conventionally tried and tested methods of rights-based strategies (Davenport 2005). Working within limited conditions, activists have organised by avoiding strategies commonly used in liberal democracies such as protests or mobilising with open and structured association (Johnston 2005).

In contrast to visible and large-scale social movements, discreet and subtle forms of mobilisation are often ignored by researchers (Davenport 2005) and more attention should be paid to how collective action can advance into different forms (McAdam 1983; Johnston 2005). Likewise, the author Ennis argued that "the question of tactical choice is a persistent one for social movements" (Ennis 1987). However, opposition voices continue to remain a challenge in navigating the socio-political terrain of Singapore.

To the courts we go

In July 2009, the Law Minister K. Shanmugan seemed to imply that the judiciary had the authority to interpret and apply 377A where it saw fit. He said, "We have the law. We say it won't be enforced. Is it totally clear? We, sometimes in these things, have to accept a bit of messiness", and he went on to state that the "government will not take the lead in repealing the law, the legal courts in Singapore have the power to decide how Section 377A is interpreted and applied" (Hor 2012).

While this could be read as the government not wanting to move and passing the buck to the courts in order to avoid being seen as the villain in both for and against camps, activists ultimately deduced, despite uncertainty, that the change they sought was to be found in the courts. Activists decided that this would give an opportunity to the legislature to sidestep the responsibility of repealing the law through Parliament. Tan Eng Hong was caught and charged on 2 September 2010 under 377A of the Penal Code for having oral sex in a public toilet. In an about turn, seven months later the Attorney General changed the charge to public obscenity which falls under Section 294 (A) of the Penal Code. Nonetheless, Tan began a constitutional challenge on Section 377A, claiming that the law in particular violated his rights under equal protection in Article 12 of the Singapore Constitution. In response, the Attorney General argued that Tan no longer had legal standing since the charge had been reduced to Section 294 (A), in which the lower court ruled in favour of the Attorney General's arguments (Hor 2012; Leong 2012).

With the aid of lawyer M. Ravi, Tan Eng Hong persisted and challenged this judgment on legal standing all the way to the highest court in Singapore, the Court of Appeal. Eventually, on 21 August 2012, the Court of Appeal declared that Tan had "locus standi" even if he was not prosecuted under Section 377A of the Penal Code and went on to state that it "affects the lives of a non-insignificant portion of our community in a very real and intimate way [...] the continued existence of s377A in our statute books causes them to be unapprehended felons in the privacy of their homes".[4]

This important judgment threw open the door of hope for LGBTQ activists to escalate their tactics. Seizing the opening of the ruling and Sayoni's efforts in 2011 at CEDAW that prompted the state to declare in the United Nations that Article 12 of the Constitution of Singapore includes gender and sexual orientation, in November 2012, LGBTQ activists quickly put forth a gay couple Lim Meng Suang and Kenneth Chee Mun-Leon to launch a constitutional challenge against Section 377A of the Penal Code alongside the first ongoing case from Tan Eng Hong (CEDAW 2011; *The Straits Times* 2012; Yahoo! News 2012). However, success was not to be; in both cases the High Court ruled that 377A was not in violation of their rights under equal protection in Article 12 of the Constitution.[5]

Despite these setbacks, LGBTQ activists knew they had to bring the fight into the highest court of the land, the Court of Appeal, and it was going to be a long-drawn-out fight. Due to their loose formation without legal status, LGBTQ activists were not allowed by the law to raise funds publicly and this placed them in a precarious situation. Once again, activists came together to look at creative ways to overcome this. Deciding that many in the LGBTQ community existed and communicated extensively online, they went back to the Internet once more and launched an online fundraising effort, using the website, indiegogo.com, which featured a video and the endorsement of community leaders with celebrities to increase credibility and legitimacy.[6] In an exceptional move never before seen in the history of collective action in Singapore, activists used the Internet and were able to raise an incredible US$80,000 in a short span of five days (The Online Citizen 2013).

On 29 October 2014, the challenge failed and the Court of Appeal ruled on both challenges that Section 377A of the Penal Code was not in violation of the Constitution of Singapore. Contrary to what the state had declared in 2011 to the CEDAW committee in the United Nations, the Court of Appeal ruled that the guarantee of equal protection stated in Article 12(2) of the constitution does not include gender identity or sexual orientation. Furthermore, the apex court reasoned that 377A did not infringe the life and liberty of homosexuals which is ensured under Article 9 of the constitution (TODAY 2014).[7]

Of particular interest was the decision clarifying the role of social order and values. It stated that even though the judgment would not have any bearing on the freedom of the individual, it was notable that "this freedom cannot, however, extend to an insistence by a particular group or individual that its/his values be imposed on other groups or other individuals".[8]

With this final judgment, the retention of 377A will continue to enforce discrimination and see hostility towards LGBTQ people by justifying policies that limit positive development and activism. Even though the state promised non-enforcement during the Penal Code review in 2007, in reality, LGBTQ persons continue to live with the sword of Damocles hanging over their heads (Chang 2015).

Because the constitutional challenge launched by LGBTQ activists was the first in the history of civil society in Singapore, LGBTQ activists were unable to read their odds for victory. Historically, the courts in Singapore lack a combination of factors such as constitutional guarantees, rights awareness and positive judicial attitudes to rule favourably in the defence of human rights. Moreover, Singapore's legal system follows a dualist model which views international law as a separate mechanism (Tan 1999).

Conclusion

As demonstrated in this chapter, LGBTQ Singaporeans have had a tumultuous relationship with the government. While they have consciously chosen to work within existing social and legal structures, LGBTQ activists have also actively sought other avenues and loopholes in these structures. In the historical framework provided, the researcher described how dedicated and creative LGBTQ activists are in their pursuit of social justice. They turned every opportunity, such as technological advancement like the Internet, opening up physical space like Hong Lim Park, the constitutional challenge in the courts or hostile reactions from the state, into an opportunity to facilitate a reconsideration of their rights in the larger socio-political structures of the country. These tactics have proven to be critical for LGBTQ activists using current institutional structures, resources or policies when seeking to challenge the incumbent regime (Phillips 2014).

However, in order to appear acceptable to the authorities by staging their activism using existing institutional structures, resources or policies and by deliberately avoiding using any human rights framework to reclaim the rights of LGBTQ Singaporeans, activists implicitly endorsed the boundaries imposed upon them by the state which in turn reinforced the status quo. Ironically, by doing this, activists continue to perform the expected and to legitimise existing limitations on a state-imposed ideological framework on nation building and socio-political rights.

This calls into question the effects of this type of organising when greater questions of civil-political and human rights are avoided. It may be said that LGBTQ activists have been successful and effective in their adoption of creative organising that is highly pragmatic instead of a rights-based approach. Activists remain mindful of staging challenges which avoided direct confrontations so as to not be seen as challenging domestic sovereignty, which according to Krasner refers to "both domestic authority structures and how effective they are" (Krasner 1999). However, without a human rights framework and submitting to the current composition of power hierarchy together with the lack of contestation to the wider systematic rights violations, whatever gains attained by the activists are limited and hinge on the whims and fancies of the state. This places activists in a precarious position where the state could also in response, pragmatically in one fell swoop, invoke its varied tools to crush the entire social movement.

As discussed previously, human rights is seen as a destabilising force from which the state of Singapore fears economic and moral decay, and the loss of domestic sovereignty from the promotion of individualism that demands civil and political rights. In contrast, the communitarian ideology that the state seeks to promote is a social order where individualism is controlled (Offord 1999). Furthermore, the framework of human rights that strives to normalise and endorse the inherent right of the LGBTQ person runs counter to the communitarian values that are deeply entrenched in the ideological rhetoric of nation building and with the heterosexual family as the foundation of the community. These fears are repeatedly on display from statements made by political leaders on Asian values and legal judgments that enforce social order in deference to community norms.

In this context of rights in a communitarian value-centric system, the Singapore LGBTQ community often adopts a pragmatic strategy away from the conventional Western LGBTQ rights discourse of "us versus them" into an assimilationist position of "us and them" (Phillips 2014). Similarly, the state employs a deliberate strategy of pragmatism by keeping law 377A and at the same time suggesting that it will not be enforced (Chua 1997; Phillips 2008). Central to this tactic was the fundamental idea of 'ambivalence' which may be seen in the course of LGBTQ engagement with the authorities and it is these contradictions that LGBTQ activists seek to organise (Phillips 2014).

A key challenge for the LGBTQ community is that an "assimilationist and homo-nationalist stance" that appeals for inclusion is unlikely to evoke change in a deeply entrenched system based on communitarian ideology (Oswin 2014). LGBTQ activists must expand their social movement beyond their identity-based status and single-issue position with broader foresight and focus on cross-cutting socio-political issues that have contributed to their oppression (Lister 2007; Paul Tan and Lee Jack Jin 2007). In addition, tactics by activists must take aim at the inconsistency and tensions in state rhetoric while building new networks and coalitions with other civil society actors in their search for social justice (Paul Tan and Lee Jack Jin 2007).

Connolly famously argued in his book *The Ethos of Pluralisation* for the diversifying of identities in which that "cultural pluralisation, critical responsiveness, and complex networks of interconnection grow together" and that,

> when the cultural conditions of pluralization are reasonably intact, differentiation along some lines opens up multiple possibilities of selective collaboration along others. To pluralise, therefore, is not to fragmentize. To dogmatize is to fragmentize. This finding discloses how self-appointed opponents of fragmentation so often work on its behalf.
> (Connolly and ebrary 1995)

In brief, Connolly argued for a new kind of pluralism, one that challenges the essentialist perceptions of identity, and for collaboration that gives birth to new possibilities.

Perhaps the way forward for gay activists is to work on the "ethos of pluralisation" to avoid being trapped within its own identity-based politics so as to act in solidarity with other facets of civil society and issues in challenging the state in its claims of itsrights and to further its political imagination (Lister 2007).

Without this, any change will also pragmatically stand on weak legs without addressing intersectional issues of socio-political rights, the protection and promotion of human rights, rights consciousness in state and non-state actors, and the support of a cross-sector network of allied social movements. Otherwise, any future expansion of the human rights discourse by LGBTQ activists with its creative organising and pragmatism will merely remain a temporal façade of success in Singapore.

Notes

1 Contributions to this chapter are based on my dissertation from the Master of Human Rights and Democratisation (MHRD) programme with the University of Sydney under the scholarship of the European Union. I would like to thank all the professors for making a difference in my life.
2 Penal Code (Cap 224, 2008 rev edn) Section 377A.
3 Constitution of the Republic of Singapore, Part IV, Article 12 (1965).
4 Court of Appeal (2012). Tan Eng Hong vs. Attorney-General [2012] SGCA 45. Civil Appeal No 50 of 2011.
5 High Court (2013). Lim Meng Suang and another vs. Attorney-General [2013] SGHC 73. T.H. Court. Originating Summons No 1135 of 2012.
6 Indiegogo campaign: Fundraising for S377A Constitutional Challenge. Available at www.indiegogo.com/projects/fundraising-for-s377a-constitutional-challenge#/ which tallied at $107,730 USD after two months.
7 Court of Appeal (2014). *Lim Meng Suang/Kenneth Chee Mun-Leong* v. *Attorney General, Tan Eng Hong* v. *Attorney General.* Court of Appeal. Singapore. Civil Appeal No 125 of 2013.
8 Ibid.

References

Berry, C. (1994). *A Bit on the Side: East–West Topographies of Desire.* Sydney: Empress Publishing.
CEDAW (2011). 49th CEDAW – Responses to the list of issues and questions with regard to the consideration of the fourth periodic report Singapore. OHCHR.
Chan, K. (2008). "Gay sexuality in Singaporean Chinese popular culture: Where have all the boys gone?" *China Information* 22(2): 305–329.
Chan, R. (2007). "Sections 377 and 377A of the Penal Code – Impact on AIDS Prevention and Control". (34): 1.
Chang, S.L. (2015). "Gay liberation in the illiberal state". *Washington International Law Journal* 24: 1.
Chong, J. (2011). *The Emergence of the Lesbian Community in Singapore.* Singapore: Asian Urban Laboratory.
Chua, B-H. (1997). *Communitarian Ideology and Democracy in Singapore.* Bristol: Psychology Press.
Chua, B-H. (2008). "Singapore in 2007: High wage ministers and the management of gays and elderly". *Asian Survey* 48(1): 55–61.
Chua, L.J. (2011). *How Does Law Matter to Social Movements? A Case Study of Gay Activism in Singapore.* ProQuest Dissertations and Theses.
Chua, L.J. (2014). *Mobilizing Gay Singapore: Rights and Resistance in an Authoritarian State.* Philadelphia, PA: Temple University Press.
Connolly, W.E. and I. ebrary (1995). *The Ethos of Pluralization.* Minneapolis: University of Minnesota Press.
Constitution (2015). *Constitution of the Republic of Singapore.* Singapore.
Court of Appeal (2012). *Tan Eng Hong* v. *Attorney-General* [2012] SGCA 45. Civil Appeal No. 50 of 2011.
Court of Appeal (2014). *Lim Meng Suang/Kenneth Chee Mun-Leong* v. *Attorney General, Tan Eng Hong* v. *Attorney General.* Court of Appeal, Singapore. Civil Appeal No. 125 of 2013.
D'Emilio, J. (1998). *Sexual Politics, Sexual Communities: The Making of a Homosexual Minority in the United States, 1940–1970.* Chicago, IL: University of Chicago Press.
Davenport, C. (2005). "Introduction". *Repression and Mobilization: Insights from Political Science and Sociology.* vii–xli.
Duberman, M. (2013). *Stonewall.* Singapore: Open Road Media.
Ennis, J.G. (1987). "Fields of action: Structure in movements' tactical repertoires". *Sociological Forum* 2(3): 520–533.
Fridae (2006). "Nation.VI to be the grand finale, Fridae to focus on web and advocacy". Available at www.fridae.asia/about/press.php?action=read&id=9207.
Fridae (2015). "Fridae timeline". Available at www.fridae.asia/about/timeline.php.
Goh, C.T. (1989). Second Reading of the Constitution of the Republic of Singapore (Amendment No. 2). *Singapore Parliament Debates, Official Report* 54: 695–705.
Heng, R. (2001). "Tiptoe out of the closet: The before and after of the increasingly visible gay community in Singapore". *Journal of Homosexuality* 40(3–4): 81–96.
High Court (2013). *Lim Meng Suang and another* v. *Attorney-General* [2013] SGHC 73. The High Court. Originating Summons No. 1135 of 2012.
Hor, M. (2012). "Enforcement of 377A: Entering the twilight zone". In *Queer Singapore: Illiberal Citizenship and Mediated Cultures.* Hong Kong: Hong Kong University Press, pp. 45–58.

Institute for Policy Studies (2013). "Our Singapore Conversation Survey". Available at www.reach.gov.sg/Portals/0/Microsite/osc/OSC-Survey.pdf.

Johnston, H. (2005). *Talking the Walk: Speech Acts and Resistance in Authoritarian Regimes*. Minneapolis: University of Minnesota Press.

Kleinwaechter, W. (1998). "The people's 'right to communicate' and a 'Global Communication Charter'. How does cyberspace change legal concepts of human rights, access and participation?" *Journal of International Communication* 5(1–2): 105–121.

Krasner, S.D. (1999). *Sovereignty: Organized Hypocrisy*. Princeton, NJ: Princeton University Press.

Lee, H.L. (2007). "Speech during the second reading of the Penal Code (Amendment) Bill". Parliament of Singapore.

Lee, Y.C. (2008). "Don't ever talk a fence down until you know the reason it was put up – Singapore communitarianism and the case for conserving 377A". *Singapore Journal of Legal Studies*: 347.

Leong, L.W.-T. (2012). "Asian sexuality or Singapore exceptionalism?" *Liverpool Law Review* 33(1): 11–26.

Lister, R. (2007). "Inclusive citizenship: Realizing the potential1". *Citizenship Studies* 11(1): 49–61.

Lo, J. and G. Huang (2003). *People Like Us: Sexual Minorities in Singapore*. Singapore: Select Publishers.

McAdam, D. (1983). "Tactical innovation and the pace of insurgency". *American Sociological Review* 48(6): 735–754.

New York Times (2003). "Quietly, Singapore lifts its ban on hiring gays". *New York Times*.

Obendorf, S. (2013). "A few respectable steps behind the world? Gay and lesbian rights in contemporary Singapore". In *Orientation, Gender Identity and Human Rights in the Commonwealth: Struggles for Decriminalisation and Change*. London: School of Advanced Study Press, University of London, pp. 231–259.

Offord, B. (1999). "The burden of (homo)sexual identity in Singapore". *Social Semiotics* 9(3): 301–316.

Offord, B. (2003). "Singaporean queering of the Internet". *Mobile Cultures: New Media in Queer Asia*: 133.

Oswin, N. (2014). "Queer time in global city Singapore: Neoliberal futures and the 'freedom to love'". *Sexualities* 17(4): 412–433.

Paul Tan, K. and G. Lee Jack Jin (2007). "Imagining the gay community in Singapore". *Critical Asian Studies* 39(2): 179–204.

People Like Us (2003a). "History of PLU: The first registration attempt 1996–1997". Available at www.plu.sg/society/?p=24.

People Like Us (2003b). "History of PLU: Moving to cyberspace, 1997". Available at www.plu.sg/society/?p=25.

People Like Us (2004). "Govt refuses to register People Like Us again". Available at www.plu.sg/society/?p=9.

People Like Us (2015, 28 July). "IndigNation: Singapore's first gay and lesbian pride month". Available at www.plu.sg/society/?p=17.

Peterson, W. (2001). *Theatre and the Politics of Culture in Contemporary Singapore*. Hanover, NH: Wesleyan University Press.

Phillips, R. (2013). "'We aren't really that different': Globe-hopping discourse and queer rights in Singapore". *Journal of Language and Sexuality* 2(1): 122–144.

Phillips, R. (2014). "'And I am also gay': Illiberal pragmatics, neoliberal homonormativity and LGBT activism in Singapore". *Anthropologica* 56(1): 45–54.

LGBTQ activism 167

Phillips, R.F. (2008). *Queering Online: Transnational Sexual Citizenship in Singapore.* Dissertation/thesis, ProQuest, UMI Dissertations Publishing.
Poore, G. (2011). "Amazing responses by CEDAW to address LGBT discrimination in Singapore". Available at https://iglhrc.wordpress.com/2011/07/27/amazing-responses-by-cedaw-to-address-lgbt-discrimination-in-singapore/ (accessed 21 December, 2016).
Ramdas, K. (2013). *Contesting Landscapes of Familyhood: Singlehood, the AWARE Saga and Pink Dot Celebrations.* Singapore: NUS Press.
Reuters. (2015). "Reuters – The opinions, and sharp tongue, of Lee Kuan Yew". Available at http://mobile.reuters.com/article/idUSKBN0MJ05G20150323?irpc=932.
Tan, C.K.K. (2009). "But they are like you and me: Gay civil servants and citizenship in a cosmopolitanizing Singapore". *City & Society* 21(1): 133–154.
Tan, K. (1999). *The Singapore Legal System.* Singapore: NUS Press.
Tan, K.K. (2011). *Stand up for Singapore? Gay Men and the Cultural Politics of National Belonging in the Lion City.* Dissertation/thesis, ProQuest, UMI Dissertations Publishing.
Tan, K.P. (2003). "Sexing up Singapore". *International Journal of Cultural Studies* 6(4): 403–423.
Tan, K.P. (2007). "Singapore's National Day Rally speech: A site of ideological negotiation". *Journal of Contemporary Asia* 37(3): 292–308.
The New Paper (2008). "'Hong Lim Green' to turn somewhat pink". *The New Paper.*
The Online Citizen. (2007). "NMP Siew Kum Hong: Turn our backs on prejudice, discrimination, intolerance and hatred". Available at www.theonlinecitizen.com/2007/10/nmp-siew-kum-hong-turn-our-backs-on-prejudice-discrimination-intolerance-and-hatred/.
The Online Citizen. (2013, 23 April). "Fundraising initiative for 377A constitutional challenge has achieved half its target". Available at www.theonlinecitizen.com/2013/04/fundraising-for-377a-challengereached-half-target/.
The Online Citizen (2014). "Christians join Muslims in protest against Pink Dot". *The Online Citizen*, Singapore.
The Straits Times (1981). "Jeyaretnam takes Anson". *The Straits Times*, Singapore.
The Straits Times (1984). "PAP wins all but two". *The Straits Times*, Singapore.
The Straits Times (2003a). "Govt should rethink hiring of gays". *The Straits Times*, Singapore.
The Straits Times (2003b). "I am disturbed by just the thought that gays are ordinary people". *The Straits Times*, Singapore.
The Straits Times (2003c). "Keep an open mind and respect differing views". *The Straits Times*, Singapore.
The Straits Times (2005). "Gay parties may have led to sharp rise in new Aids cases". *The Straits Times*, Singapore.
The Straits Times (2012). "Two launch fresh challenge to anti-gay law: Second challenge in recent years against the Penal Code's Section 377A". *The Straits Times*, Singapore.
The Straits Times (2014). "Religious teacher launches 'wear white' online campaign". *The Straits Times*, Singapore.
The Straits Times (2015). "Record 28,000 gather at Hong Lim Park for annual Pink Dot rally". *The Straits Times*, Singapore.
Thio, L. (2007). "Speech during the second reading of the Penal Code (Amendment) Bill". *Singapore Parliament Reports.*
Times, T.S. (1993). "*The Straits Times* – Tommy Koh on Ten Asian values that help East Asia's economic progress, prosperity". *The Straits Times*, Singapore.

TODAY (2014). "Apex court rejects constitutional challenges against Section 377A". *TODAY*.

Wee, C-L. (2007). *The Asian Modern: Culture, Capitalist Development*. Singapore: Hong Kong University Press.

Wong, K.S. (1993). National Library Archive – Statement by Wong Kan Seng, Minister for Foreign Affairs of the Republic of Singapore World Conference on Human Rights, Vienna – The Real World of Human Rights. *World Conference on Human Rights*, Vienna.

Wong, K.S. (2004). "Speech by Mr Wong Kan Seng, Minister for Home Affairs and Member of Parliament for Bishan-Toa Payoh GRC. Presented at the Bishan-Toa Payoh, Singapore".

Yahoo! News (2012). "Couple files challenge to S'pore law criminalising gay sex". *Yahoo News*, Singapore.

Yahoo! News (2013). "COMMENT: Why the term 'gay lifestyle' offends and is hurtful". Available at https://sg.news.yahoo.com/blogs/singaporescene/why-term-gay-lifestyle-offensive-022702704.html.

Yusop, N.B.M. (2005). *Same Sex Sexuality and Islam in Singapore*. Unpublished MA thesis, National University of Singapore.

9 Navigating through the 'rules' of civil society

In search of disability rights in Singapore

Wong Meng Ee, Ian Ng, Jean Lor and Reuben Wong[1]

Introduction

The Singapore School, initiated by the founding Prime Minister Lee Kuan Yew and subsequently propagated by Bilahari Kausikan and Kishore Mahbubani, characterises a political regime dedicated to social order and economic growth that is believed to achieve human dignity and "good governance" (Chew 1994). In this vein, the needs and rights of the community may outweigh the rights of the individual in the eyes of the government. Political and social goals, such as reducing inequality for persons with disabilities, have not been a major policy in Singapore's history (Ng 2015). Rather, economic development and nation building have been the key emphases in providing access to education, housing and healthcare. Given Singapore's economic disadvantage compounded with high unemployment rates, poverty and inadequate public housing, the priority of social welfare policy was not to place further financial burden on the state (Low and Aw 2004).

These principles continue to shape social policies in Singapore. Lee expressed the hope that Singapore would never become a Western-style, liberal, individualistic society such as the USA or the UK.

> If that happened, we would go down the drain. We'd have more poor people in the streets, sleeping in the open, we'd have more drugs, more crime, more single mothers with delinquent children, a troubled society and a poor economy.
>
> (Tan 1993)

Unlike in other developed countries, there is no purpose-built legislation or anti-discrimination act in Singapore that specifically promotes or protects the rights of the disabled. Nevertheless, the Constitution of Singapore guarantees the fundamental liberties of all citizens. For example, Article 14 guarantees the freedom of speech and expression; the right to assemble peaceably and without arms; and the right to form associations.[2] The Constitution also mentions rights covering life and liberty (Art 9), property (Art 12), equality, rights against slavery and forced labour (Art 10), and the right to freedom of conscience as articulated in the freedom of speech (Art 14) and religion (Art 15). The citizens are also protected from banishment and given freedom of movement. Since independence, these basic principles have remained intact (Ho 2000). Yet despite the guarantee of the fundamental constitutional rights and the declarations put forward by the Advisory Council on the Disabled in 1988, persons with disabilities in Singapore still have many of their human rights denied today.

This chapter argues that while the progress of disability rights has been slow, disability rights have moved from near non-existence to a less peripheral position in the human rights scene in Singapore. The 'medical model' of disability (that disability is the individual's problem, which needs to be 'solved') is still the dominant paradigm in the 50 years since Singapore's independence (Wong and Wong 2015). Tracing the historical development of disability rights, this chapter covers the post-war provision for disability and key milestones such as the 1981 International Year of Disabled Persons, the explicit disability rights captured in the 1988 Advisory Council on the Disabled, and the ratification of the 2006 United Nations (UN) Convention on the Rights of Persons with Disabilities (CRPD) in 2013.

Setting the scene

When studying disability rights in Singapore, Lee Kuan Yew's role as the nation's founding father cannot be ignored. Lee became Prime Minister on 5 June 1959 and remained Prime Minister for 31 years. The circumstances in which Lee took office shaped his style of government and the social policies that followed. Lee's immediate task upon assuming office was to build a viable economy and to negotiate terms for merger and separation from the Federation of Malaysia (1963–1965); and since independence in 1965, to ensure Singapore's survival and growth as a small, newly independent state.

The first-generation leaders were confronted with many immediate issues. Domestically, the threat of the unfavourable and volatile climate of industrial relations resulted in declining manufacturing activities and sluggish foreign investments. Adding to these economic tensions was political instability from communism and communalism (Ho 2000). In short, the government had to contend with the communist influence, raise the standard of living, and put in place institutions and infrastructure necessary for economic development. In these circumstances of national survival, the attention paid to disability rights (and human rights in general) took a back seat, in contrast to the dominant national narratives of survival and development.

The development of civil society activism on disability in Singapore

The advocacy and provision of disability rights have been shaped by interactions between government and civil society, and also by changes in the approach adopted by the international community across history. This section examines

'Rules' of civil society: disability rights 171

the approaches towards disability in the early years, the changes in social policy from the 1980s to recent years, and future prospects for change.

Historical timeline

1946 – Creation of the Social Welfare Department (SWD).
1970 – Implementation of the Voluntary Sterilisation Act (VSA).
1979 – Founding of AWWA's Handicapped Children's Playgroup.
1981 – UN International Year of Disabled Persons (IYDP); Founding of Disabled People's International (DPI) in Singapore.
1986 – Official registration of the Disabled People's Association (DPA), first advocacy group in Singapore.
1988 – Formation of the Advisory Council on the Disabled.
1993 – Implementation of Edusave (which excluded children with disabilities).
1996 – Expansion of Edusave to include children with disabilities.
2003 – Implementation of the Compulsory Education Act (which excluded children with disabilities).
2007 – Implementation of the Enabling Masterplan (2007–2011).
2012 – Amendment of the VSA.
2012 – Implementation of the Enabling Masterplan (2012–2016).
2013 – Official ratification of the UNCRPD.

Post-World War II: beginnings of the welfare model

The provision of social services to the less privileged, including the disabled, has its roots in colonial times. Early social service provision during the Colonial government era was left largely to the community and voluntary welfare organisations such as religious bodies, clan associations and secret societies (Wee 2004). Following the war, the British Empire gradually took on the role as welfare provider in response to people's expectations following the personal sacrifices made during the war. Welfare provisions served to safeguard British interests in the region, society and the colonial state (Harper 1999). The disabled were thus subsumed under welfare support and were viewed as objects of assistance.

The creation of the Social Welfare Department (SWD) by the British reflected this significant change in colonial policy (Social Welfare Department 1946). The Department's first report in 1946 spelled out its role, namely to address the "wake of human wreckage left by the war and pestilence of the Japanese occupation" (Social Welfare Department 1946). The philosophy of aid and welfare was further reflected in the 1949 five-year plan of the SWD, which declared that the government should only provide permanent assistance in specific cases like permanent disability and old age. In other instances, temporary assistance aimed at restoring the individual's productiveness in the community would be given (Social Welfare Department 1949).

To achieve this, the SWD established rural settlements to accommodate persons with physical and mental disabilities in outdoor work (Social Welfare

Department 1949). However, the responsibility to educate children with disabilities seemed secondary to the concern that contact with children with disabilities would hinder the typical child's education, as seen by the exclusionary language used by the SWD. In 1949, the SWD asserted that "[t]he normal child's education should not be retarded by association with the handicapped" (Social Welfare Department 1949).

More disparaging were remarks made by a social worker in the SWD in-house magazine of 1955, where fowls were depicted as analogous to people with disabilities. In the social worker's words, "[the] handicapped are not a problem for chickens, and that handicapped chickens make good roast dishes" (Zhuang 2010). Such shocking language, appearing in an official colonial government publication, reflected the contemporary, rather utilitarian approach towards disability – one that was degrading, even demeaning for the disabled. Zhuang (2010) explained:

> This metaphorical association with poultry represents the disabled as a transgression beyond the human to the animal, beyond what is civilised to the barbaric, from what is acceptable within the normal limits of the social to what is not.

Similarly, former President Yusof bin Ishak spoke of disability as a rehabilitation issue, claiming that "on rehabilitation, a handicapped person is an asset to himself and his country, and a testimony to those who have helped him on the road to a life of usefulness" (Singapore Association for the Blind 1968).

While the notion of welfare persisted in the 1960s, more respectful language was used when referring to people with disabilities. Then-Prime Minister Lee declared that no society could ignore the needs of the disabled and resources should be given to their "less fortunately endowed members" to allow them to live a full life (Singapore Association for the Blind 1965).

This shift in language was accompanied by the setting up of welfare-based organisations to ensure the continued provision of social services with the impending departure of the British. According to Leaena Tambyah, a prominent advocate for special education, the wives of British officials played an important role in the formation of these welfare-based organisations. For example, Singapore's former First Lady Jean Marshall, wife of Singapore's first Chief Minister David Marshall, volunteered actively with the Social Welfare Department and the Singapore Children Society in the 1960s (AWARE 2014). Another example, Shakuntala Bhatia, wife of the then-Indian High Commissioner, founded the Asian Women's Welfare Association (AWWA) in 1970.[3] Tambyah had realised that there would be a fall in the number of volunteers as the British service wives left Singapore with their husbands. In March 1979, she encouraged AWWA to offer a service to children with multiple disabilities, and care for their mothers (AWWA Educational Services 2009).

However, the disability language in the 1970s was still strongly influenced by charity overtones that were at best rehabilitative in nature. For example, with greater economic industrialisation, more industrial accidents needed to be resolved. The National Trades Union Congress (NTUC) organised workshops to provide rehabilitation and to train workers with disabilities to return to employment (Zhuang 2010). The intent to retrain workers with disabilities also led to several commissioned studies with international experts who recommended that the government take on greater roles in rehabilitation (Zhuang 2010).

Moreover, then-Singapore President Benjamin Sheares made a speech at the opening of the Fifth Pan-Pacific Conference of the International Society for the Rehabilitation of the Disabled where he emphasised that rehabilitation of the disabled should be the "earnest concern of all civic-minded citizens" (Pan-Pacific Rehabilitation Conference 1975).

The Voluntary Sterilisation Act (VSA) was implemented in 1970 to provide "legal certainty for sexual sterilisation procedures performed by registered medical practitioners, for the purposes of family planning" (Ministry of Health 2012). The spouse, parent or guardian of persons who are "afflicted with any hereditary form of illness that is recurrent, mental illness, mental deficiency or epilepsy" has the power to consent on their behalf to undergo sterilisation even though such persons may have the mental capacity of giving their own consent despite their conditions (Ministry of Health 2012). In particular, when the Act was first introduced, only one parent's or one guardian's consent was required to sterilise a child (i.e. persons under 21) (AWARE 2012b). Such policies placed persons with disability in a vulnerable position. The law gave their caregivers inordinate power to make decisions on their behalf.

1980s: milestones at home and abroad

International Year of Disabled Persons

The 1980s saw a surge in international efforts to secure and protect the rights of persons with disabilities. The UN International Year of Disabled Persons (IYDP) in 1981 (United Nations Department of Economic and Social Affairs 1981) was one such effort. The IYDP was a "plan of action at the national, regional and international levels, with an emphasis on equalisation of opportunities, rehabilitation and prevention of disabilities" (United Nations Department of Economic and Social Affairs 1981). Interestingly, this inaugural conference on disability rights was held in Singapore, a testament to how the country was seen as an 'acceptable place', economically, socially and politically.[4]

Subsequently, the World Program of Action concerning Disabled Persons implemented a "global strategy to enhance disability prevention, rehabilitation and equalisation of opportunities, pertaining to full participation of persons with disabilities in social life and national development" (United Nations Department of Economic and Social Affairs 1982).

The IYDP is significant internationally due to its recognition of disability rights, and arguably started a series of international events that eventually culminated in the establishment of the UNCRPD in 2012. On 4 December 1981, the Disabled People's International (DPI) was set up. Comprising members of the disabled community, the DPI was created as an "organisation of persons with disabilities for persons with disabilities" (Disabled People's Association n.d.), and proposed to change attitudes and policies that negatively affected the disabled in society. At the first DPI World Congress, Singaporean Ron Chandran-Dudley was elected as the first international president of the DPI. Prior to DPI's formation, Chandran-Dudley had already been an active "defender of rights" both locally and internationally, holding key positions in organisations like Rehabilitation International.[5] Despite being visually handicapped since he was 19 (Think Centre 2004), he represented persons with disabilities in conferences across the world, advocating that it was important to focus on the remaining abilities of the disabled rather than just what disabled them, saying:

> Up to this point, many of the services that existed in Singapore were organised for and on behalf of the disabled with able-bodied persons assuming the leadership role while the disabled persons themselves remained passive receivers of services and goods.
> (United Nations Department of Economic and Social Affairs 1981)

Chandran-Dudley, who had already been Chairman of the National Coordinating Committee of IYDP, played a significant role in the IYDP by championing disability rights, and unsurprisingly, DPI was one the first groups internationally to lobby extensively for the signing of the UNCRPD.[6]

Following this, the DPI's Singapore chapter – the Disabled People's Association (DPA) – was officially registered on 28 April 1986 (Disabled People's Association n.d.). In fact, it is the first advocacy group in Singapore to be officially registered (Yong 2015). DPA is unique, since it is the only organisation in Singapore that advocates for all persons with disabilities (Disabled People's Association n.d.), using a rights-based approach and "advocacy only".[7] This approach may be attributed to the historical relations between the DPA and DPI, which were both founded by Chandran-Dudley.

Together, these international efforts resulted in a greater interest in disability issues within Singapore. At the official opening of the IYDP in 1981, Dr Ahmad Mattar, then-Minister for Social Affairs, declared the government's intention to see disabled persons as equal and contributing members of society. He further emphasised the need to equalise opportunities and make services available to the disabled such that they, too, could lead a "meaningful and productive life" (National Coordinating Committee 1981).

This period also marked the formal recognition of disability in Singapore. A workshop organised by the Ministry of Social Affairs (MSA) in 1983 entitled *Towards a Better Profile of the Disabled People in Singapore: Workshop on National Definition of Disability*, brought Voluntary Welfare Organisations (VWOs) together to deliberate on disability issues on a national platform.

Mr K.V. Veloo, then-Director (Development Division) at MSA, underscored the importance of defining disability as a first step towards implementing recommendations made during the IYDP (Ministry of Social Affairs 1983).

A definition eventually agreed upon was as follows. People with disability are those whose prospects of securing, retaining places and advancing in educational and training institutions, employment and recreation as equal members of the community are substantially reduced as a result of physical or mental impairment (Ministry of Social Affairs 1983).

This was the first nationally endorsed definition of disability in Singapore that gave an identity to disabled individuals whose needs would otherwise remain unaccounted for in the larger scheme of the total population. Significantly, this definition of disability was refined to include developmental disability in 2004 (Ministry of Social and Family Development 2007). Yet, such a clear definition could isolate those with disabilities from those without.

During this period, then-Prime Minister Goh Chok Tong adopted a softer, more engaging and consultative approach to social policies, and was "on the ball" regarding disability issues and very helpful during the DPA's initiation.[8] This approach may be seen in the 1997 Singapore 21 campaign (Goh 1997) and the 2002 Remaking Singapore campaign, in which disabled individuals formed part of the subcommittees (Remaking Singapore Committee 2003).

The 1988 Advisory Council on the Disabled

With formal status now assigned to disability, the formation of the Advisory Council on the Disabled in April 1988 chaired by then-Education Minister, Dr Tony Tan, further highlighted the responsibility to integrate disabled individuals as equal citizens. This was significant for the government to recognise and consider major integral lifespan areas, including education and training, employment, accessibility and transportation, community involvement and residential care (Report of the Advisory Council on the Disabled 1988).

The aims of the Council explicitly articulated the rights of individuals with disabilities. Tan had written to then-Deputy Prime Minister Goh Chok Tong premising the Council's recommendations on the principle that persons with disabilities should enjoy the same rights as normal people to live normally and independently in society. Furthermore, caring for the disabled was the responsibility of not just the government but also the family and community (Report of the Advisory Council on the Disabled 1988).

Goh concurred, responding with the government's support for the Council's recommendations:

> I share your sentiment when you said that disabled people should have the same right as normal people to take their proper place in society and to live as independently as possible.
>
> (Report of the Advisory Council on the Disabled 1988)

However, it is not certain whether the "rights" mentioned by Goh refer to *human rights*, or to citizens' *constitutional rights*. Such a distinction may be seen in how the Singapore government prefers the use of the term "rights of persons with disabilities" as opposed to "human rights", which "seems like a pedantic distinction, but avoids a lot of issues".[9] The former arguably applies only to Singapore citizens, while the latter carries a universal connotation. Furthermore, despite this declaration of equality and integration, an attitude of marginalisation and charity still existed, as seen at a 1988 nation-planning Convention of the People's Action Party where party members were encouraged to give the disabled who needed "help to cope" the "support they needed" (People's Action Party 1988).

More explicitly, however, the view of disabled persons was captured in the 1990 Convention with a negative connotation of liability and dependence:

> Those who are physically incapacitated [...] can become *economic and social liabilities to the family and the nation* [...]. He [the disabled person] may also tie down another member of the family who may otherwise be *economically active*. Furthermore he will often have multiple hospital admissions for social and medical reasons.
>
> (Zhuang 2010, emphasis added)

Such a view captures the utilitarian perspective which had been espoused by the government that emphasises one's economic contributions. Essentially, persons with disabilities who are unable to work appear to be not worth helping, as they cannot contribute economically to nation building. However, as mentioned in the 1981 IYDP, "the cost/benefit analysis should not be the main criteria" (United Nations Department of Economic and Social Affairs 1981). The opportunity cost of supporting the disabled remains a point of tension in Singapore's focus on self-sustainability and nation building where limited human resources and the lack of natural resources were major challenges which the government faced.

First special education school

Leaena Tambyah started the first special school for children with multiple disabilities, AWWA's Handicapped Children's Playgroup, on 12 March 1979 at Damien Hall in St Ignatius Church (AWWA Educational Services 2009). Back then, no mainstream or special needs school would accept these children. Tambyah chaired the playgroup from 1979 to 1985, and then founded the Therapy and Educational Assistance for Children in Mainstream Education (TEACH ME) in March 1991. TEACH ME is an integrated programme for bright children in special schools who could be in mainstream schools (Singapore Women's Hall of Fame 2014). TEACH ME also runs mobile therapy clinics from vans that offer services to disabled students at home as well as in regular schools (Singapore Women's Hall of Fame 2014a).

Establishing services for children with disabilities was not without difficulties. For example, the introduction of the Certificate Of Entitlement (COE) system meant that the mobile therapy van could not be used unless the COE, which cost an estimated S$27,000 in the late 1980s, was paid.[10] The Ministry of Health was unable to help AWWA resolve this issue, and Tambyah eventually spoke to a Member of Parliament, Abdullah Tarmugi, who was able to get tax exemptions for AWWA's mobile therapy vans.[11] Despite the numerous difficulties, AWWA prevailed, and has since produced outstanding graduates like the Liew brothers – Liew Chong Choon and Liew Chong Heng – who were described as being "too bright for their classes" and who eventually graduated from the Singapore Management University.[12]

AWWA has also published various books to raise awareness about children with disabilities, such as *Hey Listen! We Have Something to Say* and *Hey Listen! We Have More to Say* – collections of stories about the hopes and dreams of children with disabilities – and *Three Special Friends*, co-written by Tambyah about three of her students.[13] These books have helped increase awareness of the importance of special education.

Working within the state's welfare model

Building on the events of the 1980s, a conference was organised in 1991 by the then Singapore Council of Social Service (SCSS), the Community Chest of Singapore (CCS) and the Institute of Policy Studies to plan for the future of social services. For the first time, members from various organisations, including the public and private sectors, academia and voluntary services, gathered to discuss the issues facing the community. The SCSS, CCS and VWOs were established to promote the quality of life for persons requiring social support. These early efforts were inadequate to meet the needs, as the demand for services often outweighed the supply. Worse, the magnitude of the demand was unknown, although it was estimated that the sector was meeting no more than 20 per cent of needs (Yap 1991).

Regarding services for the disabled in the late 1990s, 17 VWOs provided special education, early intervention programmes for infants and young children, vocational training, residential care, day care, employment and transport facilities for the disabled. As they were operating at full capacity, many were forced to put potential clients on long waiting lists (Yap 1991). The estimated numbers of persons with disabilities in 1988 was 12,526, based on the (now-defunct) Central Registry of Disabled Persons. This represented less than 0.5 per cent of the total population and differed significantly from the UN's estimate of 10 per cent of disability per population (Disability Information Resources n.d.). Taking a more conservative estimate based on the 3.8 per cent in Japan and Hong Kong, SCSS approximated 97,000 disabled people in Singapore. The 17 VWOs were providing services for only 7,840 disabled people, which comprised about 62.5 per cent of those identified in the Central Registry or 8 per cent of the estimated population of 97,000 disabled (Yap 1991).

Some challenges confronting the sector included difficulties in recruiting staff, acquiring premises for operations, the lack of specialised professional and technical expertise as well as a referral system for early identification and intervention (Yap 1991). Despite some developments in services for the disabled, the pre- and post-1988 services still did not reflect a rights-based approach to service provision. The historical provision of services encouraged a segregated approach to service delivery. The limited training of specialists and professionals, and the lack of cohesive cross-sector policy development, failed to meet the complex lifespan needs of the disabled. Specifically, there was under-provision of public services for disabled persons, a lack of expertise within the community, and insufficient monitoring and evaluation of services.

In terms of education policy, the Education Endowment Scheme, also known as Edusave, was implemented in 1993 to maximise the opportunities for Singapore students in schools funded by the Ministry of Education (MOE) (Ministry of Education n.d.). However, children in special schools were excluded when the policy was first implemented, for the reason that these students "did not need it".[14] This explanation was unacceptable to advocates for disabled children, who reasoned that such unfounded and unequal treatment would eventually lead to unequal future opportunities for these children.[15] With active lobbying by advocates such as Tambyah and the support of the National Council for Social Services (NCSS), Edusave eventually included children with disabilities in 1996.[16]

Furthering education and access to transportation

Exemption from compulsory education

Prime Minister Lee Hsien Loong made the following statement at the opening of the Cerebral Palsy Centre in 2004:

> Every society has some members with disabilities. How the society treats the disabled, takes care of them, and helps them integrate into the mainstream, reflects the kind of society it is. We want ours to be a society that cares for all its members; one that does not ignore the needs of those who are born or afflicted with disabilities.

The Compulsory Education Act was implemented in 2003 to ensure that all Singaporeans have a minimum of six years of education. However, similar to the Edusave scheme, children with special needs were at first automatically exempted from the system, as "the enforcement [...] may be unduly harsh on the parents of such children" (Ministry of Education 2000). Another reason for the automatic exemption was that VWOs, which are primarily responsible for providing special education with funding from the NCSS and MOE, were "not yet able to complete the building programme for special education schools, nor able to provide all the necessary teaching resources for educating such children" (Ministry of Education 2000).

In 2004, groups in the disability sphere attempted a concerted rights-based appeal for inclusive education. AWWA, together with all VWOs (except one) running special schools, compiled a report etitled *A Case for the Inclusion of Children with Special Needs in Compulsory Education* (AWWA 2004). This followed a survey conducted by a Joint Committee for Compulsory Education for All, which comprised VWOs. Despite the worry that the "enforcement [...] may be unduly harsh on the parents" (Ministry of Education 2000), the survey result showed that "95.9% of 2489 parents of children with special needs were in favour of compulsory education for their children", thus concluding that "compulsory education for children with special needs is not only viable, it is necessary" (AWWA 2004). In this submitted report, the Joint Committee argued that the Singapore government had ratified the UN Convention on the Rights of the Child (CRC) in 1995, in which the basic human right of every child is the "development of his physical and mental potential without discrimination of any kind, irrespective of the child's disability" (AWWA 2004), and thus could be held accountable for the duties described in the CRC. This is an example of how local NGOs used international rights conventions for advocacy.

There was also progress at the tertiary level. The Singapore Management University was founded in 2000 as the first disabled-friendly university, offering the opportunity of a university education to disabled students. The university included wider corridors and lifts to allow for wheelchair-friendly access. Prominent students with disabilities include national Paralympian Yip Pin Xiu (Singapore Women's Hall of Fame 2014b), as well as the Liew brothers (Baker 2008).

Access to public transportation

In 2000, the Challenged People's Alliance and Network was formed by Rethinasamy Rajasavari, who is half-blind, to request for concession rates on the trains in the Mass Rapid Transit (MRT) system in Singapore (Koh 2009). In May 2009, an online petition was started and speeches were made in Hong Lim Park to campaign for transport subsidies (Koh 2009). SBS Transit, a private bus and train operator, eventually offered concession rates for monthly passes for disabled persons in 2014 (Tan 2014).

Ratification of the UNCRPD

In 2013, Singapore ratified the UNCRPD, but did not sign the Optional Protocol that allows for complaints regarding the violation of rights to be put before and investigated by the Committee on the Rights of Persons with Disabilities. Then-Minister of Social and Family Development Chan Chun Sing explained in Parliament that there were sufficient and appropriate platforms for individuals and groups to raise concerns or complaints, such as the Ministry of Social and Family Development or the National Council of Social Service (Singapore Parliamentary Report 2012).

In addition, three reservations were also attached to the ratification of the UNCRPD: Article 12(4) 'Equal Recognition before the Law' due to the Mental Capacity Act that gives decision-making power to a pre-appointed trustee should the individual lose mental capacity in the future, Article 25(e) 'Health' as "Singapore does not intervene in the commercial underwriting decisions of private insurers" and Article 29(a)(iii) 'Participation in Political and Public Life' where an election official is to assist disabled individuals in voting instead of a "freely-chosen representative" (Ministry of Social and Family Development 2013).[17]

Ratifying the UNCRPD but not the Optional Protocol, while attaching three reservations, places Singapore in a position of reduced accountability to the international community. As disputes or complaints are addressed within a local context, it is especially important that civil society plays an active role engaging the government and citizens to ensure accountability for and protection of the rights of persons with disabilities.

Abolition of the VSA

In preparation for the ratification of the UNCRPD, the Singapore government made various changes to the Voluntary Sterilisation Act (VSA) that had been implemented in the 1970s (Ministry of Health 2012). Significantly, the Association of Women for Action and Research (AWARE) successfully lobbied for certain amendments. In particular, for persons who lack the mental capacity to make the decision, an order from the High Court or an independent committee would now be required. This was an improvement on the previous approach that only required parents', or guardians' consent (AWARE 2012a) and thus better safeguards the well-being of the mentally disabled by limiting potential abuse of the VSA.

In addition, each case involving minors (persons under 21 years old) now has to be reviewed by a Hospital Ethics Committee, which would have to "take into account all clinical, psychological, social and ethical aspects of the case" (AWARE 2012a). As the government prepared to ratify the CRPD (Ministry of Health 2012), this active and timely participation of AWARE to lobby for certain recommendations helped shape social policy so that the rights of persons with disabilities would be protected.[18]

Enabling Masterplan 2012 to 2016

To further ensure compliance with the CRPD, the government introduced the *Enabling Masterplan 2012 to 2016*, which is a five-year "national roadmap to build a more inclusive society, such that persons with disabilities can be integral and contributing members" (Ministry of Social and Family Development n.d.). This builds upon the *Enabling Masterplan 2007 to 2011*, the previous five-year plan, which covers "early intervention, education and employment" as "core developmental areas that must be addressed to enable more persons with disabilities to lead independent lives as contributing members of society" (Enabling Masterplan Steering Committee 2007). As such, the *Enabling Masterplan 2012 to 2016* aims to further "enable persons with disabilities to be equal and integral members of our society" (Ministry of Social and Family Development n.d.).

With an emphasis on better support in pre-schools, higher subsidies and more affordable services in early intervention, more training and job options to encourage employment and more help available for families to care for persons with disabilities in their own homes (Ministry of Social and Family Development n.d.), the *Enabling Masterplan 2012 to 2016* takes aspects of the CRPD into consideration and brings these to the forefront of social policy for the disabled. Focusing on equality of employment and education opportunities for the disabled, this *Enabling Masterplan 2012 to 2016* will help Singapore fulfil the requirements for CRPD.

The two *Enabling Masterplans* may be seen as a journey for both the government and society-at-large to understand what it means to be a rights-based society. However, the *Masterplan* still does not seem to fully protect the well-being of the disabled, especially those who are unable to attain employment. One recent development has been approval for the construction of a home that supports older disabled citizens whose families are unable to provide support.[19] This home, due for completion in 2017, perhaps signifies better protection of the disabled. However to ensure sustainability, continued discussions with civil society through the shadow reports in the Universal Periodic Review will be needed to improve social policy for the disabled.

Advocacy by the Disabled People's Association

The DPA continues to raise awareness about the UNCRPD by writing guides such as *Singapore and the UNCRPD*, which "contextualise[s] the CRPD in Singapore" by explaining and illustrating what social policies are in place to realise each article, and providing recommendations to bridge the gaps (Disabled People's Association 2015b). In addition, the DPA conducts sessions to educate persons with disabilities on the rights that they possess and how to advocate for them. Workshops that target the disabled are shaped depending on the current events regarding disability. For example, when the CRPD was first ratified, workshops that simplified the concepts in the CRPD were conducted to help disabled individuals understand the important concepts and what it meant for them.[20] One publication, *How to Plan and Deliver Advocacy Messages*, offers "easy-to-use tips on planning and delivering messages such as writing a complaint or feedback letter" (Disabled People's Association 2015a). Through such workshops, the DPA hopes to provide information for people to "advocate for yourself".[21]

Campaigns run by the DPA have also changed over their history. While a previous campaign illustrated a large barrier compared to a small person in a wheelchair to raise awareness on *physical barriers*, the DPA's most recent campaign addressed *mental barriers* by challenging society's norms on the use of disabled-friendly facilities such as the reserved parking lot for persons with disabilities.[22]

Conclusion

Despite the declaration of disability rights in 1988, the accompanying support structures were arguably inadequate to provide the necessary affordances for persons with disabilities to reach their potential. Granted, it is unreasonable to expect a country with limited resources to meet such comprehensive and diverse specialised needs in the light of significant competing mainstream demands; the unavoidable question then is the dilemma of choices versus rights. However, Singapore is known for its miraculous economic transformation where significant goals have been achieved despite limited resources. With good governance and active citizenry, a miracle can happen yet again.

Noteworthy is the significant shift from the medical model of disability to the social model of disability over the past 50 years. The former pathologised the disability resulting from chronic illness and impairment, resulting in an emphasis and demand on the individual with disability to adapt to society. This narrative had been used from after World War II up until the 1980s, and may be seen in enacted social policies, like the Voluntary Sterilisation Act, which assumed that mentally handicapped individuals were unable to make their own decisions. In recent years, however, the government and local NGOs have gradually shifted their approach to a social model, where "responsibility is shared within the society and it takes a lot of burden away from persons with disabilities".[23] This may be seen through government policies such as the *Enabling Masterplan 2012 to 2016* which aimed to build a more inclusive society. Such a shift from the medical model to the social model is laudable, but more needs to be done to build a more inclusive society.

Singapore is not a liberal democratic society shaped to consider the notion of rights from an individual rights perspective. While rights are declared a fundamental principle, there exists an underlying utilitarian and pragmatic set of principles shaping social policy that subsequently prioritising the needs of the majority. This points to a hierarchy of rights. Furthermore, it is virtually impossible to observe all rights, as each right will inevitably be competing and even be potentially conflicting in nature. Singapore's single-minded focus to meet economic needs before addressing social ones is a case in point. To that end, one could argue that concerns over an increasingly ageing population have probably played a significant role in the push for changes in social policy for the disabled, displaying the pragmatism that prioritises majority needs under the Singapore School of Thought, and less of a consideration for disability rights.

This notion of ensuring rights for the majority suggests the need for minority groups such as the disabled to play a greater advocacy role. Given the multiple, competing claims for rights, the voice of the disabled needs to be heard. The then SCSS (now NCSS) was the conduit between the government and the

VWOs. This was, and largely remains, the official channel that represents the voices of Disabled People's Organisations (DPOs). As recipients of government funding, DPOs are placed in a vulnerable position for advocacy. DPOs need to monitor social services while ensuring that the rights of the disabled are protected. Interaction with DPOs provides an opportunity to ensure that the voices of disabled persons are heard; thus DPOs should do more to achieve positive results on the ground. Generally, the relationship between the government and DPOs appears to be more consensual than confrontational, which arguably builds greater trust that allows for greater productivity when advocating for the rights of the disabled.

Individuals with disability need to champion the causes that they believe will improve their lives. The UNCRPD enshrines the principle "nothing about us without us" (Harpur 2012). Even though rights have been declared, there is still inadequate agency to drive the realisation of those rights. Greater participation from disabled individuals is needed to shape social policy. This necessitates a shift from passive participation to active involvement and thus requires change from within the disability community. Nonetheless, Singapore's socio-political climate remains one in which the government continues to play an active role, even in matters traditionally residing in the realm of civil society. As such, active involvement and advocacy needs to be tempered with responsibility and awareness to be effective in Singapore.

The past 50 years have witnessed disability rights changing place in society. Important milestones in Singapore's history have helped bring the issue of disability rights to the forefront, for both policy-making and civil society advocacy. The recent ratification of the UNCRPD certainly seems to bode well for the disabled in Singapore, who have had their rights infringed in the past. Nevertheless, there remains work to be done, as the disabled still occupy a disadvantaged and peripheral position in society. The progress in policies ensuring the rights of disabled persons would not have been possible without the determined and concerted efforts of individuals and organisations who fought for a cause they strongly believed in. This journey is an ongoing one, and it is perhaps apt to conclude the chapter with the following quote by Johnny Ang, former editor of Handicap's Welfare Association (HWA): "Meanwhile, we dare to dream. Without dream, there is no reality, without reality there is no challenge, and without challenge there is no success" (Ang 1990).

Notes

1 We would like to extend our heartfelt appreciation to the following individuals and organisations that have contributed to our research for this chapter: Mrs Leaena Tambyah (founder of the AWWA Handicapped Children's Playgroup and TEACH ME), Dr Marissa Lee Medjeral-Mills (Executive Director of the Disabled People's Association), Mr Ron Chandran-Dudley (founder of the Disabled People's International and Disabled People's Association), Ms Rachel Zeng (local activist for the Singapore Anti-Death Penalty Campaign) and Mr Zhuang Kuansong (independent researcher on disability issues in Singapore). Mr Ron Chandran-Dudley, one of our

interviewees, passed away on 30 December 2015 before this book's publication. As the founder of the Disabled People's Association, he championed the rights of people with disabilities. The authors thank Mr Chandran-Dudley for sharing insights required for completing this chapter.
2. Constitution of the Republic of Singapore (1999 Reprint) Article 14(1).
3. Personal interview, Leaena Tambyah, 8 October 2015, Singapore.
4. Personal interview, Ron Chandran-Dudley, 3 November 2015, Singapore.
5. Ibid.
6. Personal interview, Ron Chandran-Dudley, 3 November 2015, Singapore.
7. Personal interview, Marissa Lee Medjeral-Mills, 8 October 2015, Singapore.
8. Personal interview, Ron Chandran-Dudley, 3 November 2015, Singapore.
9. Personal interview, Marissa Lee Medjeral-Mills, 8 October 2015, Singapore.
10. The COE is a quota licence system to regulate the use and ownership of vehicles in Singapore.
11. Personal interview, Leaena Tambyah, 8 October 2015, Singapore.
12. Ibid.
13. Ibid.
14. Ibid.
15. Ibid.
16. Ibid.
17. UN General Assembly, Convention on the Rights of Persons with Disabilities, 30 March 2007, United Nations, Treaty Series, Vol. 2515.
18. See also CENTRES (Clinical Ethics Network for Training, Research and Support), "Management of menstrual problems of young female tatients with intellectual disabilities" (Singapore: NUS Centre for Biomedical Ethics), No. 11 (March 2012), Editorial, pp. 1–2, for a summary of the medical, legal, human rights and philosophical issues related to this issue.
19. Personal interview, Leaena Tambyah, 7 November 2015, Singapore.
20. Personal interview, Marissa Lee Medjeral-Mills, 8 October 2015, Singapore.
21. Ibid.
22. Ibid.
23. Ibid.

References

Ang, J. (1990). "The development of the Disabled People's Association in Singapore". *Integrator Magazine* 1(1).
AWARE (2012a). "New safeguard for minors in VSA". Available at www.aware.org.sg/2012/11/new-safeguard-for-minors-in-voluntary-sterilization-act/ (accessed 14 October 2015).
AWARE (2012b). "Sterilization Bill: They heard us". Available at www.aware.org.sg/2012/09/21542/ (accessed 14 October 2013).
AWARE (2014). "Women of impact: Transforming Singapore's social scene". Available at www.aware.org.sg/2014/09/women-of-impact-transforming-singapores-social-scene/ (accessed 14 October 2015).
AWWA (2004). "A case for the inclusion of children with special needs in compulsory education".
AWWA Educational Services (2009). "Celebrating 30 great years".
Baker, V. (2008, 14 July). "Graduation at last, against all odds". *Asia News*. Available at http://news.asiaone.com/News/Education/Story/A1Story20080714766466.html (accessed 25 November 2015).

CENTRES (2012). "Management of menstrual problems of young female patients with intellectual disabilities". Singapore: NUS Centre for Biomedical Ethics, No. 11 (March).
Chew, M. (1994). "Human rights in Singapore: Perceptions and problems". *Asian Survey* **34**(11): 933–948.
Disability Information Resources (n.d.). "Chapter 2: National-level access legislation and policy provisions".
Disabled People's Association (2015a). "Advocacy toolkit: How to plan and deliver advocacy messages".
Disabled People's Association (2015b). "Singapore and the UN CRPD".
Disabled People's Association (n.d.). History.
Enabling Masterplan Steering Committee (2007). Media Release, Ministry of Social and Family Development.
Goh, C.T. (1997). "Singapore 21: Vision for a new era". Ministry of Information, Communications and the Arts, Singapore. Available at www.nas.gov.sg/archivesonline/speeches/view-html?filename=1997060503.htm.
Harper, T. (1999). *The End of Empire and the Making of Malaya*. Cambridge: Cambridge University Press.
Harpur, P.D. (2012). "Embracing the new disability rights paradigm: The importance of the convention on the rights of persons with disabilities". *Disability & Society* **27**(1): 1–14.
Ho, K.L. (2000). "Citizen participation and policy making in Singapore: Conditions and predicaments". *Asian Survey* **40**(3): 436–455.
Koh, J. (2009). "10 years – and still no public transport subsidy for disabled". *The Online Citizen*.
Low, L. and T.C. Aw (2004). *Social Insecurity in the New Millennium: The Central Provident Fund in Singapore*. Singapore: Marshall Cavendish.
Ministry of Education (2000). *Report of the Compulsory Education in Singapore*.
Ministry of Education (n.d.). *Overview of Edusave Scheme*.
Ministry of Health (2012). Voluntary Sterilization (Amendment) Bill Second Reading – Opening Speech by the Minister for Health Mr Gan Kim Yong.
Ministry of Social Affairs (1983). *Towards a Better Profile of the Disabled People in Singapore*.
Ministry of Social and Family Development (2007). Chapter 1: "Definition of disability and prevalence rate of persons with disabilities in Singapore".
Ministry of Social and Family Development (2013). "Singapore ratifies UN Convention on the Rights of Persons with Disabilities (UNCRPD)". Available at http://app.msf.gov.sg/Press-Room/Singapore-Ratifies-UNCRPD.
Ministry of Social and Family Development (n.d.). *Enabling Masterplan 2012 to 2016*.
National Coordinating Committee (1981). International Year of Disabled Persons: Full participation and integration: Rights issue/under the auspices of the Ministry of Social Affairs and the Singapore Council of Social Service, National Co-ordinating Committee.
Ng, I.Y.H. (2015). "Being poor in a rich 'nanny state': Developments in Singapore social welfare". *Singapore Economic Review*, **60**(3): 1–17.
Pan-Pacific Rehabilitation Conference (1975). *Fifth Pan-Pacific Conference of the International Society for the Rehabilitation of the Disabled*. Singapore: Singapore Council of Social Service.
People's Action Party (1988). "Agenda for action: Convention 88: Resource materials". Singapore: PAP.

Remaking Singapore Committee (2003). *Changing Mindsets, Deepening Relationships.*
Report of the Advisory Council on the Disabled (1988). *Opportunities for the Disabled.*
Singapore Association for the Blind (1965). *Annual Reports and Accounts: 1965–1966.* Singapore: SAB.
Singapore Association for the Blind (1968). *Annual Reports and Accounts: 1967–1968.* Singapore: SAB: 2.
Singapore Parliamentary Report (2012, 12 November). Vol. 89.
Singapore Women's Hall of Fame (2014a). "Leaena Tambyah".
Singapore Women's Hall of Fame (2014b). "Yip Pin Xiu". Available at www.swhf.sg/the-honourees/22-sports/177-yip-pin-xiu.
Social Welfare Department (1946). *Annual Report: 1946.* Singapore: Department of Social Welfare.
Social Welfare Department (1949). *Five Year Plan.* Singapore: Department of Social Welfare.
Tan, C. (2014). "Bus and train fare hike offset by slew of concessions". *The Straits Times.*
Tan, L.C. (1993). "China must decide pace of change: SM". *The Straits Times.*
Think Centre (2004). "Champion of the disabled".
United Nations Department of Economic and Social Affairs (1981). "The international year of disabled persons 1981".
United Nations Department of Economic and Social Affairs (1982). "World program of action concerning disabled persons".
Wee, A. (2004). "Where we are coming from: The evolution of social services and social work in Singapore". In K. Mehta and A. Wee (eds) *Social Work in Context: A Reader.* Singapore: Marshall Cavendish Academic, pp. 40–52.
Wong, R. and Wong M.E. (2015). "Social impact of policies for the disabled in Singapore". In D. Chan (ed.) *50 Years of Social Issues in Singapore.* Singapore: World Scientific, pp. 147–166.
Yap, M.T. (1991). "Social services: The next lap". *Times Academic Press for Institute of Policy Studies.*
Yong, C. (2015). "Saving Sungei Buloh". *The Straits Times.*
Zhuang, K. (2010). "Enabling the Singapore story: Writing a history of disability". In B. Lockhart and L. Tse Siang (eds), *Monograph 42: Studies in Malaysian & Singapore History, Mubin Sheppard Memorial Essays.* Kuala Lumpur: Malayan Branch of the Royal Asiatic Society, pp. 37–72.

Index

Achtung! Productions 86
Action for AIDS (AFA) 152
Adventurers Like Us (ALU) 154
Advisory Council on the Disabled 12, 170–1, 175
Advisory Council on the Impact of New Media on Society (AIMS) 61
advocacy 6, 10, 12, 26–7, 31, 48, 59, 64–5, 102, 104, 108–9, 114–17, 119–23, 127–9, 136, 141, 145, 157, 159–60, 170–1, 174, 179, 181–3
Agence France-Presse (AFP) 20, 24
American Bar Association (ABA) 80
Amnesty International (AI) 2, 5, 20–1, 24, 28–30, 56, 58, 65, 39–41, 75
Ang, Johnny 183
Archdiocesan Commission for the Pastoral Care of Migrants and Itinerant People 119
Asian Human Rights Commission (AHRC) 80
Asian values 1, 37, 163
Asian Women's Welfare Association (AWWA) 171–2, 176–7, 179
Association of Women for Action and Research (AWARE) 5, 10–11, 13, 81, 90, 99, 102–3, 119, 137–9, 142–6, 172, 180
Au, Alex 20, 61, 127
AWWA Handicapped Children's Playgroup 171, 176

Bhatia, Shakuntala 172

Cable News Network (CNN) 155–6
censorship 54, 64, 120
Central Provident Fund (CPF) 9, 63, 96–9, 100–2, 108–9
Central Registry of Disabled Persons 177

Certificate of Entitlement (COE) 177
Challenged People's Alliance and Network 179
Chan, Chun Sing 179
Chandran-Dudley, Ron 174
Cheng, Vincent 85, 115, 118
Chiam, See Tong 86, 152
children with disabilities 171–3, 176–8; see also disability
Chng, Suan Tze 82
Chok, Stephanie 123
Christianity 118, 151
civil and political rights 6, 36, 54, 76
civil rights 24, 29–30, 74, 78; see also human rights
civil society 2–4, 6–7, 9–12, 14, 18, 24, 45, 27–9, 62, 65, 71–2, 76, 79–80, 85–90, 108, 114, 118–19, 122–3, 125, 127–8, 133, 135–6, 142–3, 145–6, 154, 162, 164
Commission of Inquiry (COI) 124
communalism 170
communism 56–7, 170
communitarian 150, 155–6, 158–9, 163
Community Chest of Singapore (CCS) 177
Community Development Council 120
Community Health Assist Scheme 100
community organisation 116
Compulsory Education Act 171, 178
Constitution 12, 36–7, 46, 54, 89, 119, 157, 159–62, 169
Convention Against Torture (CAT) 36–7
Convention on the Elimination of All Forms of Discrimination Against Women (CEDAW) 5, 11, 13, 134, 141, 143–6
Convention on the Rights of the Child (CRC) 143, 179

188 Index

Convention on the Rights of Persons with Disabilities (CRPD) 5, 12–13, 170–1, 180–1, 143
Court of Appeal 28–9, 161–2
Criminal Law (Temporary Provisions) Act 43, 70, 89
crisis helpline 121
Cuff Road Project 121
culture of fear 64, 118

deportation 123–4
disability 5, 10, 11–13, 86, 99, 145, 169–75, 177, 179, 182–3; children with disability 171–2, 176–7; disability rights 86, 169–70, 174, 182–3; mental disability 171; permanent disability 171; physical disability 171
Disabled People's Association (DPA) 171, 174–5, 181
Disabled People's International (DPI) 171, 174
DPI World Congress 174
Drug Rehabilitation Center 22

education 49–50, 96, 98, 71, 89, 120, 126, 129, 135, 137–40, 169, 172, 175, 177–81; right to 96
Education Endowment Scheme (Edusave) 171, 178
Employment Act 135
Employment Agencies Act 124
Employment of Foreign Manpower Act 135
Enabling Masterplan 12, 171, 180–2
European Committee for Human Rights in Malaysia and Singapore 80–1

Faith Community Baptist Church 159
Far East Economic Review 77
Federation of United Kingdom and Eire Malaysian and Singaporean Students Organisations 78
Films Act 84
Films Appeal Committee 87
Foreign Domestic Worker 117, 124, 135
free meal programme 121
freedom of assembly, speech and association 54, 153
"Freedom to Love" 158–9
Function 8 43, 78, 85–6

"gay lifestyle" 151
Geylang Catholic Centre 81, 87, 115–17
Goh, Chok Tong 4, 60, 141, 152, 156, 175

government 3, 5, 7–9, 11–12, 14, 18, 20, 22, 24, 26, 29, 31, 38, 40–5, 47, 54–65, 72–84, 86, 88–90, 97–102, 105–9, 115, 117–25, 127–9, 135–6, 138–46, 150–60, 162, 169–71, 173, 175–6, 170–80, 182–3
grassroots 116; *see also* civil society
Group Representation Constituency 169, 180, 183

Handicap's Welfare Association (HWA) 183
harassment 139, 142
healthcare 97–100, 169; *see also* Medisave; Medishield
Heartland for LGBTQ Buddhists 154
heterosexual family 158, 163
HIV/AIDS 152
Home Ownership Plus Education 139–40
homosexual 150–2; *see also* homosexual relationship; homosexuality
homosexual relationship 150
homosexuality 1, 150–2, 157, 159
Hong Lim Park 13, 43, 62–3, 85, 87, 108–9, 158, 162
Hospital Ethics Committee 180
Housing Development Board 97, 102–3
human rights 1–3, 5–8, 11–12, 14, 18, 21, 23, 26, 31, 37, 44–5, 47, 49–50, 56, 59, 64–5, 72, 74, 80, 85, 88, 90, 96–7, 99–100, 105, 108–9, 115–16, 126, 128, 133, 143–4, 146, 150–1, 153–5, 158–60, 162–4, 170, 176; civil and political rights 6, 76; economic, social and cultural rights 9, 96, 100, 102, 107; freedom of speech 12, 46, 54, 64, 169–70; LGBT rights 103; migrant workers' rights 11, 96, 108, 119, 132–4, 136, 139–40, 142–5, 159; press freedom 6–8, 54–6; right to work 96, 144; welfare rights 135–6
Humanitarian Organisation for Migration Economics (HOME) 5, 10–11, 44, 49, 118–24, 126–7

Immigration and Checkpoints Authority 45
inclusive education 179
inclusive society 180, 182
Industrial Arbitration Court 105
Infocomm Development Authority of Singapore (IDA) 109
Institute of Policy Studies 88, 99, 109, 145, 177
Institute for Southeast Asian Studies 18

Inter-Ministry Committee 144
Internal Affairs Office 44, 51
Internal Security Act (ISA) 18, 46, 56–7, 63, 70, 74, 80, 135
Internal Security Department (ISD) 75–7, 82–3, 117, 123
International Bar Association 80
International Committee of the Red Cross 41
International Commission of Jurists 20, 80
International Covenant on Civil and Political Rights (ICCPR) 36, 54, 62
International Covenant of Economic, Social and Cultural Rights (ICESCR) 9, 96, 100, 102, 107
International Disability Alliance 145
International Federation of Human Rights 80
International Organisations of Labour 106
International Press Institute 56, 58
International Women's Rights Action Watch Asia Pacific (IWRAW Asia Pacific) 159
International Year of Disabled Persons (IYPD) 170–1, 173
Internet 20, 59–63, 88, 109, 129, 154–6, 169, 161–2
Islam 13, 151

Jemaah Islamiyah 82–3
Jeyaratnam, Joshua Benjamin 18, 21
Jurong Industrial Mission 115

Kausikan, Bilahari 169
Kepercayaan, Aliran 80
Kuala Lumpur 24, 28–9, 56
Kuala Lumpur Selangor Chinese Assembly Hall 29

Law Association for Asia and the Western Pacific 80
Lee, Chiang Teng 125
Lee, Hsien Loong 4, 45, 63, 98, 150, 158, 178
Lee, Kuan Yew 1, 38, 41–2, 45, 55–8, 60, 63, 73, 77–8, 88, 97, 105–6, 136–7, 152, 155–6, 169–70
Lesbian, Gay, Bisexual, Transgender (LGBT) 103, 150
LGBT movement 155
Liew, Chong Choon 177
Liew, Chong Heng 177
lobbying 139, 178
Long-Term Visit Pass 139

Long-Term Visit Pass Plus 139
lorry procession 121
Love Singapore 159
Low, Peter 88–9

Mahbubani, Kishore 169
Majlis Ugama Islam Singapura 195–6; *see also* Islamic Religious Council
mandatory day-off 121
marital rape 11, 140–1
Marshall, David 1–2, 6, 17–18, 26, 39–42, 57, 70, 75, 172
Marshall, Jean 2, 172
Mass Rapid Transit (MRT) 179
Mattar, Ahmad 174
Media Development Authority (MDA) 60–2, 64, 87
Medisave 9, 98, 100
Medishield 9, 100–1
Member of Parliament 21, 142, 195
mental disability 171; *see also* disability
Migrant Voices 121
migrant workers 36, 43–4, 48–9, 89, 105, 108, 114–19, 121, 124, 126–8
Migrant Workers Council 125
Ministry of Defence (MINDEF) 82
Ministry of Education (MOE) 120–1, 178–9
Ministry of Home Affairs (MHA) 21, 77, 79, 81, 83–4, 122, 153
Ministry of Information, Communication and the Arts (MICA) 61, 84
Ministry of Manpower (MOM) 45, 99, 102, 106, 114, 119, 123–5
Ministry of Social Affairs (MSA) 174–5
Ministry of Social and Family Development (MSF) 175, 180
Misuse of Drugs Act 70

Nanyang Siang Pau 55, 57, 65
National Council for Social Services (NCSS) 178, 182
national security 1, 8, 14, 37, 85–7, 118, 126, 153
National Service 7, 132
National Trades Union Congress (NTUC) 59, 105–7, 173
National University of Singapore 12
National Wage Council 106
Newspaper and Printing Presses Act 8, 54, 58
Ngerng, Roy 9, 62–3, 98, 108
Nominated Member of Parliament (NMP) 151, 157

Non-Constituency Member of Parliament (NCMP) 21, 23
non-governmental organisation (NGO) 6, 21, 27, 44–5, 48, 119, 121–2, 145, 152

OB Markers 58, 60, 64, 96
Open Singapore Centre 21, 25
Operation Coldstore 6, 18, 39–40, 47, 63, 73–7, 83, 86, 88
Our Singapore Conversation 151

parents' consent 173
Parliament 21–2, 27, 37, 46, 54, 56, 74, 142, 157, 161, 179
Penal Code 377A 150, 161
People Like Us (PLU) 152–4, 156–7
People's Action Party (PAP) 1, 4, 12, 55–6, 59, 61, 71–2, 84, 98, 105, 107, 116, 134–5, 152
permanent disability 171; *see also* disability
Personal Protection Orders 138
persons with disabilities 12, 169, 173–4, 177, 180–2, 184
petition 21, 23, 25, 29, 62, 73–4, 77–8, 121–2, 127, 140, 157–8, 179
Philemon, Jewel 86
physical disability 171; *see also* disability
"Pink Dot" 158–9
Pioneer Generation Package 9, 100
police raids 153
poverty 26, 30, 97, 104, 169
Preservation of Public Security Ordinance 39
Progressive Wage Scheme 107
Protection from Harassment Act 142
public order 1, 8, 13, 46, 54, 72; *see also* national security

racial harmony 1
Rajasavari, Rethinasamy 179
Ravi, M. 21, 23–4, 26, 28, 31, 38, 44, 161
Reaching Everyone for Active Citizenry @ Home 111
Redqueen 154
Registrar of Societies 76, 153
rehabilitation 12, 22, 29, 101, 172–3
Rehabilitation International 174
Remaking Singapore Campaign 175
Remember May 21st 85
Return My CPF 109
rights of persons with disabilities 180; *see also* disability
rights-based approach 169, 163, 174, 178

Sadasivan, Balaji 156
Safehaven 154
Said, Zahari 56
same-sex marriage 150
Sayoni 12, 103, 145, 159–60
SBS Transit 179
See, Martyn 47, 49, 62, 83–4, 88
SG50 8
Shanmugan, K. 160
Shanmugaratnam, Tharman 85
Sheares, Benjamin 173
Siew, Kum Hong 157
Singam, Constance 5, 81, 145
Singapore Anti-Death Penalty Committee 21, 25
Singapore Association of Trade Unions 105
Singapore Association of Women Lawyers 138
Singapore Broadcasting Authority 59, 200
Singapore Children Society 172
Singapore Companies Act 85
Singapore Council of Social Service (SCSS) 177, 182
Singapore Council of Women 132, 136
Singapore Democratic Party (SDP) 24, 81, 152
Singapore Ex-Political Detainees 78
Singapore exceptionalism 7, 143
Singapore Gay News List (SIGNEL) 154
Singapore Institute of International Affairs (SIIA) 85–6
Singapore Islamic Scholars and Religious Teachers Association 196
Singapore Management University (SMU) 2
Singapore Mass Rapid Transport 10, 43–4, 107, 122–4
Singapore National Employers' Federation 106
Singapore National Union of Journalists 57–8
Singapore Press Holdings 57, 59, 62
Singapore Prison Service 17, 26
Singapore school of thought 182
Singapore Trade Union Congress 105
Singapore–Malaysia merger 70
slavery 30, 121, 169
SMRT bus drivers' strike 10, 43, 123
social liabilities 176
Social Welfare Department (SWD) 171–2
social worker 114–15, 117, 121, 172
"Speakers' Corner" 47, 158
St Ignatius Church 176

sterilisation 171, 173, 180, 182
Strategic Information and Research Development Centre 85
Suara Rakyat Malaysia 29, 80
surveillance 153–4, 200

Tambyah, Leaena 172, 176, 183
Tan, Eng Hong 161
Tan, Pin Pin 83, 97
Tan, Tee Seng 2, 8, 70, 85
Tan, Tony 175
Tarmugi, Abdullah 177, 196
The Long Nightmare: My 17 Years as a Political Prisoner 84
The Necessary Stage 50, 83–4
The Online Citizen 7, 26–8, 59, 61, 65, 84, 89, 109, 121, 157, 159, 161
Therapy and Educational Assistance for Children in Mainstream Education (TEACH ME) 176
Think Centre 5, 7, 21–5, 27–8, 47, 59, 65, 84–5, 174
Thio, Li Ann 151
Thio, Shelley 123
To Singapore, with Love 83, 87
Trafficking in Persons 142
Transient Workers Count Too 10, 114, 119, 142
Trevvy and Fridae 156
Tripartite Alliance for Fair and Progressive Employment Practices 199

UN Special Rapporteur for the Human Rights of Migrants 124
UN Women Singapore 119
United Nations (UN) 21, 31, 70, 73–4, 86, 96, 98–9, 102, 119, 121, 124, 132, 136, 141, 159, 161–2, 170, 173–4, 176
United Nations Convention for the Rights of Migrant Workers 121
United Nations Economic and Social Council 136
Universal Declaration of Human Rights 36, 54, 70, 74
Universal Periodic Review (UPR) 21, 50, 65, 83, 85–6, 89–90, 96, 181
Ustaz Noor Deros 159

Veloo, K.V. 175
Voluntary Sterilisation Act (VSA) 171, 173, 180, 182
Voluntary Welfare Organisations (VWO) 12, 174

"Wear White" campaign 159
welfare 3, 9, 12, 49, 76, 96, 108, 120, 134–6, 153, 169, 171–2, 177
Wham, Jolovan 44, 122–3, 127
Wijeysingha, Vincent 123
Women's Charter 11, 132, 134, 137–8
Wong, Kan Seng 138, 150
Wong, Souk Yee 85
Work Injury Compensation Act 135
Worker's Party (WP) 6, 18, 81, 152
Workfair Singapore 123
Workfare Income Supplement 107–8
World Economic Fund 132
World Human Rights Conference 150
World Program of Action concerning Disabled Persons 173

Yip, Pin Xiu 179

Taylor & Francis eBooks

Helping you to choose the right eBooks for your Library

Add Routledge titles to your library's digital collection today. Taylor and Francis ebooks contains over 50,000 titles in the Humanities, Social Sciences, Behavioural Sciences, Built Environment and Law.

Choose from a range of subject packages or create your own!

Benefits for you
- Free MARC records
- COUNTER-compliant usage statistics
- Flexible purchase and pricing options
- All titles DRM-free.

Benefits for your user
- Off-site, anytime access via Athens or referring URL
- Print or copy pages or chapters
- Full content search
- Bookmark, highlight and annotate text
- Access to thousands of pages of quality research at the click of a button.

REQUEST YOUR FREE INSTITUTIONAL TRIAL TODAY
Free Trials Available
We offer free trials to qualifying academic, corporate and government customers.

eCollections – Choose from over 30 subject eCollections, including:

Archaeology	Language Learning
Architecture	Law
Asian Studies	Literature
Business & Management	Media & Communication
Classical Studies	Middle East Studies
Construction	Music
Creative & Media Arts	Philosophy
Criminology & Criminal Justice	Planning
Economics	Politics
Education	Psychology & Mental Health
Energy	Religion
Engineering	Security
English Language & Linguistics	Social Work
Environment & Sustainability	Sociology
Geography	Sport
Health Studies	Theatre & Performance
History	Tourism, Hospitality & Events

For more information, pricing enquiries or to order a free trial, please contact your local sales team:
www.tandfebooks.com/page/sales

 The home of Routledge books

www.tandfebooks.com